UNEASY LIES THE HEAD

UNEASY

LIES

THE

HEAD

UNEASY LIES THE HEAD

THE AUTOBIOGRAPHY OF

HIS MAJESTY

KING HUSSEIN I

OF THE HASHEMITE

KINGDOM OF JORDAN

PUBLISHED BY BERNARD GEIS ASSOCIATES

DISTRIBUTED BY RANDOM HOUSE

THIS BOOK IS FOR
THE PEOPLE OF JORDAN

Contents

UNEASY LIES THE HEAD

1

The Murder of My Grandfather
··· My Early Days

"The greatest single influence on my life."

WHEN I WAS A BOY, my grandfather, the King Abdullah, used to tell me many a time that Jerusalem was one of the most beautiful cities in the world. His first love, it is true, was the Hejaz where he was born, that arid stretch of desert north of Yemen, with Mecca, the birthplace of Islam, in its heart. It was from the Hejaz that my grandfather first marched north in the great Arab Revolt—or as it is more properly described, the Arab Awakening.

But as the years passed and he settled in the north and his wise rule brought peace and independence to the country that is now Jordan, he grew to love Jerusalem more and more. He was deeply religious, and could never enter the city without being aware of its spiritual significance. As a boy, I

3

used to see it through his eyes. The holy places, the ancient
walls, the slim minarets, the olive trees of Gethsemane, the
bustling narrow markets that cluster around the Via Dolorosa,
have all seen tragedy and bloodshed in their time. But they
have also been the birthplace of hope and faith, and when the
sun shines above Jerusalem and the air is cool and smiling,
it is a city without peer.

Jordan itself is a beautiful country. It is wild, with limitless
deserts where the Bedouin roam, but the mountains of the
north are clothed in green forests, and where the Jordan
River flows it is fertile and warm in winter. Jordan has a
strange, haunting beauty and a sense of timelessness. Dotted
with the ruins of empires once great, it is the last resort of
yesterday in the world of tomorrow. I love every inch of it. I
love Amman, where I was born, and which I have seen grow
from a township. I am still awed and excited each time I set
eyes on the ancient city of Petra, approached by a defile so
narrow that a dozen Nabataeans could hold an army at bay.
Above all I feel at home in the tribal black tents in the desert.
But it is in fair and beautiful Jerusalem that my story starts.

It was Friday, July 20, 1951, a rather warm day, the second
of two days that my grandfather and I were spending in
Jerusalem, and it was on this day, at the El Aksa Mosque
near the Dome of the Rock, that tragedy, the cruelest of all
teachers, helped to transform me from a boy into a man.

All week the atmosphere had been tense. Apart from anything else, the end of the Israeli war had left the whole Arab
world stunned, angry and discontented. Even at sixteen I
could feel the atmosphere growing, slowly enveloping the
countryside like a cloud of poison gas. The previous Monday

the assassination of Riyad il Sulh, the great Lebanese politician, had inflamed the passions of my people. His death was quite unconnected with the murder that was to follow, but it had taken place in Jordan and had a profound effect on the country, so that now, at every street corner, one could see the sullen faces and feel the stony silences, broken by the sharp cries of argument or sudden violence that signaled a moment of crisis, the razor's edge that divides sanity from hysteria.

It was the first such outrage Jordan had ever known. It was nothing compared to the crises I have surmounted since, *but it was the first one of that type.* The sullen anger of the people was not directed so much at any one man or political party as against the unknown force that had disrupted their peaceful way of life.

And how peaceful Jordan was when I was a little boy! A smiling country, content to be left alone; its people worked hard, worshiped God, obeyed the laws, and asked for nothing more than a life that should end with a blessed place in paradise. Then suddenly an honored visitor was slain in our midst while enjoying our hospitality, and within a few days the King himself was assassinated.

I have always felt that Egypt was largely responsible, for I knew my grandfather had many enemies there. I had just returned from school in Egypt and had already witnessed the beginning of the campaign against my grandfather. It seemed to me that it was a calculated plot to disrupt Jordan, but it was not instigated by the ordinary people of Egypt. I had lived with them. I knew them. Even at that early age I could see the wicked class distinctions, the strange calm among the people presaging an explosion. The Egyptians would accept any leadership with docility—but only for a time. They are easily swayed and, as I discovered while at school there, they really knew very little about the Arab world. They accepted the word of those plotting against Jordan that my grandfather was a "defeatist" and a "traitor" (because he was so right in his warnings and someone had to take the blame for the failure of other Arab statesmen).

But internal opposition was mounting in Egypt. You cannot keep a nation ill-fed and ill-educated, as most of the rich and ruthless rulers of Egypt kept the fellahin. And as those in power saw the danger signs mount, especially after the Arab-Israeli operations of 1948, they resorted to the age-old trick of looking for a scapegoat. Jordan suited them perfectly. In the war with Israel, Jordan had taken the brunt of the fighting and most of the blame, despite the fact that my grandfather had warned his people years before what would happen. His political foresight was uncanny, but he was not always popular because he so often forecast the truth.

As we discussed the visit to Jerusalem the sense of foreboding was so strong that even my grandfather—a man not given to undue alarm—seemed to have a premonition of disaster. Three days before we left for Jerusalem we were sitting talking after a day's work, and he turned to me, for no reason that I could fathom, and said in his gentle voice:

"I hope you realize, my son, that one day you will have to assume responsibility. I look to you to do your very best to see that my work is not lost. I look to you to continue it in the service of our people."

I remember the moment perfectly. My grandfather, a Bedouin at heart, loved the desert so much that even in his palace grounds he erected tents where he used to pass some of his time. In the cool of the evening he would often recline on silken cushions, with friends who visited him, and it was in the tent, sitting beside him as I did on so many evenings, listening to his advice and wisdom, that I promised him solemnly I would do as he asked. It was a promise made with the full knowledge that one day I must redeem it. But little did I realize how short was the time ahead.

At sixty-nine my grandfather was in magnificent health. My father, though ill, showed every promise of recovery; obviously, it would be some years before my father reigned and many more, I devoutly hoped, before I succeeded him.

And yet, three days later I knelt by the dead body of my grandfather while many of those who had been around him fled. A year later I was King of Jordan; and I like to hope now that my promise to the man who was the greatest single influence on my life comforted him in his last days as it has strengthened me in all my efforts since I accepted the will of God and the wish of my people to serve them.

Throughout the week there had been ominous portents. On Wednesday morning—the day before we left for Jerusalem—the United States Ambassador requested an audience.

"Your Majesty," he told my grandfather, "may I implore you not to go to Jerusalem. I have heard there may be an attempt on your life. I beseech you, sir, to change your plans."

My grandfather looked at him thoughtfully.

"I thank you for your warnings," he replied, "but even if they were true, I would still go. My life belongs to my people and my place is among them, and I will die when I am destined to die."

During Wednesday, preparations were made for the visit. It was never originally intended that I should go, but in the evening he sent for me, and as we sat together he said:

"You know, my son, I have asked many people to come with me to Jerusalem tomorrow. It is very strange, some of them don't want to come. They seem worried about something happening. I have never heard so many feeble excuses in all my life!"

He looked at me for a long time, then added:

"Would you like to come with me, my son?"

"Certainly I would," I replied. "You know, sir, my life is worth nothing compared with yours."

It was perhaps a little theatrical, but I meant it with all my heart. My grandfather stared at me gravely and I said no more, for I could see there were tears in his eyes.

So we went to Jerusalem together. Our day began early that Friday, for we had promised to visit some friends in Nablus before attending prayers in Jerusalem. We breakfasted early and when I came to the table I was wearing an ordinary suit. My grandfather looked at me and, for no reason that I could understand, asked me:

"Why aren't you in uniform?"

There was no reason why I should be, and my grandfather, whose tastes were of the simplest, and who abhorred the extravagant trappings of office (especially at prayer time), had never made such a request before.

I had in fact only one uniform, which I had worn the previous day during a presentation of wings to the first Royal Jordanian Air Force pilots. It needed pressing and so, just before breakfast, I had arranged to have it sent to Amman in the car with some other belongings, as we were to return later that day.

"You must wear it!" my grandfather commanded.

I hurriedly sent word for the car to be stopped and my uniform returned immediately. After some delay it arrived and we drove to Nablus, there refusing all invitations from friends to remain for the day. When we returned we had some time to spare, so my grandfather held several audiences at the small two-bedroom house where we stayed. The house is now a museum.

One of the audiences was held with General Cooke, known to us as Cooke Pasha, who was a new divisional commander of the Arab Legion. He had just arrived in Jordan, and I was delighted when my grandfather asked me to translate their conversation, especially when he told Cooke Pasha:

"I am very proud of my grandson. I am going to give him the cordon of an aide-de-camp tomorrow."

We little knew that for my grandfather tomorrow would never come. But amongst us there was one man who did know. I was standing close to my grandfather when he arrived humbly for an audience.

His name was Doctor Moussa Abdullah Husseini, a relative of the Mufti, who had received his degree in Germany. He bowed low before my grandfather, looked him in the eye, expressed his loyalty, and wished him a long life and happiness. Two hours later my grandfather was dead and Husseini was so deeply implicated in the assassination that he was later executed.

My life has been very lonely since that Friday morning, and I have often wondered what lay behind the thousands of bland smiles and fervent expressions of loyalty I have acknowledged since then.

I wonder now, looking back across the years, whether my grandfather had an inner knowledge of the tragedy that was so close. All were welcome in our Jerusalem house, and

just before we set off for the Mosque, a group of friends
gathered and my grandfather was telling them about the men
who had refused to come to Jerusalem with him.

"They were afraid," he declared, and then he added words
so prophetic that I would hesitate to repeat them had they
not been heard by a dozen men alive today. He was talking
about the unimportance of life and death.

"When I have to die, I would like to be shot in the head by
a nobody," he said. "That's the simplest way of dying. I would
rather have that than become old and a burden."

Somebody looked at the clock, and my grandfather rose
from his seat. It was time to go.

Sitting together in the car, we started on the route to the
Mosque. The atmosphere was heavy with foreboding; there
were precautions everywhere. Heavily armed troops guarded
the streets and I could see more and more sullen, suspicious
faces. Nobody could have done more for the Arab cause than
my grandfather; yet, driving slowly to the Mosque, hemmed
in by thousands, one had the feeling that disaster was in the
air.

When we entered the Old City, alighted from our car and
started walking toward the Mosque, it was even worse. The
military guard was so massive that I remember turning to
an official and asking:

"What is this—a funeral procession?"

I was walking behind my grandfather, a few steps to his
right. He spoke to some men on the way down and then we
reached the door of the Mosque itself. A guard of honor presented arms.

My grandfather was almost through the door when he

turned back and told the guard commander that he did not think noisy military ceremonies should be performed in a holy place.

Then my grandfather turned to enter the Mosque, and as he walked about three paces inside the main doors, a man came out from behind the great door to his right. He did not look normal. He had a gun in his hand, and before anybody could do anything, he fired. He was only two yards away but my grandfather never saw him. He was hit in the head and fell immediately. His turban rolled away.

I must have lost my head at that moment because everything happened right in front of me. For an interminable second the murderer stood stock-still; all power to move had left him. At my feet lay a white bundle. I did not even realize what had happened. Then, suddenly, the man turned to run and I tried to rush him as he made for the inside of the Mosque.

I was near the gate. As I lunged toward him I saw from the corner of my eye—and how strange that the eye and the brain have time to notice such details in moments of agitation and despair—that most of my grandfather's so-called friends were fleeing in every direction. I can see them now, those men of dignity and high estate, doubled up, cloaked figures scattering like bent old terrified women. That picture, far more distinct than the face of the assassin, has remained with me ever since as a constant reminder of the frailty of political devotion.

All this happened in a flash as the murderer squirmed and darted this way and that. Shooting started from every corner of the Mosque and then suddenly the man turned at bay. I had a glimpse of his face; I saw his bared teeth, his dazed eyes. He still had the squat black gun in his right hand and, as though hypnotized, I watched him point it at me—all in a split second—then saw the smoke, heard the shot and reeled as I felt the shock on my chest. I wondered, is this what death is like? I waited—but nothing happened; nothing, that is, except a miracle. I must have been standing at a slight angle to the man, for—as we discovered later—his bullet hit a medal on my chest and ricocheted off. I was unharmed, and without doubt my grandfather's insistence that I wear my uniform saved my life.

As the assassin in turn fell to his death, still shooting, I turned back to my grandfather's body. I was so dazed as I knelt by his side that I could only think in a fury, at the very moment when I had lost him, that most of those he had brought up, most of those he had taught and helped, had fled.

I undid the buttons of his robe while his doctor examined him, hoping that he was still alive, but it was all over. We covered up the body in the robes that had once been white. We made a stretcher out of a carpet and carried him to the hospital. I wanted to stay, but a doctor gently urged me to leave and in the next room gave me an injection—for shock, I was told. I still could not really believe what had happened until we made our way to Jerusalem airfield.

Suddenly I felt very, very lonely.

I stood apart from the others on the airstrip, for what could those around me say at this moment of disaster other than the conventional sympathies?

Alone on the runway, how I wished that my father was not being treated for his mental illness in Switzerland at a time like this. But this was my first lesson, the first of many times I have stood apart in the midst of my fellow men.

When I think back of my life since that day, I know that

the price I have had to pay for position is not the unending work that I love, not the poor health that has dogged me, but a price much higher. It is that I have gone through so much of my life surrounded by people, crushed in by them, talking to them, laughing with them, envious of their casual, happy relationships, while in my heart I was as lonely as a castaway.

As I stood there, bewildered by what had happened, a man in Air Force uniform hesitated, then strode toward me. He had a rugged, weather-beaten face with strong teeth and sandy hair. Very shyly he said to me in his thick Scottish accent, "Come with me, sir. I'll look after you."

He steered me to a twin-engined Air Force plane, a Dove, and bade me squeeze into the co-pilot's seat next to him. Then he revved up the motors and we flew back to Amman.

The man was Wing Commander Jock Dalgleish, of the British Royal Air Force. I little thought, on that day when a page of history was turned, that two years later Dalgleish would teach me to fly, and that seven years later Jock and I, in a similar aircraft, would be fighting for our lives when attacked by Nasser's Syrian MIGs.

The next day I carried a gun for the first time in my life.

· · · · · ·

I have decided to start these memoirs with the murder of my grandfather since he, above all men, had the most profound influence on my life. So, too, had the manner of his death.

Many men were afraid of him, but not I. He loved me very much, that I know, and I in my turn loved him to the point where I no longer feared his rather austere outward appearance, and I think he knew and appreciated this. To me he was more than a grandfather, and to him I think I was a son.

I was, of course, deeply attached to my parents, for throughout my early days our family lived simply but happily. My mother, Queen Zein, who has remained by my side all my life, watched me grow up with tenderness and love. She is a remarkable woman, not only beautiful, but very wise. She still lives in Amman. Her wisdom, her courage, her never-failing advice and encouragement to me made her a major factor in my life. For our family life was far from easy. We were at times very poor. Even in 1950 my father as Crown Prince received only $3,000 a year from the State and before that it was much less. And none of us have private fortunes.

When I was only a year old my mother had a baby daughter who died after a month in the bitter cold of an Amman winter. She died of pneumonia—because we simply could not afford good heating facilities in our small house. I can just remember as a toddler visiting my cousin Feisal in Baghdad and playing with his wonderful teddy bear. I was heartbroken when I had to return to Amman without it. The next morning my mother bought me one—after selling her last piece of jewelry.

All through my life, with its crisis after crisis, her encouragement has given me strength. And it is certainly true that had it not been for my mother's patience and devotion, my father would never have been able to rule Jordan, even for the short period that he did. And if my father, with my mother by his side, had not stepped in after the murder of my grandfather, the history of Jordan might have been vastly different.

When I was a boy we lived on Jebel Amman, one of the capital's seven hills, in a modest five-room villa, with only one bathroom, and set in a small plot of land. My cousin Feisal in Iraq seemed to me, at that age, to move in a world of splendid opulence.

It was so splendid that when at the age of ten I visited Baghdad, Feisal gave me a farewell gift. It was a magnificent British-made bicycle. It shone and sparkled and I felt that never in my life would I own anything more beautiful. When the time came for us to return to Amman, arrangements were made to send the bicycle on to me. I kept that bicycle polished and spick-and-span for twelve months. In the mornings, before school, I would polish each spoke, and at the end of a year it looked as new as the day I received it.

Then one day my mother came to me.

"I know this is going to hurt," she started gently, "but our financial position is a bit difficult, so to keep going, we shall have to sell a few things. Will you be upset, my dear son, if we sell your bicycle?"

I fought to keep back the tears. My bicycle! Anything else could be sold but surely not that. . . .

"You know that all through life you will have to stand up against disappointments," she tried to console me. "Be brave; one day you will forget this bicycle when you are older and are driving big, shiny cars."

I did drive those cars, but I have never forgotten that bicycle. It was sold the next day. It fetched $15.

It does one no harm to be poor. We had never been rich, and consequently our modest mode of living meant that I could, for those first few years, lead a more normal life than later, and also appreciate the value of money, so that now I think I enjoy all the more the pleasure of helping those in need.

Poor though we were, by normal royal standards, we had

a relatively happy life. I went to seven schools in all, either
in Amman or Alexandria. I loved, more than I can ever say,
being with other boys, being treated as everybody else was
treated. But though I had many friends, I never had any who
were really close.

Perhaps this was because I changed schools so often, and
so never stayed long enough to make lasting friendships.
Opposing forces always seemed to be tugging away at my
study courses. I would be comfortably installed in one school,
then my grandfather—who, to say the least, had a domineer-
ing character—would decide that I needed special tuition in
religion, so back to the house I would go for extra private
lessons. Then my father would decide that I needed more
tuition in Arabic and I would have to change again.

Finally, however, I managed to go to boarding school, and
I was enrolled at Victoria College in Alexandria, a school
with excellent instruction in Arabic and English. A whole
new world opened up for me. Football, cricket, books, com-
panionship—how I loved my days at Victoria College. I can
see in my mind's eye to this day the long Spartan dormitory
which I shared with about thirty other boys, the cold showers
every morning, the uniform of gray flannels and college
blazer. And I can also remember sitting one afternoon on the
edge of my bed, after I had torn my blazer, struggling to
thread a borrowed needle, and finally sewing up the rip because I knew my parents could not possibly afford to buy me
another blazer.

My grandfather helped to pay for my tuition, otherwise I
would never have been sent there. It may seem odd that I
had to sell my bicycle and darn my socks yet I could go to
school in Egypt, but the reason is quite simple. My father
received a very modest annual sum, and with a large family
plus the title of Crown Prince, life was far from easy.

My grandfather, as King, also received an allowance from the State—a monthly salary if you like—which was not very large by normal palatine standards and barely sufficient for his station, but it was out of this that he helped pay for my education and aided us in many other ways. Yet, when it came to actual cash, we were often very badly off, and so the anomalous situation arose in which I was educated at an excellent school yet my weekly pocket money was barely sufficient for my needs.

All this did me some good; without doubt the habit, acquired very early in life, of having to watch every penny encouraged me later on to keep a much more critical eye on the finances of my country than is perhaps usual in responsible circles.

My two years at Victoria College were among the happiest in my life. As well as learning the routine lessons and sports, I took courses in Arabic and religion and became increasingly proficient at fencing, always the subjects my grandfather first looked for when scrutinizing my reports. During my last term at Victoria, I won a medal in fencing and got a good report, and my grandfather was so pleased he gave me the honorary rank of captain.

It was toward the end of these two years, when I was about sixteen, that I became closer and closer to him, especially during the long holidays, for to my grandfather any holiday always meant a golden opportunity for studying harder—and how he put me through my paces!

My grandfather was a full-blown extrovert who did not lightly brook refusal. Sir Alec Kirkbride, the British Minister to Transjordan, once described him as a monarch with a twinkle in his eye. He was a man of desert ways who had been brought up as a child among the Bedouin tribes. He was fierce and warlike and woe betide the enemy who crossed

him. He always felt, to his dying day, that he had been a
leading figure in the struggle for Arab independence and felt
that total victory had been snatched from him by duplicity.
Yet he was much more than a soldier. He was a diplomat—
and an extremely able one at that. He was also a classic
scholar; he recited poetry by the hour and was himself a poet;
he played chess like a master.

He was a wonderful old man, truculent and sometimes
autocratic, who transformed Transjordan, as it then was, into
a happy, smiling country—"The only country in the world,"
as one American journalist told Glubb Pasha, "where everybody without exception praises the Government."

My father, later King Talal, was utterly different. He was
the kindest of men, gentle and possessed of great charm. As
children we would sit at his feet and listen as he wove one
miraculous story after another for us. The love that united
our little family gave us enormous spiritual benefit. His
honesty was a byword and I never met a man who did not
like him. Only the terrible mental illness of schizophrenia
from which he suffered prevented him from reigning long
and wisely. Even in the short term of his monarchy he succeeded in patching up the strained relations between Jordan
and Saudi Arabia and Egypt. He was largely responsible for
our new constitution.

But alas, family differences exist between monarchs as
much as between their subjects, and the truth is that my
grandfather and my father never got on well together. The
two were separated by different lives and different ages—
and by opportunists. But worst of all my grandfather never
truly realized until the end of his life how deeply afflicted
my father was.

He could not conceive that a man at times gentle and sensible, but at other times very, very ill, was not being just awkward or difficult. My grandfather was so healthy and tough, he could not appreciate what illness was. We in the family knew. We watched our father with loving care, but my grandfather, who lived partly in the heroic past, saw him from outside. He had wanted a brave, intrepid Bedouin son to carry on the great tradition of the Arab Revolt. He was incapable of accepting an invalid in place of his dream. It was the bitterest disappointment of his life.

I remember one incident illustrating this, and which I hesitated for some time to include in these memoirs, because it is so personal, but I think it should be mentioned. It was the day the Lebanese politician was assassinated, the Monday before my grandfather's death. Our visitor was killed in my grandfather's car. My grandfather's aide-de-camp was with him at the time. I heard the news in the afternoon and rushed up to the palace. Never had I seen King Abdullah in such a towering rage. That a visitor should have been killed in Jordan! As the details trickled in, and my grandfather became more and more enraged, his aide-de-camp, who had escaped death, dashed in. My grandfather looked at him scornfully and cried:

"How dare you remain alive!"

My uncle, Prince Naif (the younger half-brother of my father), was supposed to be in attendance. At one crucial moment he was not present and my grandfather shouted to me:

"Where's your uncle? Go and find him."

I rushed out to look for him. I found him, but a few minutes later he disappeared again. More and more people came in, and suddenly my grandfather looked around and cried to me:

"He's vanished again! Where the devil is your uncle?"

Once again I ran for him, and when the crisis was over and I alone remained, my grandfather looked at me with a face torn by suffering. He put his hand to his forehead and cried, as though to the gods:

"This is the cruelest blow of my life. One son ill—and another who can't even stand still in a crisis."

Looking back now, I can see how and why, toward the end of his life, my grandfather lavished such affection on me as he grew older. I had possibly become the son he had always wanted.

Once he took me in hand, especially during that last holiday, he was relentless. My grandfather always rose at dawn—a habit useful to me in later life—so most mornings I got up about six, had a quick wash in our little villa and drove to the King's palace by 6:30 A.M.

Everything was ready for me. One room in the palace had been reserved as our schoolroom. But my tutor was to take second place, for my grandfather invariably started our day's work himself.

"Now, my son"—he would open a volume of Arabic or religion—"we will start at this page!" And then, with a frosty look at the teacher, "Make sure the Prince learns the lesson well." Having finished my two hours of lessons, my grandfather would either fetch me himself, or I would go to his office and watch him at work. He had already accomplished much of his day's work and expected me to have done the same, and he was so expert in most of my curriculum that one could never bluff him. One day I was learning Arabic under a tutor chosen by my grandfather, when, like a school principal, he bustled into the room and started to question me. He was so dissatisfied with my answers, he ended up by cross-examining the teacher instead.

Some days we shared a modest breakfast around 8:30 A.M.
—Bedouin coffee flavored with the delicate scent of carda-
mom, or tea with mint and some flat cakes of bread without
butter or jam. My grandfather believed one worked better on
a nearly empty stomach.

Many times at his office in the palace he would honor me
by asking me to act as translator, for though he understood
English, he did not speak it. I always liked this duty, but I
had to be very wary, for though he did not speak English,
many a translator was caught out during diplomatic conferences if so much as a word was changed. My grandfather had
an uncanny ability to seize on one single word which a translator altered, perhaps because he thought it was better that
way. I did a great deal of translating for him. But he never
caught me out.

It was this part of my education that has served me so well
since, for most days I returned to the palace before evening
prayers and dined with him, so that over the evening meal I
would listen to him talking about the subtleties and pitfalls
of the hazardous profession of being a King, or I would sit at
meetings with notables, or listen to him dictate or, fascinated,
watch him play chess until long after dark, when he would
say, looking at my drooping eyes, "Go to your home, my son,
sleep and prepare for the morrow."

He let me accompany him everywhere; it was he who
taught me to understand the minds of my people and the in-
tricacies of the Arab world in which we lived. He taught me
the courtly functions, how to behave and—perhaps because
he was a sadly disappointed man who had been deceived by
the British and French—he taught me how to come to terms

with adversity as well as with success. And he taught me above all else that a leader's greatest duty is to serve.

I also remember the devastating way he would crush people when he was angry. He was dining one night with a visiting diplomat and the talk turned to Saudi Arabia. My grandfather often had differences with the Saudis and the visitor asked my grandfather if he did not think it would be better for the cause of Arab unity if the quarrel with Saudi Arabia were patched up.

"How old are you?" asked my grandfather.

"Er—about forty-five, sir."

"And may I ask"—my grandfather's voice became increasingly sarcastic—"how old you were at the time of the Arab Revolt?"

"I suppose about nine, Your Majesty." The visiting diplomat began to look pale.

"At that time," my grandfather retorted, "I happened to be commanding the Eastern Army liberating the Arabs. And now you tell me how to serve the Arab cause!"

What an astonishing man he was! He had all sorts of talents hidden from the world. One morning I wanted his advice and went to his palace earlier than usual—it must have been before seven o'clock. I walked into his bedroom for the first time. He was still in bed, but awake. To my astonishment I saw some scientific equipment with which my grandfather had been experimenting. Against the walls was a formidable array of scientific books.

He also had a wonderful sense of humor. He always used snuff, and one day mislaid his small snuffbox. As I brought it to him I examined it with the normal curiosity of a boy.

"You seem very interested." He looked at me.

I said nothing.

"You had better try it," my grandfather urged me, and took a pinch himself.

I had no idea how strong snuff was; I think I must have sniffed half the box. For an hour I could not stop sneezing. For an hour my grandfather could not stop laughing. It cured me—I have never used snuff since.

It is true that I was not afraid of him for I loved him and respected him, but I did have one secret. Though I was only fifteen, I had managed to learn to drive a car, squeezing in a few lessons in my spare time.

I was not sure whether or not my grandfather knew; I rather fancy he pretended ignorance, but I was afraid that if I mentioned the matter he would object, so I never told him. He discovered my secret shortly before his death. I drove to his palace for dinner and then prepared to leave. I always took my leave inside the palace and he never accompanied me to the door.

I walked out, closed the doors behind me and jumped into my car. I was just starting to drive off when my grandfather came out. I simply froze. I got out of the car and went around to him.

"I see you are going home," he said.

"Yes, sir," I stammered.

"Well, take it easy—be careful," was all he said.

I drove home. I had not been in the house a minute when the telephone rang. It was my grandfather.

"I just wanted to make sure that you'd got home safely," he said. "Good night."

This was the man who taught me so much, who loved me so dearly, and to whom I owe more than I can say, the man who sat facing me one evening and told me:

"Remember, the most important thing in life is to have

the determination to work, to do your very best, regardless
of all the setbacks and all the difficulties that will occur. Only
then can you live with yourself and with God."

Now, at the age of sixteen, I was on the threshold of a life
in which one day I would have to try to put into practice all
the principles he had taught me; and if, as I say, his influence
on my life was profound, it was his death which taught me
the ultimate lesson.

The Arab lands are not like other lands. Life is all too often
held cheaply, and death often passes unheeded. Yet his murder was the first time that violence had touched me personally and on that terrible day I learned much, even if I did not
immediately realize it. First of all, I learned the unimportance
of death; that when you have to die, you die; for it is God's
will. Only thus have I found that particular inner peace
granted to those who do not fear death.

If you believe this, if you believe in fate, it behooves a man
to give of his utmost in the brief span which can end as
swiftly as my grandfather's, as swiftly as the puff of smoke
from the killer's gun was lost in the shimmering air above
Jerusalem.

I believe I must live with courage and live well, serving and
abiding by my principles in life, regardless of any difficulties
I face, so that when the time comes for me to lose my life, I
will at least have done my best.

These beliefs have helped me greatly to bear the loss of my
grandfather, and they have served me well in moments of
crisis and danger. Without doubt, it was the death of my
grandfather that brought me face to face with myself and
made me clarify my philosophy of life for the first time.

I learned one more thing. If life is cheap, man is cheaper yet. For the rest of my days, nothing can ever blot from my memory the falseness of man as I saw it on that day; many of those whom my grandfather had defended, government officials and members of his entourage whom he had trusted, had placed in positions of importance, at one moment so staid and so faithful as they clustered around his person, slowly marching to the Mosque, yet the next second scurrying like cowards and leaving only a few of us to mourn my grandfather's death.

I was very bitter at that time. The behavior of my grandfather's so-called friends distressed me so deeply that I had no wish then to reign as King of Jordan and it was with relief that I learned that my father, who was being treated in Switzerland, appeared to be recovering. On his return I hoped I could go back to Victoria, away from the power lust and avarice that followed my grandfather's death as rapacious politicians fought for the crumbs of office, sullen, determined, hating each other, like the money-hungry relatives who gather at the reading of the will.

Within a matter of hours the politicians were starting to fight. There were those who whispered, Was my father well enough to succeed to the throne? They were the ones who hoped he would never reign, simply because they themselves wanted power. Powerless for the moment, I was forced to watch how some of his former friends changed without a thought for our country; I saw his great work jeopardized by weakness on the part of those around him, by the way they permitted opportunists to step in, even if it meant the ruin of little Jordan.

2

A Prince at Harrow

"I was rather unhappy at first."

MY GRANDFATHER had wanted me to go to Harrow, but shortly before his death I managed to persuade him that I would do better if I stayed on at Victoria College in Alexandria where I was already settled so well. I had been there for two years and was almost ready to take my school certificate in the summer of 1951 and wanted very much to pass. So after much discussion, my grandfather agreed.

When he was killed so suddenly, however, everything changed. It was felt that the antagonistic Egyptian attitude toward Jordan had played its part in Jordan's crisis. Cairo's continued attacks on Jordan had made relations between the two countries bitter and angry. As Crown Prince—which I had become automatically—it was impossible for me to return to school in Egypt. So I had to start all over again.

My father was still in Europe and until he could return it was necessary for me to remain in Jordan. I could not stomach the squabbling I saw around me, the politicians jockeying for position, arguing as to whether or not my father should be King. I ignored most of them as much as possible. My uncle, Sherif Nasser, returned from Iraq, and with a cousin, Sherif Zaid, we formed a trio and concentrated on meeting the people of my country. We toured everywhere and spent many nights in the desert. It was much more rewarding, and most enjoyable.

Eventually my father returned and then, with a heavy heart, I set off for England to a new school, attended by boys I did not know (except my cousin Feisal), who played Rugby instead of football, and whose colloquial English was bound to complicate the strain of fitting into a new educational pattern.

The school chosen was Harrow, and I was, in fact, rather unhappy at first during my early months there in 1952. I do not think it was entirely my fault. I could not fit in with the other boys easily. I immediately discovered that my English pronunciation was far worse than I had imagined. After two years at an English-speaking school in Egypt, I found that an entirely different language was spoken at Harrow. In Alexandria we spoke English with a lilt and at a leisurely pace. At Harrow, everybody seemed to gabble at double speed. On the few occasions when my schoolmates deigned to talk to me in those first few weeks, I could not understand them half the time.

In class it was even worse. I had done well at Alexandria and now I tried my best. But the difficulties were so great that frequently I could not even start to learn my lessons properly. In Alexandria my main subjects had centered around the Arabic language, but now I had to start to *think* in English. My best subjects at Harrow were history and English literature, but at first the extra strain of trying to understand as well as learn was enormous.

Psychologically, too, I was at a disadvantage. Most youngsters learn gradually how to be a public-school student. In
using the term "public school," I am, of course, referring to a
type of institution that, in England, is more or less equivalent
to the private schools of America. Preparatory schools in England lay the foundations, and the whole process of becoming
a senior public-school boy follows a well-defined pattern. But
I had never even seen the inside of such a public school until
I was sixteen. I knew nothing of the rigid codes and shib-
boleths that existed among the boys of Harrow. At sixteen I
was more "raw" than the newest drudge. Yet paradoxically I
was far more adult than they were in non-scholastic matters.
Because of my grandfather's teaching, my position at home
and what I had been through, I was a man among boys.

Perhaps this was the reason that I was not immediately
accepted; or maybe this is an attitude that all boys take to
newcomers. I felt it more keenly than most because sixteen
is so late to join Harrow or any English public school. I
also imagine they regarded me as a bit of an oddity. It may
seem a trifling reason for being a fish out of water, but Feisal
and I were just about the only two boys at Harrow who did
not have surnames. English public-school boys are sticklers
for protocol (they are much more rigid than we are in our
palaces in Amman!) and they could not accustom themselves
to switching from names like Smith, Minor or Brown, Major
to just Hussein—and so very rarely called me anything at all.

As I struggled to settle down, wandering alone in the corridors of that wonderful school, trying to grapple with my
study assignments, searching for a friendly smile in the sea of
faces at meals, I tried to analyze what separated us. They all
seemed so sure of themselves; they all had their own sets of
friends, and actually many of them seemed to me to be rather
snobbish. In those first weeks, my conversations consisted

almost entirely of "Good morning," "Good afternoon" or "Good evening," and I sometimes felt lucky if anybody bothered to answer me at all.

Even the food was different and, though not bad by ordinary public-school standards, I longed occasionally for some Arab dishes, such as tea that tasted like tea, and coffee that tasted like coffee. Britain was still severely rationed. We needed coupons for sweets and I seem to remember that we were allowed only one egg a week.

But youth is resilient. Oddly enough, the first thing I began to enjoy was this very food I had begun by despising. I suddenly realized how much I liked the eating habits of the English, especially the regularity with which food appeared—breakfast, a snack at eleven, lunch, tea and supper. One wonderful day, canned peaches were de-rationed. We wallowed in them, and to this day I never eat peaches without remembering the tins I used to take into my room in the evenings.

Gradually everything began to sort itself out, almost without my noticing it. One day I seemed to be lonely, the next I was surrounded by friends. I enjoyed playing Rugby enormously. I played scrum half, and I remember the glow felt one day when a boy threw me a long, low pass, shouting, "Get moving, Hussein! It's all yours."

I escaped "fagging," the British public-school institution in which younger boys perform various menial chores for the seniors, such as making toast or shining shoes. I was too old for it by the time I arrived, though too young to have such service myself.

I had a small room, on one wall of which I carved my initials. It was a funny little room, containing the most extraordinary bed I have ever seen. Made of rope and canvas, it fitted into the wall during the day so that when I had made it up each morning it would be pushed back and hidden while I used my room as a study. As extra furniture I was allowed to buy a small wooden desk and a strip of carpet. Otherwise I had one upholstered armchair, and a cupboard in which I kept my clothes and an assortment of tinned food to supplement school meals.

I arose about seven o'clock each morning and after my "tosh" (cold bath), which I rather disliked, I tidied my room, polished my shoes and made sure my trousers were neatly pressed. (I achieved this by putting them under the mattress during the night.) I enjoyed looking after myself. I have always been neat, though I hope not finicky, and I liked polishing my shoes and took great pleasure in keeping my study spotless. I think I was subconsciously starting to live more of the life for which I yearned—that of an independent man making his own way.

I liked the challenge, and the knowledge that the results were entirely up to me.

In addition to our regular lessons, I took extra courses in the Arabic language, and fencing, for my grandfather had always been very proud of my ability at this sport.

I also found, a little to my surprise, that I was in need of extra tutoring in another subject. This was dancing. A special course was arranged for me with a lady instructor near the school. One afternoon a week I went to the dance studio where a lady partner was awaiting me. An elderly lady provided the only accompaniment on a rather tinny piano, beating out a steady rhythm as I plodded my way through the fox trot, waltz and the South American dances.

But above all else, at Harrow I first enjoyed a pleasure not included in the curriculum. A friend of my father's presented me with my first automobile. It was a sky-blue Rover. I had

learned to drive in Amman but it had never been satisfactory
since I had always to borrow the family car. Now at last I had
my own, and almost the first thing I did was to get a driving
license. Ridiculous though it may seem, I could never get a
license when driving in Amman. Nobody would take the responsibility of authorizing me to drive. They knew I was driving, but giving permission for me to do so was another thing.
In fact, I had to go all the way to Britain to get a license to
drive in Jordan! For with my British license, I had the right
to an international license—which included Jordan. So when
I returned as King, it was with a British driving license.

Garaging the new Rover posed a problem. It could not be
garaged at school, but after a day in London, the Jordanian
Ambassador, who was driving me back to school, suggested
that we look for a garage as near Harrow as possible.

We found it at a place called Sudbury, about a mile from
the school. There for the first time I met Maurice Raynor,
who has worked in Jordan almost ever since. Raynor was a
man whose only interest in life was cars. I was a boy who
shared exactly the same passion. We got on together fa-
mously from the first moment. Raynor found a little lock-up
near the main garage where he had just been appointed manager. I got into the habit of going down to Sudbury just to
sit and chat with him. I was allowed a certain amount of
leave and together we invented new ideas for making my
beautiful car even more attractive. We put little lights everywhere; we fitted eagles on the sides which lit up at night. I
became so enthusiastic that if I could not go to the garage
I would telephone Raynor and he would come out to me,
so that we could talk about the car.

When I had received my English driving license, I said to

Raynor, "You're an expert, do you really think you can drive faster than I can?"

Raynor looked a bit startled and said with some caution: "Sir, I really cannot tell."

"Let's find out," I said. "Come on, get the Rover out."

We drove until we came to a stretch of road not far from Sudbury. I drove from A to B. Raynor timed me with a stop watch. When I got to point B we turned the Rover around and I timed Raynor as he drove the car to A.

This was the start of my love for fast cars and very soon I began to think of bigger and better ones. Then I had a stroke of luck. I received another wonderful gift—this time a Bristol, a beautiful maroon sedan (the color known as Bristol Red) that would do ninety miles an hour without trying.

I took my cousin Feisal out in it once—strictly against orders. We naturally became very close friends at Harrow. We were both a little different from the other boys and that threw us into each other's company. But poor Feisal was never allowed to leave school during term. It seemed to me a wicked shame, so one weekend I smuggled him out of Harrow and we went for a drive. He loved cars, but as his father had been killed in a car crash, there was an absolute veto on speeding when Feisal was in a car.

With this in mind I thought it better not to drive Feisal myself, so I let Raynor drive and sat with Feisal—and kept my eyes off the speedometer as we raced along the flat road past Northolt Airport.

Life at Harrow, however, did not consist solely of driving fast cars or eating canned peaches. We had to work hard. But what I liked about Harrow was that, though the discipline was strict in some respects, a boy of sixteen was allowed considerable liberty and given many privileges as long as he didn't abuse them. I am all in favor of teachers allowing boys to discipline themselves so that a boy growing to manhood is given the opportunity to prove himself capable of behaving like a man, and so earn special privileges. If he worked hard at Harrow, and made progress, he earned the right to use his leisure as he thought best. Without doubt this is why the best British public schools have such a formative influence on character in later life. It is no accident that so many national leaders come from the British public schools.

The academic side at Harrow was first-class and I received an enormous amount of attention. Equally important, however, was the fact that I was not only expected to work hard, but to learn how to accept punishment and to face up to the difficulties in life. A young boy had to do the menial jobs according to custom, however rich he was. An older boy had to learn tolerance in his treatment of younger boys serving him. This is good training. So, too, is the fact that at a school like Harrow everybody is equal. My youngest brother is now at my old school. I believe profoundly that boys who may one day inherit responsibility must learn to mix and see all the facets of life.

I do not see how a man in these modern times can rule a country unless he knows something more of its people than what he learns from his advisers. Nor can a man be a good officer unless he has gone through the ranks and so understands the problems of, and sympathizes with, the men in his command.

I look back on my schooldays at Harrow as one of the most vital periods of my training for the responsibility I was later to assume.

Nowadays I number many old Harrovians as my friends. I still feel great pride because I went to Harrow. It gives me real pleasure to wear my Harrovian tie and I shall always be glad that I attended one of the greatest schools in the world.

If I have any criticism of the British public-school system, it is this: I believe the way in which boys are cut off from the outside world each term tends to increase any natural shyness and thus makes them too remote from everyday life. You cannot expect a boy of sixteen to live like a monk for several months, be let loose into the world for a few weeks and then be returned to the monastery. It is too unsettling. School life is a preparation for the battle for existence and only the strong can overcome this unbalanced life. But there are run-of-the-mill boys at school as well as potential leaders and they would benefit if they were given more preparation for the future instead of being kept so isolated.

I know I longed for a breath of the real world, not only to enjoy myself, but as a contrast to the make-believe of Harrow. I know, too, that Feisal felt the same way.

I think also, on reflection, that there is on the whole too much "roughing it" at Harrow and other British public schools. This sort of thing can be overdone. I do believe in youngsters being toughened so they can cope with what is in store for them, but without exaggeration.

The only time Feisal or I ever experienced a privilege denied the others was when a visiting diplomat interrupted our lessons. Our names would be called out in class—and how welcome each visitor was as a break from the routine of French or math!

Once, too, we escaped our lessons when we were interviewed by a group of Egyptian journalists. This sort of conference was arranged by our embassies; we only (very willingly) did as we were told.

The newspapermen first went to see Feisal and one of them asked him if I had a nickname.

"He certainly has," replied Feisal. "The boys here call him Hussie."

Next the journalists came to interview me. I took them to my room, showed them my wonderful bed (which intrigued them as much as it did me) and then one of them asked:

"I hear the boys call you Hussie."

"Hussie? I've never heard the name," I replied.

"That's what we heard," said one.

"Who told you?" I asked.

"Feisal," said another journalist.

"Oh, did he?" Some boys happened to be passing and I shouted to them, "What do you call me?"

They all answered "Hussein."

"And what do you call Feisal?"

"Fuzz," one replied.

And "Fuzz" was what King Feisal became in an Egyptian newspaper the following morning. I did not think it prudent to tell the other boys that "fuzz" in Arabic means "aloof."

Most of our visitors, however, were on a diplomatic level. I was now heir to the throne, and so Jordanian government leaders would come to see me whenever they visited England. Invariably I was kept fully informed about the state of my father's health, and at first I was very hopeful that his mental condition was improving.

At forty-one he had everything to offer his country. Born

in Mecca, he had studied at Sandhurst, learning to be a soldier, and then joined the Arab Legion as a cavalry officer. After a period as a judge of the Tribal Courts, he had at times acted as deputy in my grandfather's absence.

How wonderful it would be if his health permitted him to rule. But the occasional warning filled me with doubt. Once I had to be excused during a period in order to receive a personal telephone call from the family in Amman asking whether I would meet them in Paris. It was obvious my father's health was causing deep concern, and I knew that if anything happened I would have to return.

I hated the idea. I loved my family. I loved my country, but I felt the responsibility of leading Jordan and serving it was far too much for me to undertake. At this time I did not want to be King. Not only was I disillusioned by the way I had seen men react to my grandfather's death, but I wanted, before it was too late, to live a normal life. I wanted to finish my education and then get a job on my own merits. It did not matter what it was; I wanted to prove that I was capable of holding down an ordinary job, not to impress other people. It was a dream I never realized.

The summer term ended at Harrow, and though I was by now enjoying myself, like any other schoolboy I was delighted at the prospect of the holidays. As soon as we broke up, I went to the Beau Rivage Hotel on Lake Geneva where my mother, who was receiving medical treatment, and my brothers and sister were due to meet me. The first few days were heavenly. The summer of 1952 was glorious and world affairs seemed remote from that corner of Switzerland where everything marches in such orderly fashion.

On the morning of August 12, my mother and the others went out shopping in the arcades that branch off the Place St. François. I was alone in my bedroom looking at the swans on the lake and the white steamer coming into port, when there was a knock on the door and a hotel page came in with a cablegram on a silver tray. I did not need to open it to know that my days as a schoolboy had ended. One glance at the envelope was enough. It was addressed to "His Majesty, King Hussein."

I looked out of the balcony, holding the envelope in my hand. For a long time I did not open it. What I had always feared had come to pass. The very title on the envelope told its story with such brutal frankness that the message inside was superfluous.

It was still nine o'clock in the morning and the heat had not yet seized upon the day. With a sigh, I slit open the envelope. The message was from the Prime Minister advising me with that cold courtesy typical of diplomacy that he regretted my father had abdicated and I was now King of Jordan. The decision, he informed me, had been taken by the two Houses of Parliament and my presence in Jordan was expected as soon as possible.

There it was, the moment I had dreaded. At seventeen I knew the end of a dream. I would never be a schoolboy again. Would I ever even live the life of a private individual? All my hopes were shattered by that cablegram, and I shall never forget the shock from the fateful envelope the page so casually handed me.

How hard my father had struggled to overcome his mental illness! How brave had been his efforts, not only for his own sake, but because he knew his country needed him. My imagination flew from the stilted furniture of the Louis Quinze bedroom, the big windows looking out on the unruffled waters of the lake, and suddenly I was back in Amman—so different, brown instead of green, high in the mountains, the dust swirling in the streets, the motley crowds. I could imagine the turmoil in the Basman Palace where I would shortly be. How wicked of me to wallow in self-pity when my father, so far away, had suffered so much.

It was hard to realize the drama and the desperate sadness of what must have taken place the previous day. Only later did I learn the truth about August 11. I had known in my heart—we had all known—that my father's mental condition was such that he could not rule the country much longer. He was a victim of schizophrenia, which had grown increasingly worse during the twelve months since he ascended the throne.

But we had still dared to hope. Like any wife and son, my mother and I had hoped until all hope was gone that he would recover. Now we knew at last what we had refused to admit. His reign was at an end. Only a month before, I received the cable telling of his return to Amman after seeking treatment in Europe. His popularity as monarch was enormous, but even before he returned he must have known that his future was in doubt, for he sent a cable—and in retrospect how honest yet pathetic it sounds—to the Prime Minister saying, "I am coming back to my country to put myself sincerely at your disposal."

On the morning of August 11, both houses of the Jordanian Parliament met in private for ten hours while the King rested in his palace. The Prime Minister at that time was Tewfik Pasha Abdul Huda. Gravely he told the House that the King, my father, was no longer fit to exercise his constitutional powers. "Much though I hate to say so," he said, "I fear that there is little use in waiting for His Majesty's recovery from his schizophrenia." The Prime Minister submitted to the two houses of Parliament reports on my father's health made a month previously by two foreign doctors and other reports made by three Jordanian doctors.

Our constitution contains an article specifically stating that in the event of any Jordanian King being incapacitated by mental illness, the Council of Ministers has the right to invite Parliament to meet. If the illness is confirmed, the Parliamentary body has the right to depose the King and transfer the royal prerogative to his heir.

That is what had happened. The Committee's decision was adopted and by a majority vote they resolved to terminate the rule of my father. So, at the age of seventeen, I became the King of Jordan after only a few months at Harrow. I was too young to be a king in anything but name and in my absence a Regency Council of three was formed.

Even so, I had to return swiftly to Amman. Putting the envelope in my pocket I went downstairs to the hotel courtyard and into my car. It took me only a few minutes to reach the Place St. François in the heart of Lausanne, and I parked my car and looked into one or two shops until I found my mother.

"It's come." I handed her the cable.

She put her arm on my shoulder and then returned with me to the hotel. I sat down in front of the small French writing table and composed a cable to the Prime Minister advising him that I would return as soon as possible and that I would be pleased and honored to serve my country and the Arab world to the best of my ability.

Within a matter of days I said good-by to Europe and flew back to Amman.

3

A King at Sandhurst

"Only once did I get C.B."

I FLEW BACK to Jordan in a BOAC Argonaut after the news of my father's abdication, and when we touched down at Mafraq airstrip I hardly knew what to expect from my new life. I had left Jordan a prince, I returned a king.

It was a very hot afternoon and a vast number of officials jammed the airfield to receive me. I inspected the Guard of Honor and shook hands with scores of my country's leaders. I remember seeing Glubb Pasha of the Arab Legion standing there telling his beads.

This was my official welcome home. It was genuine and warm but inevitably protocol and formality dominated it. I thought, as we walked in solemn procession toward the waiting cars, "This is what it will always be like now that I am King. People will never be able to unbend." Then I remember also thinking, "All the same, I'm going to have a jolly good try at getting them to unbend."

How different only a few days before, driving unrecognized along the shores of Lake Geneva! How different, only a short while before, a schoolboy eating canned peaches after study hours. That life had ended. Never again would I be able to escape the barriers that surround a monarch. But there again, I was determined to remove as many of those barriers as possible, and try to bring about more of a family spirit in my country.

The royal car was awaiting me, and I climbed in, driving slowly up the short airport road and turning left for Amman.

As my car swung out of the airport, which had been very closely guarded, and we set off toward the capital, something happened. Though Arab Legion troops lined the streets, I suddenly found myself in the midst of frenzied crowds screaming, shouting, dancing and crying, "Long live Hussein! Welcome to Hussein!" They knew nothing of protocol or diplomatic niceties. As they cheered, some tried to stop the car by clambering on the running boards. Then the troops, powerless to keep order any longer, joined in the melee. It was a fantastic welcome.

Lausanne and England seemed very far away from the pale brown stone houses and desert sweeping to the skyline. On the flight out I had felt lonely and depressed, but all my miserable forebodings evaporated as I drove toward the Basman Palace. I could not have explained why, for though the cheering excited me, I was not then as well versed in crowd psychology as I am now. Since that day I have had much experience with crowds—ugly or otherwise—and can instinctively and quickly judge the temper of a mass of people. But I was unable to analyze the reason for my sudden happiness. I did not realize that the crowd was not only cheering, but sending out waves of sympathy and encouragement to a boy of seven-

teen suddenly a king. It was a very curious, exhilarating emotion, as though my subjects were sharing the day with me
rather than merely applauding me.

The Prime Minister was sitting next to me and as we
turned up the hill to the palace I remarked, "No man could
receive a welcome like this without promising himself and
God to do everything to justify the people's faith. I hope they
realize I am going to do this."

Though my journey from Lausanne had been both men-
tally and physically exhausting, I retired to bed that night a
very happy man and awoke the following morning refreshed
and eager to face any problem.

I did not know what my immediate duties would be, for I
had to wait several months before assuming my constitutional
powers at eighteen—actually, just before eighteen, as my age
was determined by the Arabic calendar. In the intervening
months, the Regency Council would continue to rule, and I
decided that I would profit from this period by getting better
acquainted with my people, mastering the technical intri-
cacies of my new life, though without wielding any power.

In the beginning, this is exactly what happened. In order
to meet my subjects at close quarters, I made a three-weeks'
tour of my country in which I visited every major city and
town, and scores of villages, and met thousands of Jordanians. I traveled, sometimes by air, sometimes by car, to the
remotest corners of my kingdom. It was a wonderful experience to see for myself, among the people who formed the
backbone of Jordan, how devoted they were to their King and
country.

At one Bedouin encampment where I attended a *mansef*

(an Arab feast), hundreds of tribesmen danced, fired their guns in the air and made me join in the dancing, and as I stood there, the brown tents merging into the desert, I thought to myself, With men like these, Jordan will always be secure.

But when the tour was over, what next? I am a restless individual who cannot bear idleness. What could I do? What did happen was the one thing I had dreamed of, but could not believe would ever occur.

One morning my uncle, Sherif Nasser, and the Prime Minister came to see me. We talked at first of unimportant matters. Servants brought in small glasses of sweet tea with mint leaves floating in them. Then my uncle, a very kindly and wise man, who has stood four-square by my side throughout my reign, turned to me and said:

"Do you think, Your Majesty, you will employ your time profitably, staying here till your accession to the throne?"

"Can you suggest anything better for me to do?" I asked him.

"Yes, I can," he replied. "Something far better. Something I know your father would like you to do—and something your grandfather would have wished."

Suddenly I realized what my uncle was driving at. My heart leaped.

"You mean—Sandhurst?"

My uncle nodded. "Why not?" he asked. "Your father went to Sandhurst. I remember him telling me that Sandhurst is the greatest military academy in the world and the finest place for a man to learn to be a king."

My mind flashed back to a day many years before. I was playing soldiers on the hearth rug, and my father turned to

me and said (and this was many years before he was king):
"No man can rule a country without discipline. No man can
be a good soldier without discipline. And nowhere in the
world do they teach men discipline like they do at Sandhurst."

What a wonderful chance! Though I was prepared to do
anything my country demanded, my accession had been so
sudden, and I was so young, that I was overjoyed at the prospect of living just a little longer as an ordinary man. It was a
respite, a breathing space. And at seventeen, six months is a
long, long time.

The Prime Minister and General Glubb attended to the
details and arranged with the War Office that I should have a
special shortened course, cramming the regular curriculum
into six months. Almost exactly a month after the news that
proclaimed me king had reached me in Lausanne, I changed
my royal title and became Officer Cadet King Hussein of the
Royal Military Academy, Sandhurst. I remember I was allotted room 109, Inkerman Company, the Old College. It was
September 9, 1952.

A new world opened up for me at Sandhurst. Looking back
on those carefree days (carefree providing one did not flout
discipline) I think in many ways they were the most formative of my life. There was a great difference between Harrow
and Sandhurst. I had liked Harrow but there I had been
treated as a boy. At Sandhurst I was treated as a man—an
ordinary man. I was given responsibilities and trusted. I had
to study hard, yet my studies were more interesting than at
Harrow. We Arabs are a martial people, so perhaps I took
easily to the tough life of a cadet. I enjoyed the discipline; I

liked my military training and the atmosphere of Sandhurst.

On my first day the Commandant welcomed me and gave me a short lecture on the traditions of Sandhurst and hoped I would benefit from them. Then he looked me in the eye and said:

"I would like to give you one of two choices. Sandhurst is a very tough place. Men who come here have to work hard—harder perhaps than anywhere else in the world. The courses are arduous. The life here demands enormous reserves of strength and will power. Do you think you can take that—or would you rather have a special course without the rough-and-tumble we give to other cadets? But I must warn you that if you choose the hard way, you will be treated like everyone else."

Of course, I chose the hard way. I never dreamed of anything else, for I was determined to make the best possible use of this heaven-sent opportunity. Because of my short course I even had extra spells of drill and marching. I took part in night assaults across rough country. I learned to fire modern weapons and did my utmost to understand the essentials of military science.

Just over two months after that first morning, I was summoned to the Commandant's office. It was 10:30 A.M. and, because I had already entered into the life and spirit of Sandhurst (which meant fun as well as work), my first thought was, My God, what have I done? The sly innuendoes of my fellow cadets did not reassure me.

Nervously I went in and saluted. He looked very stern, but perhaps he was only preoccupied, for suddenly he said:

"Hussein, I am very happy with your work. I've been watching you and I think it's time you were promoted to an intermediate cadet. At this rate, you should become a senior in another two months. Keep it up. You are doing very well."

I did keep it up, for though I had a great deal of fun at Sandhurst—what cadet doesn't?—at the back of my mind I always realized that there was one difference between the other cadets and me. They would rise to be officers, perhaps even generals. But I would very soon be commander-in-chief of my country's entire military forces and I was determined to learn so much about army affairs that men of the Arab Legion would not easily bluff me.

I knew, too, that the discipline of Sandhurst was nothing to the self-discipline I would need to keep my throne in the years to come. Discipline and work. I had seen enough of Europe, even at seventeen, to know that its playgrounds were filled with ex-kings, some of whom had lost their thrones because they did not understand the duties of a monarch. I was not going to become a permanent member of their swimming parties in the South of France.

But the wonderful thing about an academy like Sandhurst is that, though the discipline is strict and one must work hard, once a cadet is off duty he can forget it. It has never been possible since, for as a monarch I can almost never be off duty. But at Sandhurst, the moment a spell of leave started, all cares were forgotten until the moment I reported in.

Some of my short leaves were semiformal, for I was always offered special facilities to learn about the outside world, occasionally with highly embarrassing results, as when I found myself sitting on the left-hand side of the judge at the Old Bailey in London. I was delighted to have this opportunity of seeing British justice in action and settled down to watch attentively as the judge tried a case.

The defendant stood in the dock; the atmosphere was charged with the dignity of the law as the case proceeded. The judge was stern. At times he turned to me kindly to explain a point of law.

All went well until the case was reaching its dramatic climax. One could sense the tension, and as one counsel sat down, there was a hush of expectancy; then without warning, the shrill bell of an alarm clock tore the silence to shreds.

I caught a glimpse of the judge's startled, incredulous face beneath his wig. The barristers started as though they had been shot. And since it was obvious where the ringing came from, all eyes were frostily turned toward the King of Jordan.

How I must have blushed! I stammered out an apology to the judge while with my right hand I tried frantically to switch off the bell of my prized possession, an alarm wrist watch.

As order was restored I looked furtively at the watch—it was *always* set for the time I had to get up. Why was it set now to ring at 11:30 A.M.?

Some cadets, knowing I was going to the Old Bailey, had fixed it. I learned later that while I was having a shower, they had set the alarm for a time when they knew I would be sitting in court.

I had to wait, but I got my revenge. It happened in this way. We all had bicycles at Sandhurst, either rented or issued to us. We had wheel locks so that other cadets could not borrow them. We used them to cycle to classes from one building to another.

One morning I had allowed myself a bare two minutes to reach a lecture on military science. I ran for my bicycle only to find its tires flat. One look at the valve—the unscrewed valve—and it was clear that this was somebody's idea of a joke. I ran all the way to the lecture hall, arriving puffing and blowing—and late. The lecturer looked at me.

"Ah, Hussein! Good morning. How nice of you to come!" he said sarcastically.

After the lecture I tried to discover who had done it, but not a hope. So that evening, when there was no one about, I crept down from my little room and, under cover of darkness, undid the valves of at least thirty bicycles—taking the precaution of hiding my own behind the guardroom. I might have been suspected, but nobody ever proved who did it.

Only once did I have a spell of "C.B." (confined to barracks) at Sandhurst. I managed, however, to get out of it by confessing to a crime I did not commit.

The trouble started on a Friday night. I was not even at Sandhurst, but spending the evening in London celebrating my birthday. It was near the end of the term, which the cadets were celebrating with mock battles and—accidentally or deliberately—one cadet rang the fire alarm at the college.

There was pandemonium. Within a few minutes a fleet of fire engines sped in from Camberley. Others rushed in from neighboring fire stations. Soon the Old College at Sandhurst was ringed with fire apparatus of all sorts. Eager firemen in helmets and hip boots panted for action. The only thing lacking was a fire. Instead there was the biggest row Sandhurst had had for years. The College Commander was furious. By the time I returned late at night and signed in, the fire engines had gone, Sandhurst was asleep, everything looked normal, and I did not have the faintest idea of the wrath that was to fall on us all the next morning.

Early parade, breakfast, the first lessons proceeded in a

state of uneasy expectation. As it was a Saturday, all of us had weekend passes and most of us had made plans.

During the last period before lunch (and leave), the blow fell. We were all ordered to parade in front of the College Commander at one o'clock.

Looking sterner than I can ever remember him, he came straight to the point.

"Will the officer cadet who rang the fire alarm please step forward?" he demanded.

There was silence. Not a man stirred.

The C.O. waited, growing visibly angrier, but managing to control himself.

"Please step forward, the man who rang the fire alarm," he repeated.

Still no answer.

"Very well," the C.O. said briskly. "The entire college will be confined to barracks as of midnight until the cadet responsible owns up. Gentlemen, you are dismissed."

Nobody knew who had done it. We all waited, anxiously counting the minutes and still hoping to get off to London. But nobody owned up.

I felt it was a little hard on cadets like myself—and there were quite a few of us—who had been elsewhere when the incident occurred and could not therefore be guilty. But there was nothing we could do about it.

All Sunday morning we waited. Finally, by the afternoon it was obvious that nobody was going to own up, and I decided something had to be done about it. I requested permission to meet the College Commander. I donned my smartest uniform and was shortly afterward summoned to his presence. As I walked in and closed the door, I gave him the best salute Sandhurst had taught me and said: "Good afternoon, sir."

"Well, Hussein, what do you want?"

"I did it, sir!" I blurted out.

"You did what?"

"I rang the fire alarm, sir."

He looked at me in amazement. "What on earth do you mean?"

"I rang the fire alarm," I insisted.

"May I inquire, Hussein"— his voice took on a sarcastic edge—"how it was possible for you to ring a fire alarm when you were in London?"

"That's perfectly true, sir," I replied, "but if that's the case, sir, there were a lot of other cadets in London as well."

For one moment I thought he was going to explode. Then he saw the humorous side of it.

My "confession" resulted in victory for all those cadets known to have been out of college at the time, for our "C.B." was canceled. It was considered a great victory by some cadets at Sandhurst. I am still pleased with myself when I think of it.

I had a special reason for wanting leave, for I was preparing to try out my new car at Goodwood race track. I had progressed a long way since the Rover and the Bristol. I had kept in touch with Maurice Raynor, who used to run the garage near Harrow, and it was with Raynor that I acquired the fastest car of all.

I rather fancy that when I left Harrow, Raynor thought we would never meet again. He certainly could not have realized that he would shortly leave his garage in Harrow and start life afresh with his family in Amman. When I settled in at Sandhurst I telephoned him.

"Why don't you come and see me?" I asked him.

He was a little surprised, perhaps because Sandhurst is about forty miles from Harrow, but as I still had the Rover garaged at Harrow, I suggested he should drive over. And when he arrived, I said to him: "I think we should try to buy an Aston Martin."

His face lit up. He had never driven an Aston Martin and was delighted when I asked him to look after it. I arranged for the registration number plate, B3 (to denote it was my third British car), and when it arrived, black and beautiful, capable of 120 miles an hour, I sent for Raynor again.

"Why don't we race it?" I asked. I knew Raynor had always dreamed of racing cars.

"Make all the inquiries," I told him, "enter it in my name, with yourself as driver, at the next Goodwood race meeting."

Raynor took the car to Goodwood and did some practicing. Then a week before the race, I unfortunately suggested having the car super-tuned for the big event.

Something went wrong. Raynor insists that the Jordan Embassy, afraid of the speeds at which I drove, exerted pressure with the garage and told them to slow it up. It was certainly in perfect condition when we put it in for super-tuning, but when Raynor phoned on the Thursday morning before the race, the garage told him the car was not really good enough. Raynor was crestfallen. "I was hoping to show you, sir, how good I am," he told me glumly as we went to the track together.

I drove it round a few circuits, but we never did race the Aston Martin. Perhaps it was just as well.

The car I kept at Sandhurst became known as the "People's car," because most weekends it was jammed with cadets going on leave. In fact, I became a chauffeur for them and the "People's car" was a highly popular institution at Sandhurst.

On the whole I drove carefully, though I did have one big crash—and as with my "C.B." I took the blame, though I was not driving.

It was half term—three whole, glorious days without drills or marches or lessons. A few of us decided to visit London. Among the party were some Malayan cadets, very likable chaps. A friend asked me for a turn at the wheel.

"Of course," I replied. It was well after midnight, and it was raining as we drove along Knightsbridge delivering friends to their flats or homes. Suddenly the "People's car" slithered on the oily surface and I saw ahead of us a lamppost or a bus stop. I leaned over and grabbed the wheel, at the same time shouting, "For God's sake jam the brakes on!"

Unfortunately, the accelerator was applied instead.

The car spun round in the middle of Knightsbridge—happily the roads were empty—and utterly out of control, went head-on toward a billboard. There was nothing to be done. We ducked and the car smashed its way straight through the wooden structure. The car lurched to a stop. I had banged my legs badly.

"Change places quickly!" I cried. "If anybody asks any questions, remember, I was driving. It'll be easier."

We scrambled over each other before the police arrived. We seemed to be in a deserted brickyard. I tried the door to see if it was jammed, but it opened.

"I'd better see how we stand," I suggested, and stepped out—straight down into a ditch half filled with water. I climbed out, my dinner jacket covered with mud. The bill-board concealed an old bombed-out site, and I had fallen into it feet first.

Covered with mud and slime, I watched apprehensively as two policemen arrived and began to question us. By sheer coincidence, one of them had served in the Palestine Police and had even met my grandfather, so after answering questions I spent several minutes signing autographs at three o'clock in the morning.

The police were very obliging and appreciated the truth—that nobody could have prevented the skid (though I thought it better not to mention the difference between an accelerator and a brake). But one thing really worried me. There would be an awful hullabaloo when the press got hold of the story, as they certainly would.

I racked my brains for a solution. Incredibly, the car could still move. The front was smashed in, but it was possible to drive slowly. After we got it back on the road, I decided on a course of action.

Very gently I drove back to the Dorchester and as soon as I got to my room I telephoned to Raynor, where I still garaged the Rover.

"I've had a smash-up," I announced. "No time for questions. Can you get the Rover ready? I'll collect it in half an hour."

Raynor said he could. I had a quick shower and several cups of coffee, then drove the wreck slowly out to Raynor's garage. There I took out the Rover—noticing that it had a small dent on one side. I drove back to the Jordanian Embassy. What I expected had happened. The steps were crowded with reporters. The Ambassador came out to meet me.

"Are you all right, sir?" he asked.

"Of course!" I replied, and turning to the newspapermen, I added, "Gentlemen, as you can see, it was nothing but a dent."

Much though I loved fast driving, it always had to take second place to slow marches. Actually, I had very little spare time at Sandhurst apart from weekend passes. I had to do so much extra work to catch up with the others that frequently I had extra classes when they were off duty, especially toward the end of term, when we had in turn to undertake various tasks to see how much we had learned.

For weeks I had dreaded the moment when I would be appointed orderly corporal. To me, this was a miserable job, and when my two weeks as orderly corporal started, it meant rising before 5 A.M., arranging the sick list before breakfast, collecting and distributing mail, opening offices, and several other jobs. I also had to be on hand all day to deal with unexpected problems.

The first evening I learned quite unofficially that there would be no early parade the following morning. This meant cadets would have an extra hour in bed and go straight to breakfast—all except Senior Cadet Hussein, who had to be up at five o'clock.

Well, nobody informed me officially of this change and as a good cadet I knew that an army runs only on official instructions. Since nobody had told me—rumor was my only guide—what could I do?

At 6:45 A.M., having already finished my general office work, I stamped up and down the corridors and yelled, "Six forty-five! Inkerman Company, time to get up. Six forty-five! Come on! Out of bed!"

A steady stream of abuse greeted me, but I ignored it with dignity.

I kept up my calling at five-minute intervals until 7:10 A.M. The abusive language was followed by a hail of boots and shoes—anything which angry cadets could grab in a hurry. I ducked as they flew around me and ran for the door. My Sandhurst-trained voice had not only awakened my own company but also the one on the floor below.

I had also wakened the senior sergeant, and after breakfast he sent for me. He looked at me stonily while I stood at attention before him.

"Hussein," he announced sarcastically, "it is quite obvious you do your job too well. You have nothing to learn as orderly corporal. You may return to your regular duties."

And that finished my five o'clock mornings at Sandhurst.

Toward the end of my time at Sandhurst, I completed a course of motorcycle driving. As a senior cadet it was always my ambition to borrow a Sandhurst motorbike and ride it to London, but I never achieved it. However, a few weeks before the term closed—just before my passing-out parade— I was driving a motorcycle across country in very bad weather. As I tried to turn a corner too soon, I skidded and the machine fell on top of me. When I untangled myself I was in great pain. I had hurt my left arm, yet I did not dare to say so; I was afraid I would be put on the sick list and miss the passing-out parade. As we reached the end of term, the arm got steadily worse. On the morning of the parade Company Sergeant-Major Cullen could see I was in trouble.

"Hussein," he said, "you'll never get through the parade like that. Wait a minute and I'll fetch you something that'll fix you up."

He returned a few minutes later, announcing, "It's a special mixture, you know. I'll not tell you what's in it, but I'll guarantee it'll last the parade."

It certainly did.

I never knew what was in the "special mixture" but it knocked the pain right out of my system for three hours.

In fact, my arm was far worse than I thought. After I left Sandhurst, I went on a tour of England, Scotland and Wales with my uncle, Sherif Nasser, and by the time we reached the Lake District, the pain was so bad I had to send for a doctor. He found a blood vessel was smashed and immediately put my arm in plaster.

"It will have to stay in plaster for a month," he declared flatly.

My left arm in a cast looked very impressive, but it was a confounded nuisance. I had worked hard for six months and now I wanted to enjoy my first holiday.

"It's no good," I said to my uncle after only one day, "I can't keep this thing on any longer."

"The doctor will certainly not take it off."

"Well, then—we will take it off. It can't be as difficult as all that. Wait till we get to the next stop."

When we reached a pleasant hotel, we signed in and then, in what I hoped was a deceptively casual manner, I asked an attendant:

"Could you lend me a pair of pliers or garden shears, please?"

He looked at me in astonishment, and I added, "I shan't need them for long."

After a while some workmanlike tools were brought.

"Perfect, thank you." I turned to my uncle. "And now, please, will you cut it off?"

His Majesty King Hussein I in his official uniform

With my mother

My enthusiasm for fast cars showed itself early.

My first privately owned airplane

My grandfather, King Abdullah, photographed when
the Arab armies entered Palestine

At Harrow in 1951

My cousin, the late King Feisal of Iraq, and his uncle, the Regent—a photograph taken during a visit to Sandhurst followed by a bitter quarrel

I become a crack shot at Sandhurst.

Ready for the passing-out parade

My father, the former King Talal

Two men who have served Jordan well. Sitting down next to me is Maurice Raynor who runs the royal garages and whom I first met at Harrow. In flying kit is Wing-Commander Jock Dalgleish, who taught me to fly.

President Nasser comes to
visit me in Jordan.

The late King Feisal and King Saud visit Amman for policy talks.

Inspecting the Arab Legion with Glubb Pasha

I talk to General Ali Abu Nuwar, a one-time friend who plotted my death.

One of Jordan's greatest patriots and one of my firmest friends, Prime Minister Hazza Majali, brutally murdered in a bomb outrage in 1960

The Treasury at Petra, one of the archaeological wonders of the world

The Camel Corps of the Arab Legion on parade

I give my wife a start in a Go-Kart race.

Wild Scenes in Amman on our wedding day

Muna and I shortly after our wedding

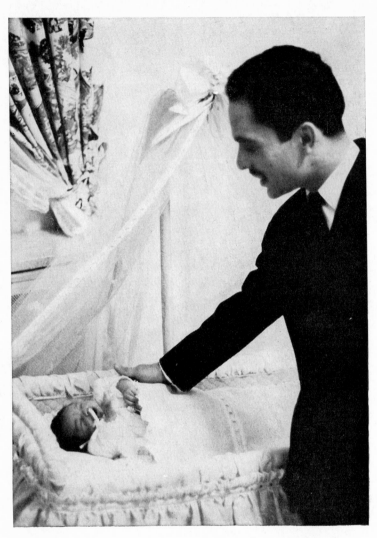

My son and heir

We cut the plaster away while the man looked on in horror, and I had a much more enjoyable tour without it—the last few days of what I call the Sandhurst phase of my life.

Soon it was time to return to Amman for my inauguration and we drove to London to prepare for the flight and the start of a new life.

But if the doctor in the Lake District who put me in plaster happens to read these words, I can assure him he was right. That arm still troubles me—because I did not obey doctor's orders.

4

My Inauguration as King
... Life in Jordan
... My First Marriage

"Most of us live very simply."

I WAS NOT quite eighteen when I assumed my constitutional powers on May 2, 1953, the same day that my cousin King Feisal assumed his responsibilities in Baghdad. But I was eighteen in the Moslem calendar. Nearly a year had passed since my father's reign ended, when I took the oath in the Parliament building at Amman as the first step in my inauguration as King. Great arches, gaily colored, had been erected over the main streets from the Palace to the Parliament building. Long before I got up, thousands of people had already started to line the streets for the procession. Flags flew from every building.

I awoke early that morning and lay in bed a little while, content to be alone with my thoughts. Ahead of me was the most momentous day of my life. When it ended I would be charged with the responsibility of leading and serving my country. I remember thinking, as I lay there before breakfast, "Am I any different than I was yesterday? Yesterday I could make no decisions. From today my life will consist of making one decision after another, all vital to Jordan." I prayed I would make the right ones.

At breakfast I could hardly eat. It was not excitement alone that took my appetite away; it was more a feeling of the immense implications of the step I was about to take. My life could never be the same again.

My uniform was laid out for me, and I started to dress. My ceremonial uniform is made of a heavy material, white for summer and dark blue for winter. It has golden epaulets, to be used only on State occasions. Soon after nine I was ready, and at nine-thirty I stepped into my car at the Basman Palace and set off on the procession. My car was escorted by cavalry of the Royal Guard, armed motorcyclists and other escorts. Slowly we made our way through cheering thousands of Jordanians to the Parliament building. The enthusiasm was tremendous and the troops lining the streets could hardly hold the crowds back. I knew that on an occasion like this I had to act with composure, but I must admit I had a lump in my throat all the time.

Once inside the Parliament building, the Prime Minister, the Regency Council and the Cabinet sat on my left, while my younger brother, my uncle and the chief officers of the Royal Palace ranged themselves on my right. The Prime Minister and the President of the Senate both expressed their wish that I should enjoy a happy and prosperous reign and then I stood up and took the oath of Jordan: "I swear by the name of God that I will preserve the constitution and be faithful to my people." I hope that I shall never forswear this oath. My promise of allegiance given, a salute of 101 guns from the Arab Legion announced my accession and full constitutional powers.

From the Parliament, I went to the Mosque for prayers and immediately afterward to my grandfather's tomb. Then I went to see my mother to receive her congratulations. She embraced me and told me how proud she was of me and what hopes she held for me.

"You will never forget this day," she said. "When you face difficulties in the future—and they're bound to come sooner or later—look back on this day. Remember then how the people of Jordan—thousands and thousands of them—showed their loyalty to you and their love and trust. But remember, my son, never let responsibility and power go to your head. God be with you."

This was only the first day of the celebrations. A short time later I was again greeted by enormous crowds, this time on the brown airfield that stands on the plateau only a few miles from Amman itself. A hundred thousand people jammed the field as I drove there to take the salute while five thousand troops of the Arab Legion passed in review. I could not help contrasting the differences between Sandhurst and this parade, the striking contrast between old and new as I saluted men with field guns and armored cars, wheeling in perfect formation, followed by troops of the desert patrol lumbering along on camels. Cavalry on white horses, armored vehicles, artillery, even boys from the Arab Legion schools— all had their part in this splendid review, the first of so many I have saluted since I became King.

As the march finished, I declared, "Jordan acknowledges

the brotherhood which links together all the people of the great Arab nation. Jordan is but a part of that Arab nation and the Arab Legion is only one of its armies."

Much of a monarch's work is routine. I started my reign as I meant to continue—by going each morning to my "office" in the Basman Palace just like any man with a day's work to do, and staying there until the day's work was done. The work is extremely varied. Since I planned from the very start to become the head of a family as much as the king of a country, I made myself accessible to all. A great deal of my time is taken up with a large variety of audiences from all walks of life, and at regular intervals contingents of tribal leaders visit me. All are welcome.

Not so long ago a group of Bedouin visited me and one by one shook my hand. Toward the end of the long, brown straggling line, I spied a little boy.

"Sir," he cried breathlessly when his turn came, "will you please help me? I want to go to school."

He had come with the other Bedouin. There was some dispute about his age, and a local school had refused to admit him. Since most of my Cabinet Ministers visit me regularly, it was not surprising the Minister of Education was present that morning. Such is the intimate, family feeling in Jordan that the boy was at school in three days.

The routine of the Palace works very smoothly. In charge is my Chief of Diwan. One might describe him as Chief of the

Royal Cabinet—my own Cabinet and my link with the government. But Diwan means other things. Originally, of course, it meant sofa (hence divan), then it became a room with sofas, then an office. Finally it also became a meeting in an office or a reception room. Thus I can say, "I am going to the Diwan," meaning "I am going to my office"; or "Where is my Chief of Diwan?"—"Where is the head of my personal Cabinet?"

Requests for audiences are filtered through my chief of protocol, but since he occupies an office in the palace next to mine, *anybody* can climb the steps of the palace and ask him to request an audience, or telephone for one.

If a request for an audience is refused, one can be sure that it is only because I have a full program. And that I do have! Sometimes I hardly know which way to turn. On a typical day recently I breakfasted at home, helicoptered to the Basman Palace—my office—and by nine o'clock received the first of three Ambassadors. At 10:30 A.M. I held a meeting of government and department heads to discuss Army and Air Force matters. I then discussed problems of our broadcasting station, and at one o'clock—when I was thinking of lunch!— my chief of protocol coughed gently and reminded me that a party of forty British university students had been promised an audience. I shook hands with each one and said a few words. By then lunchtime had passed, and I was due to hold a Cabinet meeting to hear plans for economic development. Before I left at 7 P.M. several visitors had briefer audiences with me. Letters had to be signed, documents studied. It was already dark, so I could not fly, but had to drive fifteen miles to the cottage where I live.

A great deal of nonsense is written about the opulent palaces of the Arab world. The truth is that most of us, descended from the frugal life of the Bedouin, live very simply. I myself have no personal fortune and, as you will presently read, my real home, where I return to my wife each night, is a two-story house where my wife and I cook breakfast on alternate mornings.

The King's palace does not of course belong to him. It belongs to the government and therefore it is bound to have an impersonal air. The Royal family in Jordan has three palaces. The first was built by King Abdullah when he first came to Jordan and is called the Raghadan. My grandfather also started building the Basman Palace, where I work now, but he never lived in it. My father is now living in Turkey, and my mother, the Queen Mother, has a palace which she shares with my brother, His Royal Highness Prince Mohammed, and the younger members of the family. This is called the Zahran Palace, and this one is our property. I live in my small house at Hummar and we also have a small winter villa at Shuna, built by King Abdullah, in the Jordan Valley. Here I occasionally spend an odd day in the winter—if I can spare the time.

But do not imagine that our palaces are vast like those in Europe. Basman Palace is divided into three sections. One is where I used to live before I married. The private quarters are very simple—a master bedroom and four small guest rooms, a dining room, three salons, one large enough to hold a reception for twenty-five people. The other two salons are very small. The second section is my office where I go each day, with rooms for those who work with me. The third section was added later and consists of a large dining room for official ceremonies, or when I have banquets for important guests such as foreign kings or potentates. We can seat between a hundred and fifty and two hundred for dinner.

In this section there is another hall used for collective audiences or for press conferences, and sometimes in the evenings we use this as a private movie theatre.

The Zahran Palace is just as simple and so is the Raghadan Palace. This was my grandfather's original palace, and I still use half of it on occasion—especially the Throne Room where I receive ambassadors presenting their credentials. It is also used occasionally for national feasts when large groups come to greet me. The other part of this palace is used by my grandfather's widow.

Soon after I settled in Jordan I asked Maurice Raynor, who had run the garage near Harrow, to come to Amman as head of the palace garages. He was slightly startled and at first demurred. But his wife persuaded him at least to try life in Jordan and so he asked his employers for a year's leave without pay. They agreed to let him return to his post as manager at the end of twelve months, but Raynor never went back. He has stayed in Jordan ever since, living in a house in the palace grounds—where once, as you will read, I spent the night after an attempt on my life.

Looking back on those first years as King, I suppose what irked me most was the difficulty I had in getting closer to my people. Because I was so young, my advisers tried to run my life for me. I wanted exactly the opposite—and got it! How could I even try to be a good King if I did not know my subjects well? I looked forward to my periodic trips into the desert, visiting my tribes. What a different life! I was still their King, but with them I did not feel lonely, I felt one of them. To them I was "Hussein." The only protocol was that of the Bedouin, whose life is based on three virtues—honor, courage and hospitality. We believe that to be an honorable man you must have the courage to defend your honor. We believe that you must always show hospitality. What is yours belongs also to your guests. Even an enemy has the guarantee of shelter and food once he reaches the camp of any enemy tribe.

When I visit my tribes I sit at the head of the tent, with the other guests around me. Members of the tribe stand in front, dancing their traditional dances and singing. When my name is mentioned in a song they shoot their rifles in the air as a salute. (Before the rifle and pistol era, they used to wave their swords or lances.) After I sit down, coffee is served. Then the chief of the tribe makes his traditional welcome speech, composing it as he goes along. It is considered very impolite not to improvise speeches or songs. Soon a poet appears from the crowd and makes up poetry as he talks. Then comes dinner—usually a *mansef*, consisting of rice and lamb cooked in large pots. Literally, *mansef* means "a big dish," and sometimes a score of lambs will be slaughtered. We recline on silken cushions in tents fifty yards long. No women are allowed, and no members of the tribe—even the chief—eat until all the guests have finished.

I love these visits, such contrasts to the dignity of court life. I try to do what I can to help. I think I keep a special watch for anything the Bedouin need—especially wells, schools and clinics. Many of them are very poor, but even so one has to search to discover their needs and deal with them, for they are too proud to ask for help. Tribesmen sometimes present petitions when they hear I am visiting them, and most are so simple I can deal with them on the spot. One needs work, another medical treatment—and always schools, clinics and water supplies. I like this simplicity of approach. It means that the Bedouin consider me the head of their tribe. Whatever the Bedouin want, they think of only one way to get it—to ask me.

I have tried, with some success, to settle the Bedouin—to stop them traveling from place to place in search of water and grazing land—by initiating a program to give them land to live on and to assist them in building modern settlements where there is water all year round. I hope that in the not too distant future most of the Bedouin will be settled.

But those first months were not easy. In many ways it was a perplexing time for me, perhaps because I had no yardstick by which I could measure my progress. Was I making a success of my task? Was I starting the right way? At eighteen it is hard to know, and as a king it is even more difficult to get an unbiased opinion.

Sometimes, however, a man or a king gets a word of encouragement from an unexpected quarter. One day I visited a small village that had been attacked by the Israelis and spent the night in a camp. The moon was high and I went for a short walk unattended, just to breathe in the night air. Through the walls of the tent in which I knew some of the older Jordanians were resting, I heard the murmur of voices. They were talking about me. Suddenly a phrase was pronounced clearly. You can imagine my pride and gratitude as that unknown voice said, "Abdullah would have been proud of his grandson."

But the Bedouin were only a portion of my people. How could I get to know those of the towns? How could I discover what they were thinking about? I went out among them whenever I could. I mixed with the youth in their schools. I went to villages and talked to the people. And I made every effort to penetrate the group one finds in any country—the "in-betweens"—so that I could talk to the genuine, representative core of the people.

Yet I always wanted to do more. One night, alone in the palace, I had what seemed like a good idea—to disguise myself and move more freely among my people. But how? Naturally I could not tell anybody, not wanting to risk the horrified official reaction. Then it came to me. I would become a taxi driver.

I decided that the best district to cruise for fares would be between Amman and Zerqa, the military area, seventeen miles from the capital. Even in summer, the nights can be cold because of the altitude, so I muffled up in an overcoat and put on a red *shemagh* (headdress) wrapped well around my head and face. I was completely unrecognizable. And anyway, who looks at a taxi driver?

About eight o'clock on two successive nights, I left the palace, driving an old green Ford with taxi number plates, returning at about midnight and giving the guards the slip. They thought I was in my room reading. For two nights I drove my "taxi" on the Zerqa road, and I learned a great deal.

I wanted to know what the people really thought about me and the government, and I certainly found out. It is curious how people talk in taxis as if the driver were not there.

I always like to talk to people in different walks of life who do not know me. I remember once, I was driving to

Jerash and met a Bedouin carrying a heavy sack of vegetables. Thinking my car was a taxi he signaled me to stop, and I did. After bargaining about the price, he climbed in and I asked him, "How is the season? Have you had good crops?"

"Thanks to God and the King, everything is wonderful," the Bedouin answered.

"What do you think of this King Hussein?" I asked him. "What sort of a man is he? Is he any good?"

"He is our man after God; he is protecting us and giving all the help we need. We love him."

"I'm not so sure about that," I replied, whereupon the Bedouin got furious and shouted:

"Don't you dare to say anything against my King. If you do I'll beat you black and blue with my stick!"

At this moment the guards, who had spent half an hour chasing me, caught up with my car. They may have saved me from a beating!

I also traveled whenever I could in those first years. I did my utmost to establish the best possible relations with our sister Arab states and our friends in the free world.

On one occasion I visited Saudi Arabia to see King Ibn Saud, shortly before his death. He was very infirm and could no longer walk along the interminable corridors of his palace, so he used a wheel chair.

I stayed in one of his palaces and on one occasion he came to visit me. I went out to the gates to greet him. Saudi palaces are rather large and have long, wide corridors leading from the gates to the actual reception rooms. The King arrived in his wheel chair. At this moment a servant arrived with a second wheel chair. Nothing was said, but he pushed it discreetly toward me.

"I beg your pardon?" I was genuinely puzzled.

"It's for you, Your Majesty," somebody said.

"Thank you very much," I replied, "but I'm perfectly all right. I don't mind walking a bit."

Then it suddenly dawned on me. It was beneath the King's dignity to sit while I walked. The hall was filled with nobles and members of my entourage. I had to climb into the wheel chair. I sat down and was pushed sedately along by the side of the King. I found it very difficult to meet the eyes of my aides, especially as they could hardly prevent themselves from laughing.

Thus life went on in this happy little country, and thus I learned more and more about my people. We continued to have serious troubles with the Israelis but not until 1955 did our enemies first try to break up my country.

Before that, there occurred an event on which I would like to dwell briefly. This was my first marriage. On April 19, 1955, I was married to Sharifa Dina Abdul Hamed, a member of the Hashemite dynasty, who lived in Cairo. She was a distant cousin.

She was a highly intelligent woman with an M.A. degree at Cambridge, and was a few years my senior. At first I was very hopeful that I could build a happy family life around this marriage and I was overjoyed when our baby daughter Alia was born.

I have always wanted to live the life of an ordinary man. But it was not to be—not then. The marriage was a failure. It was just one of those things that did not work out. Despite all efforts, it was not possible to share the same life, so it was far better, and only fair to both of us, to end it. It was a very sad and difficult period. There have been many criticisms about the divorce, but the basic principle in life is to live it in the best way one can, and honestly, regardless of people's opinions. How much better to meet such a crisis with courage and frankness. Eighteen months after our marriage we separated, and my former wife returned to Cairo.

5

I Learn To Fly

"In the cockpit I shake off my problems."

AS LONG as I can remember I have wanted to fly. When I was a boy, years before I went to school in Egypt, I was never interested in the hobbies of most boys. My chief enthusiasm was pictures of aircraft. I collected them all, the latest fighters and bombers, even the different types of passenger aircraft, pasting them in books during the evenings in our house on Jebel Amman.

But if I love flying, it is certainly not because I have a passion for speed or am merely mechanically minded. Flying for me has an attraction far deeper than merely pressing knobs or pulling controls. Now that I am a pilot it has opened up a wonderful vista before my eyes. The moment I climb into a cockpit I shake off my problems and worries. Once in the air the restrictions that inevitably surround the monarchy seem to vanish. I am a man alone.

I never climb away from the end of a runway without

breathing a sigh of gratitude. In an aircraft, if nowhere else, I am the master of my fate. The beauty of flying high in the skies will always, to me, symbolize freedom.

On land my duties are manifold, and to be truthful, some are monotonous. I have heavy burdens of responsibility or wearisome tasks to perform day after day—and in moments of crisis, night after night—and I would hardly be human if at eighteen I did not occasionally feel a desperate need to escape, if only for an hour. Flying provided just that safety valve.

There was another reason, too, why I wanted to fly. I mentioned earlier that I had always longed to make a life of my own and was deeply disappointed when I had to assume my responsibilities so young and, to my mind, ill-prepared. I have tried to be a student of life, learning day by day, year by year. It is calamitous for a man with responsibilities to reach the point where he believes there is nothing more to learn. That is why I always wanted to strike out on my own when I was young. Anything you can do on your own, to prove something to yourself, is a source of added strength. Flying provided just that, for in the ultimate, a pilot's final standard is the ability to survive. Each time I fly a jet I feel that here is something I have achieved entirely on my own merit.

There was another reason. I felt strongly that there was a big gap in Jordan's ability to defend herself due to the policy prevailing at the time. We had an excellent army—the best in the Arab world—but no real air force. While the Arab Legion (as it was then called) would defend us on land, we had to call on the British Royal Air Force for air support. I did not want Jordan to have to rely on help from abroad. Anything could happen to prevent help from coming. With

Israel threatening us constantly, it was most unwise to be at the mercy of another country (however friendly) whose policy could change for reasons unknown to us.

My grandfather tried hard to rectify this anomalous position, and formed the nucleus of a small air force, but all attempts to make it strong had failed. The old aircraft we bought were no good, and when I came to power the government was even considering selling the few old planes that constituted our air force.

Something had to be done about it, yet it was understandable that against this background, young men did not easily take to flying. If they wanted to belong to the armed forces, they joined the Legion and exchanged horse or camel for a Land-Rover or Bren gun carrier. I hoped that if their King became a pilot, others would seriously follow suit. How right I was!

I can clearly remember the day in 1953 when I decided to overcome the opposition I knew this decision would arouse. The Jordan Air Force was commanded by Colonel Jock Dalgleish, the same man who had flown me to Amman the day my grandfather was murdered in Jerusalem. ("Colonel" was his Arab Legion rank; he was a wing commander loaned to Jordan by the Royal Air Force.)

I realized the opposition would be serious, but I was determined to get my own way. It would be a good thing for me as a person and for my country. I had talked about flying with Dalgleish and many a time I had flown in the co-pilot's seat with him. One day I called him in and told him:

"I'm going mad in this office. You must teach me to fly."

Even Dalgleish, a dour Scot, was taken aback.

"But sir-r-r! You'll encounter all the opposition in the world!"

"I don't mind," I told him. "I'm going to fly. We will face these objections one by one. But I'm going to become a pilot."

For a time there was intense opposition, but gradually I wore it down. For a week or two I received almost daily deputations from political and other groups, from my family, from friends. I insisted there was no particular danger in flying; nothing in life is dangerous if one approaches it carefully; and I repeated what I deeply believe: that if you must die, you will die, whatever precautions you take.

In the end, I overcame all opposition and started to learn, though I was not told at first that I would not be allowed to fly solo. Flying with a co-pilot was one thing, but nobody would take the responsibility of letting me fly solo. (Shades of my youth—when nobody in Jordan would take the responsibility of giving me a driving license and I had to drive without one!)

The day of my first flight arrived. The Colonel planned a trip over Amman in a tiny Auster. I do not know whether the Colonel's idea was to make me give up my ambitions but he certainly gave me everything in the book on that flight. The Auster is a tiny aircraft, not very powerful, and he took me up for the most intensive hour of aerobatics I have ever experienced. I suppose it was in an effort to deter me. We looped, we rolled, we stalled, and as we came down to land I suddenly felt very, very sick. It was the one and only time I have ever been airsick. Many times since, trying out other aircraft, Dalgleish has, I rather fancy, done his best to make me ill again but I was always able to grin and say, "It's no use, Colonel. You'll never make me sick again." He never has.

Somehow or other I managed to climb out of the Auster, but to tell the truth, I did not know whether I was standing on my head or on my feet. The whole world swam in front of my eyes.

Dalgleish jumped out without turning a hair and everybody looked on as he asked me, in a voice deceptively casual:

"When do you wish to fly again, Your Majesty?"

I replied, swallowing hard:

"Tomorrow afternoon."

It was partly a sense of pride, perhaps a stubbornness in my make-up, that made me say that. But though I loathed that hour in the air I was determined to continue.

I returned to the palace and awaited the next day. Almost immediately I forgot what it was like being airsick. Still, I determined there should be no recurrence of such unseemly conduct, and my duties that afternoon consisted largely of acquiring the best antisickness pills I could find. For quite a while after that first flight I used to fill up with pills in order to fortify myself and thus appreciate Dalgleish's intricate maneuvers.

All through June and July I was down at the airfield five days a week. The Colonel has said that I was a born pilot, but I disagree. Some people find it easy to master flying. Not I. I tried very hard to relax but I had a great deal of trouble with instrumentation. It was difficult to do so many things at the same time, and at first I was worried by my physical reaction. Flying did not help the sinus trouble from which I have suffered since boyhood.

What a wonderful time that was, learning to fly! In many ways I had been very lucky—I managed to spend a few months at Harrow, then six months at Sandhurst, and now when learning to fly I was escaping, for a short time each day, from my official duties to the free and easy life of a young cadet again—this time in the Jordan Air Force. But more important than this was the fact that I was already helping to build the morale of that tiny group of fliers who provided the nucleus of a fine Air Force. It was a long, hard fight, and a difficult task getting our first fighters, but we succeeded and the day arrived when the Jordan Royal Air Force had its own jets—and the men to fly them.

I flew about ten hours in that little Auster before we transferred to the larger and more comfortable twin-engined Dove. And I remember at one stage becoming very miserable. I started with excellent landings and then suddenly everything went wrong. I had a bad patch; my landings were not very good. I fretted and worried until one day Dalgleish said to me, "Don't worry, Your Majesty, you can never make good landings unless you make bad ones."

Some months later, in January, 1954, I think, my Air Force procured its first Viking, and naturally I flew in it. Dalgleish was converting to this new type of aircraft and as he learned the ropes, he made several bad landings. Then he made a particularly bad one. I had been waiting a long time for this moment. Looking at his downcast expression, I patted his shoulder and reminded him, "Don't worry, Colonel, you can never make good landings unless you make bad ones!"

After a month I was ready to fly solo, but I still did not know that this was forbidden. On the third trip in the Dove, however, Dalgleish got out of the co-pilot's seat as I was handling the aircraft, and as he moved back, told me:

"Right, Your Majesty, will you please land the aircraft."

Whereupon he went back to the cabin and firmly closed the door behind him.

I was slightly alarmed. Then I took a grip on myself and reflected, "Well, if that's the way he feels about it, I'm going to have a try at it."

And land her I did—and though I say it myself, landed her very well.

But though I was alone in the cockpit when we came down, it was still a far cry from flying solo. As we unzipped our flying suits, I asked Dalgleish:

"That was as good as solo, wasn't it? So when can I go up alone?"

He looked embarrassed. "I'm afraid, sir, we'll have to wait a bit."

"But why on earth—" I began.

"I'll have to explain, sir—"

"But there's nothing to explain," I remonstrated. "In point of fact I was flying solo, wasn't I? If I'd crashed with you in the cabin, you could never have helped me."

Dalgleish sighed, buttoned up his Air Force uniform, and then out came the whole story, which I had sensed though nobody had told me. He had been instructed that I must never fly solo.

I was too upset even to be angry. I returned to the palace crestfallen. And then I began to think it over. It was utterly ridiculous. It was like telling me I could not drive a car at a hundred miles an hour without a chauffeur in the back seat. Yet I could not insist because, if anything did go wrong, the blame would naturally fall on the Air Force.

I decided the time had come to deal with this problem in my own way. The aircraft I flew was always under guard and everybody, from the mechanics to the control-tower officers, knew that in no circumstances could I fly solo. I bided my time and then suddenly my chance came.

I arrived at the airfield one afternoon to find everybody

very busy. An aircraft had overshot the end of the runway. It was not a serious accident, but everybody was far too occupied to notice me and there was nobody near my Dove. Like lightning I got in and revved her up. I shouted to the engineer who ran toward me, "I'm collecting the co-pilot on the way."

This was good enough for him, but of course there was no co-pilot. In a few moments I was airborne. Soon everybody was in the control tower watching me. I enjoyed myself immensely. Now I was really a pilot. I circled the capital, looking down from my lonely cockpit on the city I loved so well. I felt no fear—I was probably far less frightened than the men in the control tower. I stayed aloft a considerable time and then came in and made a perfect landing.

That did the trick. There were no more restrictions, and I have flown solo many times since.

By now I have flown well over a thousand hours and in many types of aircraft. Soon after I flew solo, I converted to jets and started flying with the Jordan Air Force, adding an entirely new excitement to my life. I became one of a team taking part in firing competitions, aerobatics and formation flying. This is perhaps the most exhilarating flying I have done. The intricate maneuvers forced one to think and act at double speed. We flew together in battle formation, in low-level attacks, and when each flight was over, what fun it was, back in the pilots' mess, pulling off the flying suits, hanging them up, discussing the day's work, then waiting impatiently for the next day's exercise.

In all my flying hours I have been in many tight spots but only two slight mishaps. The first occurred just before I was ready to solo in a jet. We had a couple of Vampire T-11 jets and Dalgleish and I had just landed and were halfway down the runway when the port wheel collapsed. The aircraft slewed around and we slithered to a stop on our drop tank.

I had often anticipated a moment like this and wondered how quickly it would take me to react. I need not have worried. We were out of that aircraft in seconds.

The damage was not serious, but the R.A.F. Commander in Amman rushed up to the scene. He was a group captain, and he arrived just as we were trying to fix the wheel.

His comments were, I thought, a trifle patronizing. How had we crashed? Perhaps, he suggested, we had made our landing too near the end of the runway and had to retract our undercarriage to stop in time. The wheel had collapsed and that was all there was to it.

However, the group captain had a little trouble of his own before long. He had flown an R.A.F. Pembroke from Amman to Mafraq and on the return journey left Mafraq at 2 P.M. For hours nothing was heard of him. Finally, at 8 P.M., a search was started. Soon afterward the gallant group captain was discovered, feeling rather sorry for himself. On the way to Amman he diverted and decided to land on some mud flats near Azraq to see if there were any ducks around.

The only thing wrong with this landing was something that could happen to any pilot—he forgot to put his undercarriage down!

The second mishap occurred when I was flying my Dove back from Jerusalem with my aide-de-camp. Over Amman airfield I suddenly found I could not get the undercarriage down. Obviously there was a leak in the mechanism. I tried again and again but could not get the undercarriage to work. Finally I used the last resort—a compressed-air bottle that jolts the nose wheel out of its housing. If that had failed, it would have meant a forced landing, but fortunately the air bottle worked. I have since had flame-outs in jets, and flown under some very tricky conditions, but it has all come out all right.

After jets there seemed to be nothing else to learn—that is, until 1958 when I decided to master the helicopter. It seemed a good idea to have a helicopter at the back of my palace, not only for my convenience, but because I like to pay surprise visits to military camps or civil programs, and I like them to be *real* surprises so that I can see my subjects as they really are and not after they have made elaborate preparations. A helicopter seemed the ideal aircraft for moving about the country unobtrusively and easily. I did not want to be dependent on a pilot, however, so I took a conversion course, and I was more than pleased when I learned to fly a helicopter solo after only two and a half hours.

The months I spent learning to fly were among the happiest in my life. I have always believed that one must draw a sharp line between the official and private life of a monarch, but sometimes it is not easy.

But once on the airfield I was no longer a monarch. I became a cadet again and the free and easy camaraderie that belongs especially to fliers exists for me to this day. Inevitably I became on friendly terms with many men at the airfield, and soon with the Air Force when I started to fly with them. It is perhaps not difficult to understand how a reigning monarch, hemmed in by protocol, can experience in those hours at the airfield a glorious escape from the discipline of kingship.

I would drive myself to the airfield and very often slip into the house on its edge where Jock Dalgleish lived with his wife and two children. Sometimes we would have to wait for a flight, and so I would arrive unannounced to inquire about favorable conditions.

Occasionally these unofficial visits led to amusing incidents. I drove to Dalgleish's house one afternoon and his five-year-old son Bruce was playing outside. The Colonel's wife told me later she had assiduously instructed her son how to greet me, by walking forward, bowing and then saying, "How do you do, Your Majesty?"

We were just drinking a cup of tea when the door burst open and in ran little Bruce. He stopped dead when he saw me. I could see him struggling to remember what he had been told. Then his face cleared, he smiled happily and walked toward the armchair before the fireplace, gave me the briefest possible bow, shot out his hand and shouted, "Hullo, King!"

I loved it—just as, years later, on my first visit to the United States, I loved those ever-recurring cries of "Hi'ya, King!" But then I genuinely love informality. I need it as an antidote to restriction—which flying has provided.

Once when an R.A.F. plane was reported missing near Amman, I went out with Dalgleish on a dawn search for it. We decided to meet at Dalgleish's house at 4:30 A.M., but I was early, and when I opened the door Dalgleish was shaving.

I shouted out, "Am I too early?"

The Colonel's wife told me she was making tea and sandwiches.

"Good, I'd love some," I cried. Then I added: "You make the sandwiches. I'll make the tea."

With that I headed for the kitchen. Despite a lot of argument she could not stop me. There is a moral somewhere in the fact that I wanted to brew a pot of tea at four o'clock in the morning. Perhaps it is that I believe so strongly that a king is really just the head of a family, and a servant of his nation. Right from the beginning of my reign I have fought to remove all barriers and live as a member of a family, or the team that is Jordan.

And when I offered to make that cup of tea, just before dawn, I had been accepted as a member of a team of fliers. The barriers were down. I had been allowed, for the moment, to forget I was a king.

6

Problems of the Arab States

"The crisis has not yet produced leaders."

VERY SOON after my accession to the throne, I was plunged into the traps and hazards of Middle Eastern politics that lay ahead. The chapters that follow demonstrate how serious were the threats both to my country and to my person. Almost unceasingly, enemies sought to destroy our small country; small, yet vital because of its strategic position, not only geographically but because of our unswerving, uncompromising stand for freedom and against communism, and our struggle to serve the principles and objectives of the Arab peoples and the great Arab Revolt.

Yet when trouble erupts in the Middle East, the Western world rarely understands the basic causes behind it. It tends to reduce our troubles to black and white, to oversimplify them. A complex Arab problem is all too often reduced to a label by the West which blames communism, the Palestine Question, Nasser, Kassem, or just "the Arabs," instead of realizing that many forces tugging in different directions cause our difficulties.

We are perhaps partly to blame for this lack of knowledge, but it is also very true that an astonishing number of bad books have been written about the Arab states. It seems to me that few authors from the West have yet been capable of writing balanced, intelligent books about our problems. Often the press is biased or improperly informed. Yet if one is to understand the reasons for the violent upheavals, and the bitter personal hatreds that I shall presently describe, some background knowledge is necessary. I propose now to describe that background and explain briefly the events that have brought the Arab world to the point where it stands today, to set the scene for the events to follow.

There is an Arabic proverb which says that "Peace comes from understanding, not agreement." Agreements are more easily broken than made; but understanding never. It is urgent, therefore, and in the interest of peace, that there be better understanding among nations. As people we are one, seeking the same goal. As nations we lose each other down the different paths we choose to fulfill our national objectives.

Unhappily, I must refer only to free nations. We have a different relationship with the nations of the Communist bloc, where freedom of thought and of action does not exist, where unrelenting attack is waged to deny all people the right to any personal goal save slavery to the State, and the right to any national aim except dictatorship by a foreign power.

That is why we must understand each other better. Communism survives only by dividing people and nations against each other. Communism penetrates the gaps that are opened by unhappy internal conditions and drives a wedge between nations whenever they lack understanding of one another's political aims and aspirations. In the case of small nations, such tactics expose them to destruction. In a crisis, the clarity with which they assess the danger seems to vary with their size and their distance from the powerful free nations. However, prior understanding of the problem of the nation in distress might *prevent* the crisis. In the past, awareness of a threat has frequently come too late to be of much use. We know this well in Jordan, because time after time we have barely escaped destruction.

The feeling of being alone or misunderstood greatly affects the potential strength and morale of the many small nations that form freedom's front line. The larger nations well understand our strategic importance, but not always our national aspirations. This understanding is important to survival and to the better future for all. That is the common interest and aim of the world's free nations.

In the Hashemite Kingdom of Jordan, we are eager to carry out our duties toward other free people, to justify our existence. A nation once divided, we are now bound together by daily strengthening ties, inspired by need, by common interests, by patriotism and, above all, by what is known as Arab nationalism.

I must attempt to define Arab nationalism as it really is, and explain its development and aims. In doing so, I present as well the case of the people of the Arab world. I present it as a person who has inherited the responsibility of serving a proud people on the long, rough journey toward its objectives.

The true nature of Arab nationalism has been obscured, sometimes by us Arabs and sometimes by others who believed that Arab nationalism threatened their interests. As a result, many of the past actions of some of the more powerful

Western nations, particularly Britain and France, have lacked foresight and have been contrary to their own interest.

Arab nationalism is a potential force for good. It binds Arabs together even when they are split into many factions. It drives them toward a more cohesive Arab world, regardless of explosive changes in rulers or regimes.

Arab nationalism was born when the rest of the civilized world was slumbering in the Dark Ages and when Arabism was contributing greatly to mankind's progress. Isolated Arab civilizations had long existed in Yemen, Mecca, Petra, Palmyra, Southern Syria and Iraq, but Arab history really began with Islam about A.D. 611. Morally, the influence of the new faith was great, but its political influence was due chiefly to its concept of equality among individuals, irrespective of race. That is a first principle of Islam.

We express this ideal in the word *takwa,* which embraces tolerance, love of God, love of good deeds, a deep-rooted sense of justice. In brief, the concepts of morality and behavior of Islam are the principles for which we in the free world stand. These immortal concepts led Arabs to establish an Islamic empire extending from Spain to China. It molded different races and civilizations into a progressive and creative movement based on all the good from their pasts as well as from our own. It spurred development of the most advanced civilization of its time, and opened new fields in science, medicine, art and philosophy; Islam's contributions are enjoyed today. This tradition, rooted in Islam—and not some new political concept—is the foundation of today's Arab nationalism.

Unfortunately, the Arab empire, beset by rivalries, was destroyed by Mongol invaders and, while Europe was enjoying its Renaissance, the Arab nation slipped into darkness. Yet through almost four hundred years of Ottoman domination, pride and dignity survived.

After Napoleon invaded the Middle East, Arabs began to be influenced by European nationalism and colonialism. But even that might not have stirred the Arabs had not a new nationalist movement been launched by the Young Turks. Early in this century they began to change the Moslem Ottoman empire into a Turkish empire, in which the Arabs were to be deposed as co-rulers and to become completely subjugated. Intent on wiping out Arab opposition, the Turks in 1916 hanged Arab leaders in Beirut and Damascus. This, more than anything, spurred Arab nationalists.

The Arabs turned for leadership to Mecca and to the Hashemite dynasty. Descendants of the Prophet Mohammed, the Hashemites were respected all over the Moslem world. About the time the Turks joined the Germans in the First World War, leaders in what are now Iraq, Syria, Lebanon and Jordan urged Sherif Hussein, leader of the Hashemite dynasty, to act. Through his sons, contact with the Allies was established and terms for Arab alliance with the Allies and Arab revolt against the Turks were agreed upon in what is known as the Hussein-MacMahon Correspondence. The British, on behalf of the Allies, recognized Hussein as the leader of his people, encouraged his determination to liberate the Arab world and promised their support in creating a free Arab nation.

The Arab Revolt began in June 1916, under the supreme command of Sherif Hussein. The leaders were his sons Ali, Abdullah and Feisal. In conjunction with British operations under General Allenby, Arabian forces marched northward from Mecca and reached Aleppo in 1918, realizing their dream of liberation and fulfilling their pledge to help bring about the Turkish-German defeat and Allied victory in Arab Asia.

What thereupon happened to the agreement between the Allies and ourselves? The answer is important because it explains much about the Arab attitude toward the West today. Unpleasant reading though it may make for Westerners, we must examine the record, from the day of our joint victory in 1918 until the sad day in 1948 when the Palestine tragedy reached its peak.

In that record will be found reasons for bitterness toward the outside world, for an occasional apparent loss of sound judgment, for the backward conditions in certain Arab areas. In that record will be found the basic reasons for the relative success of communism in parts of our homeland, the resentment over Jewish existence in the present state of Israel, and the unfortunate conditions in Algeria. As a direct result, the Arab world and Arab nationalism may appear to be hostile, negative and confused.

None of this would have occurred had it not been for the shocking actions of our allies—actions indicating that their leaders lacked foresight and even principle. At the conclusion of the peace treaty, two documents whose existence was unknown to the Arabs came to light. One was the secret Sykes-Picot Agreement between the British and French, made in 1916 only a few months after the conclusion of the Hussein-MacMahon Correspondence (which had bound the Allies to quite different actions). The second was the Balfour Declaration in which the British declared that they "Looked with favor" upon the creation of "a national homeland for the Jews" in Palestine.

The Sykes-Picot Agreement and the Balfour Declaration—and actions arising from them—reflected dishonor on Western ethics and were a shock and bitter disappointment to the Arabs. First, instead of winning complete and united Arab independence, Arab Asia was divided into regions under French and British mandates. Second, without the knowledge of the Arab people, who then comprised ninety-three per cent of its population, Palestine was promised as "a national home" for the Jewish people. The final result was the creation of Israel, in complete violation of the principles of self-determination. And King Hussein the First, who refused to bargain over a single square foot of the Arab homeland in Palestine, was forced into exile for six years.

In Syria another promise was broken. The French marched on Damascus and forced King Feisal I to leave the country. In Iraq, the situation was much the same until a revolt forced the British to give in, and Feisal the First became King of Iraq.

In Jordan, King Hussein reacted by dispatching his son Abdullah with all available forces to advance northward and help stem the French advance on Damascus. Abdullah left Medina, in the Hejaz, at the end of October 1920 and arrived in Ma'an, in Jordan, on November 21. It took him twenty-seven days traveling by train to cover the few hundred miles —partly through lack of fuel, partly because the railway had been destroyed in places. But by the time Abdullah reached Jordan, the French had liquidated the Arab kingdom in Syria.

On March 20, 1920, Winston Churchill (then Colonial Secretary) held a conference in Jerusalem with my grandfather. As a result Transjordan was formed as a British Mandate with my grandfather at its head as Emir. By April 21, Transjordan had its first cabinet.

It was a small country of about 350,000 people. The landscape was rough and spectacular, partly mountainous, partly desert, with only a small fertile strip along its western boundary, the River Jordan. Not until 1924, when my grandfather incorporated southern Transjordan, did the country even have an outlet to the sea at Aqaba. There were few schools, virtually no police, and most of the country's forests had long since vanished as ties (or even fuel) for the fantastic Hejaz Railway. But such was the magnetism of my grandfather that thousands flocked to his banner. The Bedouin loved him as a father. The Syrians in the north, bitter at the French annexation of their country, turned to him for help. He set up his court in Amman, then a town of three thousand people in the Edomite mountains, and where Og, King of Bashan, last of the race of giants, had left his bed of iron in the book of Deuteronomy.

When World War II came, Transjordan immediately offered to fight side by side with Britain, and the Arab Legion played a valiant role in the Middle East theatre, taking part, among other engagements, in the liberation of Damascus from Vichy France. It is to my grandfather's credit that he never wavered in his principles or his friendship with Britain, though he always felt deeply hurt at the way she had broken her promises to the Arabs after World War I—breaches of faith that led even Churchill to describe British conduct as a "confusion of principles"; which Lawrence described as "a despicable fraud," and which George Antonius, the Arab historian, felt were the "product of greed, leading to suspicion and so leading to stupidity."

But with determination and faith he served his nation. Then in May, 1946, the Transjordan Mandate was abolished and the independent Kingdom of Jordan was created. My grandfather ruled wisely and well as King, working tirelessly to find a solution to the Palestine problem. After the Palestine war, as I shall describe later, that part of Palestine saved by Jordanian forces was joined by its people's consent to Jordan. Thus, when I came to the throne, the population had grown to a million and a half.

All this explains why today we have, instead of a single Arab state, separate Arab states as well as Israel. And one million Arab refugees are paying for Israel's creation. The inevitable fact is that Israel, governed by the present expansionist policies of Zionism, can only spell injustice, danger and disaster. It would behoove the world to become used to this fact: that without a just solution to the Palestine tragedy, there can be no stable peace in the Middle East. Those nations which base their policies on the *fait accompli* of Israel's existence forget that the relationship that enabled Arabs and Jews to live together for centuries as neighbors and friends has been destroyed by Zionist ideas and actions. So long as Zionism is the dominating political force in Israel, that friendship can never be rekindled.

The consequences of dividing up the Arab homeland are visible for all to see. One of the most unfortunate aspects of it is the sorry picture presented to the world of what must eventually be the salvation of the Arab world—true Arab nationalism. Nationalism properly means the ultimate loyalty of the individual to the Arab world as a whole; it demands that a Jordanian be an Arab first and a Jordanian second, an Iraqi an Arab first and an Iraqi second. Loyalties to lesser concepts have seriously weakened our ability to pursue constructive policies. They have slowed our progress toward improving our economy, standard of living, education, and other measures for the general good.

My own concept of Arab nationalism, for example, is quite different from what I understand President Nasser's to be. If I interpret his aims properly, he believes that political unity and Arab nationalism are synonymous. Evidently he also believes that Arab nationalism can only be identified by a particular brand of political unity. If this is his belief, I disagree. It can only lead, as it has in the past, to more disunity.

The seeking of popular support for one point of view or one form of leadership in countries other than one's own has fostered factionalism to a dangerous degree, splitting countries to the point of revolution. It is nothing but a new form of imperialism, the domination of one state by another. It makes no difference if both are Arab states. Arab nationalism can survive only through complete equality.

Nor can worthwhile future objectives be achieved by unprincipled, immediate tactical maneuvers. This preoccupation with shortsighted objectives, usually attributed—perhaps wrongly—to political ambition, has brought three attendant evils. It has diverted Arab energies from sound, peaceful pursuits into wasteful political intrigue. It has split people into factions, and thus has provided the gap into which communism has driven a dangerous wedge. And it has hampered the Arabs in dealing with the greatest political problems confronting us: the Palestine question and the Algerian tragedy.

It is in our power as Arabs to unite on all important issues, to organize in every respect and to dispel the frictions between us. It is not the fault of the Arab peoples that they are burdened with the Palestine problem, or that they have been unable sufficiently to aid their brethren in Algeria, or that Arabism is held in low esteem. The fault lies partly in the situation created by the policy of divide-and-rule, and partly in the lack of sincerity and honesty in some Arab leaders. Every Arab problem suffers from the irresponsibility of the dominant Arab class.

It is indeed unfortunate that, having been victimized by the shortsighted, disheartening and deceitful policies of the West, we have been able to do nothing but divide ourselves further. There was a time when we could unite, in spirit at least, against the imperialist enemy. But we have as yet been unable to unite properly against our two most potent enemies: communism and Zionism.

I believe that slowly but surely we are overcoming these difficulties, which have been due to a variety of reasons, not the least being the fact that the crisis has so far produced no real leaders.

Ambitious men have made claims without foundation and promises they could not keep. They have been aided indirectly by outside forces which seek control over this area, both the Communists and those who attempt to preserve their interests in ways that have failed them before. The few sound attempts aimed at practical unity came from Jordan and were led by the late King Abdullah, my grandfather. He proposed the unity of larger Syria (Syria, Lebanon, Jordan and Palestine), or the unity of the Fertile Crescent (Iraq, Syria, Lebanon, Jordan, Palestine and Kuwait), or even the unity of Syria and Jordan. Recently we had a go at what turned out to be the short-lived Arab Union of Iraq and Jordan.

My grandfather's attempts were thwarted by the divide-and-rule tactics of the British and the French, who mistakenly believed that they would gain by keeping the Arab world disunited. The Iraq-Jordan Union was disrupted by the murder of my cousin Feisal and his family, during the Iraqi revolution. It is an object lesson in the fallacy of pursuing short-term objectives, that Kassem, its leader, has since been bitterly attacked by Nasser, who was the first to recognize and support him.

The Arab League, which came into existence over fourteen years ago, for a time appeared to be a step toward a better, progressive Arab world. But the upper echelon of Arab irresponsibles soon destroyed its high hopes and it became a puppet, its strings pulled by a few ambitious self-servers. In his memoirs my grandfather likened this creature to a sack into which had been forced seven heads (the original seven Arab countries which formed the League) tied by ribbons of foreign domination and Arab ignorance. Such a creature could breathe; but if it attempted to move, it would choke itself to death. It is still tied together; but it is bound, not united.

Given sincerity and sound leadership the Arab League has great potential. It is the anvil on which Arab nationalism must be forged. But it must weld together its strong links with the past, with Islam, and with the Moslem world. The Arab nation has a common tongue, a common cause, a common future and a common challenge of survival. Combining the best of its past and the best it can absorb from modern civilization, it should prosper.

If this is the goal and progress of Arab nationalism, to what practical ends should it address itself? First, it can only be the enemy of communism. Communism denies all faiths and thus the very principles on which Arab nationalism is based. Arab nationalism, given the chance, the respect, the support and the understanding of others in this free world, can only side with those who are free and who believe in God.

How then can anyone who believes in true Arab nationalism defend a policy that is a form of neutrality, whereby a country pretends to maintain good relations with both the free world and communism? This is the announced policy of Nasser and some others. The exponents of "neutrality" in the Arab world, as possibly elsewhere, describe Arab existence as in peril of destruction by the outside world, mainly by the free nations. At the same time, although originally they denounced the theory of communism, they seem gradually to implement its practices and accept its help. The salvation of the people, they declare, is to follow their lead in a movement they created. Those who openly declare themselves to be part of the free world, as we do in Jordan, are represented as being hostile to Arab nationalism, a course which in fact strikes at the root of nationalism.

In Jordan we denounced such demagoguery. We believe that to be neutral, the third power has to be so powerful as to need no support from either of the conflicting sides. If threatened by either, it must be able to defend itself. Then a constructive, positive neutrality could exist which could per-

haps prevent a conflict. But is this the case between international communism and the free nations? Is it the case between the Arab states and the Soviet Union or Communist
China? Would Arab nationalism ever be respected by communism? Is Arab so-called neutrality, in fact, a method for
preserving Arab existence, let alone a way to prevent such
a clash?

And finally, is it in Arab self-interest to earn the animosity
of the free world, even if such intolerable situations as those
in Palestine and Algeria have resulted from misunderstandings? We believe it is not, because there can be no life and
future for Arabism under the alternative to freedom: local
or world-wide communism.

There is no future for Arabism without the teachings of
Islam and without the faith in God which unites us in the
free world. There is no basis to the theory that local communism and international communism differ. There is no
validity to the belief that we can accept Communist help and
support because communism respects our principles or ad-
mires our aspirations.

We Arabs regret that some powerful states in the free
world have not been wholly honest with us. The answer, however, lies not in embracing communism but in our power to
implement our own principles and to defend our own freedom. The power that should strengthen us should be Arab
power, and it is the duty of the upper echelons in the Arab
world to organize Arab development through unity of purpose. Then we can engage in strong, sound, dignified international relations to remove misunderstandings that impede
our progress. Then we can enlist to our just cause, pursue in
Arab dignity our dealings with other nations, and develop
pride in our accomplishments.

As for the Hashemite Kingdom of Jordan in the Arab world, we are devoted bearers of the ideals of the Arab Revolt. We believe, and will never cease to believe, in the basic need for Arab freedom, unity, equality, strength and progress. Jordan's main strength lies in holding to those ideals bravely.

We are Arabs first and Jordanians second. As Jordanians, we have learned one lesson that contributes daily to our progress: we have clarity of purpose. Having escaped death as a nation, we must make our life as a nation worth living.

Jordan has borne the brunt of the burden laid on the Arab world by the unsound policies and emotional judgments of Arab leaders. We are not prepared to do so again. We will pursue our own policies, in the militant democratic tradition. We will preach among our brethren in the Arab world the spirit of Jordan.

There are in the free world different interpretations of the term democracy. In the Arab world we have learned that to copy one system of government or another completely, and to attempt to apply that to a newer state with a different background and history, is unwise, even dangerous. The older democracies continually discover that they must make adjustments to deal with changing times. Some nations in the Arab world have so-called democratic parties, but many of these groups, for reasons of selfishness or subversion, link themselves with elements outside their country. In such cases the party system embodies the reverse of democracy. So communism entered the Arab world under the guise of nationalism. Almost every party proclaims the same slogans of unity, freedom, development. Few, however, have real programs. The slogans are merely the means by which an individual or group hopes to gain power. As a consequence, democratic though Jordan's government is, we do not feel we can yet

afford the luxury of these "parties" in our democratic process
—at least not with this concept.

To my mind, the problem of the Arab world is to define
itself clearly and positively through united actions in the
Arab League in a manner that would be respected and ad-
hered to on all issues. We must no longer talk with a confusion of angry voices.

In the need for Arab unity, there is no difference of opinion. So instead of debating an accepted principle, let us debate a practical plan. There are four great natural units in
the Arab-speaking world: the Fertile Crescent, the Arabian
Peninsula, the Nile Valley, and the Maghrib, including Algeria.

Let the countries in these natural units associate themselves in whatever way they choose as a step toward the great
goal of an Arab nation. Let their association be voluntary, and
let it embrace only what the people of each country want it
to embrace—whether it be culture, economics or defense. Let
political alliance, if it is desirable at all, be the last step. Let
all of this be undertaken through an active, respected Arab
League, in which equality and sincerity of joint purpose
would be assured, and in which danger of domination by any
member of the family would be eliminated.

To such a proposal Jordan pledges the full weight of its
power and strength. It would subscribe immediately to any
practical step designed to realize it. Our only plea is for well-
considered action.

Jordan seeks to play only one role, that of a model state. It
is our aim to set an example for our Arab brethren, not one
that they need follow but one that will inspire them to seek a
higher, happier destiny within their own borders. We pro-

pose to devote, without ever losing sight of the ultimate goal
of a united Arab nation, our full time and energy to the creation of a way of life that we hope in time all Arabs will
achieve. We are supposed to be an underdeveloped country.
But we are not underdeveloped in those attributes that will
eventually make us great—pride, dignity, determination, courage, confidence, and the knowledge that nothing can be
achieved without work.

In a short time we have more than doubled our national
output and quintupled agricultural output. We are in the
process of further development in five major areas: our vast,
uncharted mineral resources; our water resources; light industry; internal highway communications; and tourism.

Mindful that ignorance is the enemy of the Arabs, we will
continue to develop our rapidly expanding school system.
Our immediate goal is the technical training of our youth.
Eventually we will achieve for all Arabs an Arab university
in the Holy City of Jerusalem.

We are aware of the great part which labor plays in the
successful development of a truly democratic state. We propose to raise the standard of living of all workers to the maximum possible extent. We will continue to improve our health
services, so that no one ever again shall suffer or die from
ignorance or neglect. To that end, we are expanding medical
and nursing training, and establishing clinics and hospitals.

We will continue to improve our system of government. We
are still a very young state, but administrative reforms are
constantly being effected and will continue as part of our
efforts to achieve a truly efficient, democratic government.
We will fight as well the disease of corruption, another old
enemy of the Arab world. It has no place in a state whose
foundations are the precepts of Islam and faith in God.

When I think of my family, I think with pride of everyone

in Jordan, who, standing by me as we faced the storms, inspired me in serving them. When I think of the tribe to which I belong, I look upon the whole Arab nation. My life is dedicated to a cause, just as the Hashemites have been throughout history; that cause is to be an Arab worthy of Arab trust and support. I fear only God.

Our hands are stretched in friendship to all who may join us to work toward Arab greatness and unity with sincerity, devotion and sound principles. We challenge all who claim to have Arab interests at heart to meet us along this course. We belong to one nation and the nation does not belong to individuals. Finally, as always, we pray to God for guidance and support.

Arab nationalism has a clear message that can be heard all over the Arab world. Respect us and you will be respected. Correct injustice and we will be grateful. Help us to build our strength and it will be that of freedom. Remember that we are masters of our homes, and we were born free.

7

The Baghdad Pact Riots

"At first I was impressed by Nasser."

THE YEAR 1955 saw the decisive turning point in the postwar history of the Arab world. If the cold war between Egypt and Jordan was born well before my grandfather's assassination, it came to a boiling point in 1955. It was the beginning of three dangerous years in which Jordan as a country nearly perished. Time and again our country was saved by nothing short of a miracle, and almost everything that happened can be traced back to 1955, a year which saw the signing of the Baghdad Pact, the sudden spectacular arms deal between Nasser and the Soviet bloc, our discussions on entering the pact, and finally the riots that all but split Jordan in two.

The Baghdad Pact was the start of it all. It was based on a concept of a "northern tier" of defense against Communist pressures. Indeed I had myself sometime previously put forward tentative suggestions for a similar free pact to unite the Arab world in the face of mounting Communist pressure. But there was not much point having a northern tier if people could step over it and build behind it. During my state visit to Turkey in 1954, I had talks with both the President and the late Mr. Menderes, the Prime Minister, on the possibility of forming some alliance which would include all the Arab states. True, there were difficulties. The Turks were understandably worried about the presence of Soviet troops on their northern frontier, but even though Turkey's relations with Israel began under the previous regime, they could not be easily accepted by us Arabs.

That obstacle had to be dealt with to the satisfaction of the Arab world. I was careful to point out to Menderes that if any mutual agreement were ever signed, it would have to include most of the Arab states at once. I warned him that if any Arab state formed a pact with the free world without prior consultation and agreement between sister Arab states, it would be disastrous.

Yet this is exactly what happened. When the formation of the Baghdad Pact was announced in 1955, the Arab world was stunned. The immediate reaction—and whether it was correct or not is immaterial—was that Britain, because of its vast oil interests in the area, and its influence, had "got at" Iraq.

I knew that something was in the air, for sometime after visiting Turkey, I went to Britain. I heard rumors, but the negotiations were so secret I did not realize how far advanced they were. I was in Rome, on my way back to Amman, when I heard the news, and at first I refused to believe it. It was a fatal mistake on the part of all countries involved to rush into an agreement with Iraq only.

The immediate outcome was a bitter feud between Cairo and Baghdad. Almost overnight they were at each other's throats. Nasser was furious, partly because he was annoyed with any rivals for power and prestige in the Arab world, and partly out of pique because he was not approached before Iraq. Iraq was rich and powerful, Turkey even more so. He had to attack the pact if only to prevent other Arab states joining and so diminishing his growing prestige. Night after night Cairo Radio fulminated against "this traitor to the Arab cause" and "the cat's-paw of the imperialists."

As James Morris says in *The Market of Seleukia*, "the alliance . . . so infuriated the Egyptians that most of the Arab world was roused against it. . . . So hostile was public opinion, thanks chiefly to the malignant competence of the Egyptian propagandists, that no other Arab government dared to join it. In the eyes of the extremists, it was a device to maintain Western (especially British) ascendancy in the Middle East. It compromised the sovereignty of the Arabs. . . . It was a slap in the face to Colonel Nasser. It was meant to divide and weaken the Arab world. In short, said the Egyptians and their advisers, speaking very loudly, it was intolerable. Their views were not only misleading, but also pitiably parochial."

Soon Nasser widened the scope of his propaganda attacks and I came in for a share of the general invective merely because Glubb Pasha was still commanding the Arab Legion, and because the Anglo-Jordanian Treaty still existed. So I, too, was "a tool of the West." But the propaganda at first was not directed mainly at Jordan, possibly because Cairo was so busy attacking Baghdad for forming an alliance "with those responsible for creating Israel." Any part that the Communist camp played in this creation was and is, of course, never mentioned.

Nonetheless I was highly alarmed lest this breach between Egypt and Baghdad should widen. If it did, and if the Arab states were weakened by division among themselves, what was to stop the Israelis from attacking?

Naturally I looked at this problem from a Jordanian point of view. Jordan is a very special kind of country that depends on good neighbors for its existence. But what was happening to those "good neighbors"? They were squabbling, maneuvering for position, just as they had done in the past whenever the Ottoman Empire showed signs of breaking up. Where was Arab solidarity? Where was the unity of the Arab League? And what would happen to Jordan if she remained friendless while those around her quarreled?

Saudi Arabia had an eye on Aqaba, our only port, which she claimed as part of the Hejaz, for so long the seat of the Hashemite dynasty. (Saudi Arabia has since quieted her demands.) Syria was coming increasingly under the influence of Egypt, and if the Arab states started fighting, might not Syria seek to "protect" us? If that happened, Iraq would never stand idly by, for, in addition to the Hashemite cause which bound us together, Iraq would never let a hostile Syria march along her western frontier. But above all, there was Israel. If the quarreling that Nasser had started developed, Israel would without doubt use the confusion to conquer the enclave on the West Bank and straighten out her frontier along the Jordan River.

In the years since my accession, Israel had directed most of its aggression against Jordan, and if any attack were to be launched, my country would without question bear the brunt of it. I doubted very much whether we could hold them alone. Numerically and as far as equipment was concerned, the balance was most uneven and we had by far the longest battle front with the enemy. (Of the six hundred seventy miles of the Israel-Arab border, Egypt has to defend one hundred eighty miles, Syria forty-five, Lebanon just over fifty, leaving Jordan with the colossal task of defending nearly four hundred miles.)

I tried my best that summer to help Iraq and Egypt come to a better understanding. I visited Baghdad, but my cousin King Feisal was virtually powerless, and though I argued with Nuri Said, the Prime Minister, there was no ground for maneuver. I admired Nuri Said very much, but his attitude was expressed in one sentence:

"Sir, we are in the Baghdad Pact, that's that, and we are certainly not backing out of it."

I also paid a visit to President Nasser. I had for a long time been impressed by Nasser. I felt in those early days that he was a new element in the Arab world, an element that could bring about much-needed reforms. If he worked for the people of Egypt, he could accomplish a great deal. He had the resources, a vast population, and a leading position in the Arab world. I had been to school in Egypt and even then realized that something would have to be done to change conditions. The problems of the Arab world are almost always the fault of its leaders and politicians, not of the people, and so I had a lot of faith in Nasser and tried to support him as much as I could.

I asked Nasser about the Baghdad Pact and he said the hasty way in which it had been conceived, involving one Arab country only, was most unwise. I agreed with him, and I believe that had Nasser been consulted in the preliminary stages, the results might have been very different.

But now things had gone too far. The Baghdad Pact was a *fait accompli* and Nasser made it clear that it was not possible to remain friendly with Iraq. He was quite frank. Though he did not like the pact (he doubtless saw it as a threat to his own prestige), he added, "As far as the King of Iraq is concerned, I have nothing but affection for him. I wish him every success and I have great hopes for him. But still, I don't like the way it was done. I've nothing against the pact as such, but we should have been consulted properly."

I had to think of Jordan. The fact that Nasser was extremely polite to me did not stop Cairo Radio from abusing me. I asked Nasser why he insisted on keeping up his radio campaign against Jordan.

He smiled charmingly.

"But this is the first I've heard about it!" he replied. "I'm glad you mentioned the matter; I'll look into it straight away."

Needless to say, nothing was ever done and the radio propaganda campaign went on.

As the summer wore on, I became more and more worried. The ties between Iraq and Jordan are so strong (partly because of our Hashemite dynasty) that Cairo more and more linked our two countries in its attacks. (In fact, Iraq and Jordan did not always see eye to eye. The Iraqi policy-making group considered themselves superior and rarely discussed matters with us.) Still I took no action.

Then the bombshell fell on the Arab world. On September 25, 1955, Nasser announced his now historic arms deal with the Soviet bloc. In an instant everything changed.

Hundreds of thousands of Jordanians, listening avidly to

the propaganda on Cairo Radio, saw in Nasser a mystical sort of savior and—as so many, including myself, at first wrongly thought—their best bet for the future against Israel. It never entered our heads that Nasser had linked himself to the Communists. All we saw was the reverse of the coin—that Nasser was the first Arab statesman really to throw off the shackles of the West. I must admit I sympathized with that point of view to a great extent.

The ordinary people of Jordan rejoiced, and I took in my stride the increasing abuse that was hurled at me for continuing to let my army be run by Glubb and other British officers. But my task of trying to keep order was not made easier because of niggling problems which Cairo seized upon avidly as propaganda. For example, Britain was paying for the Arab Legion, yet despite entreaties from my Prime Minister, Britain refused to pay the money directly to the Jordan government, but to a special Legion account, controlled by Glubb. Thus Jordan had virtually no say even in the finances of its own forces.

Always afraid that other Arab states would join the Baghdad Pact, Cairo quickly seized the initiative. Not only outright lies, but dangerous half-truths were hurled over the radio to every coffeehouse in the country. Expert propagandists lashed the emotions of everybody and the theme never varied: "Get rid of British officers in the army!" or "Get rid of the King who is keeping Jordan as a tool of the West."

As the full significance of Nasser's economic tie-up with the Communists became more evident, Soviet Russia, with a typical switch of policy, abandoned outwardly its support of Israel. Immediately the Israelis started getting arms from France to put their country on an even stronger war footing. With Iraq and Egypt still at loggerheads, with Israel poised for war, with pressure mounting against Jordan, something had to be done.

On November 2, the Turkish President paid me a state visit. Immediately Cairo Radio launched a bitter attack on Jordan—to make sure, no doubt, that we did not join the pact. Naturally the question of Jordan joining the pact was discussed. I kept an open mind at first, while considering every point for and against in the light of conditions entirely changed by the Egypt-Czech arms deal.

Finally, on November 7, the eve of the Turkish President's departure, we held a conference at my house in Shuna in the Jordan Valley. I told the President I realized the advantage of the pact, but that in fact we needed economic aid as much as a military alliance. The Palestine War had all but ruined us, and we had half a million refugees. But we also needed a revision of the Anglo-Jordanian Treaty.

"I understand your difficulties," the President replied. "Why don't you write to the British government and explain the additional help you need? We will write at the same time and support your case."

I decided to do this, and on November 16 handed the British Ambassador a note explaining our difficulties and needs. I mentioned our conference with the Turks.

Early in December, General Templer, Chief of the British Imperial General Staff, arrived, ostensibly to discuss questions "concerning the defense of Jordan and the Arab Legion," but during his visit he raised with me privately the question of our joining the Baghdad Pact. I realized that if Jordan joined, the free world would gain an enormous moral victory. I felt that if we joined we should receive more arms and economic aid, and the Anglo-Jordanian Treaty should be changed and its duration shortened so that Jordanian officers would have more opportunities to rise in the Arab Legion. I told Templer the time had arrived when the Jordan Army should be Arabized quickly.

One thing I was resolved upon. I would enter no alliance without first informing President Nasser and seeking his views. Though I was worried by Communist infiltration and the increased threat from Israel, I would do nothing behind Nasser's back.

I did not approve of what he had done, I was upset by his propaganda campaign, but I believed him to be a man of his word, and when our discussions were well advanced, I sent him a personal message with full details by his commander-in-chief, General (later Field Marshal) Abdul Hakim Amir, who was visiting Jordan at the time.

I explained our close nationalistic, economic and geographical ties with Iraq. I pointed out the real danger from Israel. I knew Nasser was astute. He would not relish the idea of Egypt defending our four hundred miles of frontier if Jordan could not do so. I fancied he would prefer to let us carry on so that he would have a scapegoat in case of an Israeli victory. But, as I told him, we needed more arms and so I outlined to him the Jordanian conditions for entering the pact.

Officials had drawn an outline of our immediate requirements, should we enter the pact. These included more arms, economic aid and guarantees of support in case we were subjected to attack, and a definite pledge that Britain would shorten the time of the Anglo-Jordanian Treaty and that a new treaty would be signed with improved conditions, including an acceptable plan for the Arabization of our armed forces.

When this outline was complete, I sent a copy of it to President Nasser. Nasser immediately sent one of his top officials to Amman to discuss the matter with me. Then a message came from Nasser himself, giving the idea his blessing. In his message he echoed specifically the words of his right-hand man, General Amir, "Any strength for Jordan is a strength for the Arab world. Therefore I can see no objection."

Here was good news! Nasser had seen the force of my arguments, and I was delighted at the response to my letter. We proceeded to draft a confidential note, not yet binding us to join the pact, but getting down to details.

Then suddenly, everything changed. Without warning, the Egyptians launched a heavy barrage of propaganda against Jordan. Within a matter of hours Amman was torn by riots as the people, their senses blurred by propaganda, turned to Nasser, the new *mystique* of the Arab world. "Hussein is selling out to the British!" screamed Cairo Radio. "Egypt is the only really independent Arab country—thanks to Nasser!" The Egyptian Embassy, as we discovered later, worked overtime on persuasion. There was money for anybody who would work for them.

Propaganda poured out of Cairo Radio. One story insisted that the Baghdad Pact was a trick and that Israel would be linked with it next. We knew no country could join without the agreement of every existing member, so it was impossible. But it was equally impossible to get the truth across to everybody, and this and countless other stories were accepted by thousands of people.

I stuck to my guns. Then on December 13, four members

of the Cabinet resigned. Under pressure, Said Mufti, the Premier—a good man, but old—resigned and the government fell.

Immediately the rioting flared up again. By innuendo, the Ministers who had resigned let it be known they had only taken this extreme step through patriotic motives and that perhaps Cairo was right about a "sell-out to Imperialism and the Jews."

In the vanguard of the rioting was the Ba'ath Party. Ba'ath stands for Al Ba'ath al Arabi, meaning the "Arab Renaissance," and though technically nothing more than a group of left-wing socialists originating in Damascus, they had since 1954 been led by a group of opportunists and during that period aligned themselves from time to time with communism.

They organized demonstrations in all the major cities. Political agitators, financed, in my opinion, by Egyptian money, stormed buildings from one end of Jordan to another, while Cairo Radio never ceased to declare, "The Baghdad Pact is an imperialist plot! Get rid of Hussein, the traitor!"

As the mobs roamed the streets, I brought in Hazza Pasha Majali, who had been Minister of the Interior under Said Mufti. He was a man of courage and not afraid to shoulder responsibility. He announced publicly that he was in favor of the Baghdad Pact, and between us, this great patriot and I did everything we could. But we were virtually helpless. This was no ordinary rioting. Though some demonstrations were spontaneous, most of them were cold-bloodedly organized and led by avowed Communists who ran the riots with the authority and discipline of well-trained officers.

Still we might have held on, but on December 19, the Minister of the Interior and two others of Majali's government resigned. Majali tried to find replacements but in vain. There was nothing I could do but dissolve the government, letting a caretaker government carry on with the promise of elections in three or four months.

There was an immediate calm over the country and I believe this calm would have continued but for a most unfortunate factor. Some Deputies, possibly fearing they would not be returned in the election—or for other motives—claimed that the government action in dissolving Parliament was illegal. The law proved them right, for the decree dissolving Parliament lacked a sufficient number of signatures. I had signed it and so had the Prime Minister, but the signature of the Minister of the Interior was missing, for he had resigned just before the decree was made. The Jordanian High Court ruled the decree was unconstitutional and the old Deputies had to be reinstated.

Now all hell broke loose. Riots such as we had never seen before, led by Communists again, disrupted the entire country. This time bands of arsonists started burning government offices, private houses, foreign properties. I had no alternative but to call out the Legion, who with tear gas and determination met force with force. I imposed a ten-day curfew on the country.

Looking back on those days I am quite convinced that the ordinary Jordanians, unaware they were duped by the Egyptians, were profoundly thankful when the Army appeared. Without doubt it saved the country.

What on earth made Nasser change his mind? How could he possibly send such fulsome compliments and assure me of his support and then, in a matter of hours, try to tear Jordan apart? I cannot recall another incident in world history where a statesman has made such a *volte-face*. At one moment President Nasser encouraged Jordan to take this step, he gave it his blessing, he even sent his trusted experts to help me; and then at the critical moment he turned against us and nearly destroyed my country. That was the end of Jordan and the Baghdad Pact. It was not the end of double-crossing by Nasser!

I was so deeply upset at what had happened, and so fearful of Communist infiltration, that I decided to invite the heads of all Arab states to a conference in Amman. I issued personal invitations to all the leaders, but my plan was foredoomed to failure. Iraq and Lebanon agreed to attend, and Saudi Arabia almost agreed, but was influenced against accepting when Egypt refused point-blank to attend unless each state publicly repudiated the Baghdad Pact. This was obviously something Iraq could not do and so the conference fizzled out.

8

The Palestine Issue

"We will never sacrifice principle for expediency."

JORDAN TODAY is an avowed and active member of the comity of free nations, despite the fact that it faces a complex pattern of hostilities. On one side we have Israel, which Jordan as much as any other Arab nation regards as a hostile force unjustly created in our midst, and helped by some nations of the free world on many occasions since. On the other side are our sister Arab states, comrades against the common foe of Israel, but also frequently hostile to us.

The outward reason for their antagonism to Jordan has been that, in our fight against communism, freedom's worst enemy, we are automatically in close association with other free nations, some of which were largely responsible for the creation of Israel. Our association with the free world, on which the fight against communism depends, has been used at times as a means of almost splitting us from our Arab neighbors. As we seek to strengthen ourselves and stand

114

firmly against the infiltration of communism, we are subjected to the ever recurring jibe, spoken or unspoken, from
friend and foe alike, "What about Israel?"

To our friends we have always said clearly that Jordan will
never give an expedient answer to any such question. No part
of the world is as much a test of men's principles as the Middle East today. Everywhere one sees men of ambition, opportunists sowing dissension, using the unfortunate Palestinian
refugees as political pawns. We in Jordan will never sacrifice
principle for expediency. And I suggest that what is good
enough for a small country like Jordan is good enough for the
rest of the free world. In our opinion, this is the only hope
for future peace. Yet the trouble today is that the world too
often accepts a *fait accompli* as a moral justification for its
continuance.

It is as well to remind ourselves of the origin of the Palestine problem. When one strips away the emotional considerations that invariably cloud the issue, the blunt fact is that
the Palestinian Arab people (ninety-three per cent of the population of Palestine) were denied the basic political right of
self-determination expounded by President Wilson. It may
be that other human rights have been denied the Palestinian
Arabs since then, but this was the basic wrong, the original
sin on which others have been compounded.

We realize how grievously the Jews suffered in Europe during World War II, and we can understand their desire to seek
a better life. As George Antonius says in *The Arab Awakening*, "Posterity will not exonerate any country if it fails to
bear its proper share of the sacrifices needed to alleviate Jewish suffering and distress." But he adds, "To place the brunt
of the burden upon Arab Palestine is a miserable evasion of
the duty that lies upon the whole of the civilized world. It

is also morally outrageous. No code of morals can justify the persecution of one people in an attempt to relieve the persecution of another."

The recent history of events which led to the present situation, in which about a million Palestinians have become refugees, is well known, but it may be of interest to trace, even briefly, a curious succession of incidents over the past hundred years which laid the foundations of modern Israel.

All too often one imagines this to be a relatively recent problem, and it is true that it only became a *major* issue within living memory, but it is not generally realized that as far back as 1838, Lord Palmerston, in appointing the first British Vice-Consul in Jerusalem, instructed him "to afford protection to the Jews generally."

Two years later Palmerston wrote to the British Ambassador in Istanbul, "It would be of manifest importance for the Sultan to encourage the Jews to return to and settle in Palestine, because the wealth which they would bring with them would increase the resources of the Sultan's dominions; and the Jewish people, if returning under the sanction and protection and at the invitation of the Sultan, would be a check upon any future evil designs of Mohammed Ali or his successor . . . bring these considerations confidentially under the notice of the Turkish Government, and *strongly recommend them to hold out every just encouragement to the Jews of Europe to return to Palestine.*" The italics are mine. This was in 1840!

In 1909 the American geographer Ellsworth Huntington wrote that the fellahin of the fertile parts of Palestine "see in the Jew their greatest enemy," and in 1912 there was an angry scene in the Ottoman Chamber of Deputies when Arab members protested at the way Jewish families were grabbing large tracts of land from absentee landlords.

But it was toward the end of World War I that the most shattering blow against the Arab world took place. On November 2, 1917, the British government issued the Balfour Declaration, in which they stated that they viewed with favor the establishment in Palestine of a national home for the Jews. It was a vaguely worded document. The second paragraph read, "It being clearly understood that nothing should be done which may prejudice the civil and religious rights of existing non-Jewish communities in Palestine." Whatever the British might have meant by this, the Zionists had already made up their minds. Dr. Weizmann stated their thoughts bluntly—"to make Palestine as Jewish as England is English." The Balfour Declaration was an iniquitous document and to my mind the root cause of almost all the bitterness and frustration in our Arab world today.

The immediate reaction was so serious, and the Zionists were so active, that in 1919 President Wilson sent a study group, called the King Crane Commission, to the Fertile Crescent. Their object was to test the reaction of the local people to the mandate proposed by Britain, and though according to one writer they "began their study of Zionism with minds predisposed in its favor," when it came to writing a report for President Wilson, facts caused them to change their opinions considerably. They advocated a serious modification of the extreme Zionist program. They reported that in conferences with Zionists it became apparent that they planned completely to dispossess the non-Jewish population of

Palestine by various means. They found the entire non-Jewish
population of Palestine deeply against the Zionist program.
Seventy-two per cent of the petitions received by the Commission in Syria were against the Zionist program. Every
British officer they interviewed insisted that the Zionist
program could never be carried out without force of arms.

The King Crane report was one of the most important
documents ever compiled on the Palestine issue. But what
happened to it? The United States government quietly
pigeonholed it. It was too frank, and was only published unofficially after Wilson had ceased to be President (when
nobody could be blamed for its frankness).

As the Zionists started to take advantage of the Balfour
Declaration and more and more Jews entered Palestine, my
grandfather, then Emir of the newly created Transjordan,
became increasingly worried. Palestine and Transjordan
were both by then under British mandate, but as my grandfather pointed out in his memoirs, they were hardly considered as separate countries. Transjordan being to the east
of the River Jordan, it formed, in a sense, the interior of
Palestine. It produced cattle, cereals and other crops, while
Palestine managed commercial transactions with the outside
world through its ports on the Mediterranean.

They were peaceful, well-ordered countries, working
happily together, until Jewish immigration started building
up. But as thousands of Jews arrived in Palestine, disrupting
life, the Arabs in Palestine from time to time rose against
them. The British, not really knowing what they were trying
to do, found themselves fighting the Jews on one hand and
the Arabs on the other.

In 1931, the League of Nations sent a committee to investigate, and my grandfather wrote to the High Commissioner bluntly that the incidents and fighting "have put an end to every hope of friendship between the newly arrived Jews and the Arabs in Palestine, which has for thirteen centuries been inhabited by the Arabs." Again and again in 1933, 1934 and 1935, my grandfather warned the British that the continued Jewish immigration would have disastrous results, and demanded a new and just policy for Palestine. In 1936, just before Britain sent the Peel Commission to Palestine, King Ibn Saud, King Ghazi of Iraq and the Emir Abdullah of Transjordan issued (on October 9) a proclamation urging the Arabs in Palestine to stop violence, and "rely on the *bona fides* of our friends the British Government and their wish to provide justice."

How vain were their hopes for justice! The Peel Commission declared in favor of partition. There were demonstrations in Amman and other towns in Transjordan. Fighting against the Jews in Palestine increased.

My grandfather still hoped in his heart that some solution could be found whereby the Arab and Jewish struggle for existence would not end in disaster. He alone, of all the Arab statesmen of the thirties, realized that unless a solution was found, the situation would inevitably get worse for the Arabs. He realized that once partition became a *fait accompli,* the disaster would continue for a long time.

He therefore suggested to the British government the establishment of a state comprising both Transjordan and Palestine. The main points of his memorandum to the British were: (a) the Jews in such a Union should be given local

autonomy in certain areas; (b) they should have full administrative powers in these areas; (c) they should be represented
in Parliament on a pro rata basis, and the state should have
Jewish ministers; (d) Jewish immigration should be restricted
to a reasonable number.

For this plan he was bitterly attacked by other Arab states,
but as he wrote on June 5, 1938, in reply to one critic: "The
number of Jews in 1921 did not exceed one hundred thousand. There are now nearly half a million. They own the most
fertile lands and have infiltrated everywhere. Zionism is built
on three pillars—the Balfour Declaration, the European nations trying to get rid of the Jews, and Arab extremists who
will not accept any solution but only weep and wail while
they appeal to those who will never help them.

"I am informed that the Jews have demanded the continuation of the British mandate so they can buy more lands and
bring in more immigrants. Palestine is falling into the hands
of other people. The only remedy is to act quickly, stop the
danger, limit the attacks, and think later how we can remove
these threats completely. Procrastination will kill Palestine.

"I believe complaints are of no avail. I believe that by
uniting Palestine and Transjordan, I could put an end to the
catastrophe. We would be able to run the administration
capably; we would have an army to defend ourselves; we
would close our doors to illegal immigration. I would like to
know whether you have a more efficient solution than I have
been able to foresee."

Nobody had. But nobody would listen to the advice of the
only man who did foresee the perils that lay ahead.

In January, 1939, the leading Arab leaders attended a conference in London to discuss the Palestine issue. Within a

few months Britain issued its White Paper stating that an independent state of Palestine was to be established after a period of ten years.

When he read this White Paper, my grandfather wrote to Britain, "If there is any value for the Islamic East from Burma to Tangier, then it is the obligation of Mr. Attlee and Mr. Bevin to correct the situation."

As this unhappy and sordid story drifted toward its bitter conclusion, the kings and presidents of the states in the Arab League met at Anshass in Egypt in 1946. Here a vital principle was declared, that "The Palestine question is the problem of all Arabs and not Palestinian Arabs alone." From this moment onward the Palestine issue was one that would be shared by Arabs the world over. Yet this significant warning went unheeded. Within a year, Britain gave up the struggle and decided to terminate its mandate.

Immediately the United Nations sent a Special Committee on Palestine to investigate partition. Its report was submitted in August. It was far from unanimous. Seven members recommended partition, three supported my grandfather's plan for a Federal Union with Jewish and Arab cantons; one member voted against making any recommendations at all. It is significant to notice what happened after this. The U.N. appointed an *ad hoc* committee to study the report. This committee rejected by twenty-five votes to nineteen, *with eleven abstentions,* an Arab proposal that the Balfour Declaration should be submitted to the International Court of Justice. Thus, more than half the committee refused to vote against this vital Arab resolution.

Worse was to follow. When the committee finally voted on whether to adopt the Special Committee's report in favor of partition, the proposal was adopted by twenty-five votes to thirteen, *with seventeen abstentions.* So out of a committee

of fifty-five members, only twenty-five voted for the proposal!
It was a moment of disaster for relations between the West
and the Arabs. How right was Sir Muhammad Zafrullah Khan,
Foreign Minister of Pakistan, when he warned the free world,
"Remember that you may need friends tomorrow, that you
may need allies in the Middle East. I beg of you not to ruin
your credit in those lands."

While awaiting the General Assembly vote in November,
the Zionists lobbied furiously for supporters. They have acknowledged publicly the aid given to them by President
Truman (who possibly had an eye on the Jewish vote). They
succeeded in winning the Soviet bloc votes. On November
28, the General Assembly voted in favor of partition by
thirty-three votes to thirteen, with ten abstentions.

It was the end of all hope. Sir Muhammad Zafrullah Khan,
in a post-vote statement, summed up what many members of
the U.N. felt: "In the words of the greatest American, 'We
have striven to do the right as God gives us to see the right.'
We did succeed in persuading a sufficient number of our
fellow representatives to see the right as we saw it, but they
were not permitted to stand by the right as they saw it. We
entertain no sense of grievance against those of our friends
and fellow representatives who have been compelled under
heavy pressure to change sides and to cast their votes in
support of a proposal, the justice and fairness of which do
not commend themselves to them. Our feeling for them is
one of sympathy that they should have been placed in a
position of such embarrassment between their judgment
and conscience on the one side, and the pressure to which
they and their governments were being subjected on the
other."

Now the die was cast. On May 14, 1948, the British Mandate ended, and the State of Israel was proclaimed. President Truman and Soviet Russia immediately recognized the new state. On May 15—the date the last British troops left Palestine—the Arab states sent their troops into the country to restore order and protect the Arab population, already under attack.

The Arab states at the last moment nominated my grandfather as Commander of all Arab forces. Unfortunately, this was a nomination only, as he soon discovered. He was never given proper authority to control the troops of other Arab states. In some cases, he was even refused permission to visit them.

I remember a friend of my grandfather's telling me that he saw him on the day war started. The King said: "I am going to lead my troops into battle myself. I will fight as bravely as I hope I fought for the ideals of the Arab Revolt." Then he was silent. The past, and all his vain efforts for peace, must have passed through his mind, for he added sadly, "I shall fight to the end, but how I wish I may die on the field of battle with a bullet in my head."

He was, happily, saved for further great service to the Arab cause, for it was during the final stages of this war that my grandfather showed more than ever before his strength and wisdom. As the Jews, flushed with victory against the unprepared poorly co-ordinated Arab effort, turned here and there to grab what land they could, hundreds of thousands of refugees, brutally uprooted from their homes, fled in every direction. Many went to Gaza, some struck north to Syria, but most looked to the east, and hundreds of thousands of bitter, disillusioned, hungry and tired refugees crossed the frontiers into the lands of my grandfather.

A man who was never afraid—he once came out of the

Palace and personally dispersed a demonstration!—my grandfather visited every refugee camp. His stocky, tough, bearded figure, handsomely dressed, was known to every refugee who came to him for succor; his was the banner to which they turned.

Just as the fighting was ending, over two thousand Palestinians held a great meeting in Jericho and decided to unite the rump of Palestine and Jordan under King Abdullah. This was perhaps my grandfather's greatest triumph of humanity. While the other Arab leaders sat waiting, watching, hoping, blaming each other, my grandfather acted. A man of great foresight, blended with realism, and a true Arab nationalist, he formally agreed to incorporate into Jordan that part of Palestine which Jordanian troops of the Legion had saved for the Arabs. It was a stretch of country leading up to the West Bank of the River Jordan, until then the frontier of Jordan. My grandfather gave nearly one million Palestinians, many of them refugees and destitute, full citizenship. This is how the West Bank of Jordan came into being, an important part of the Hashemite Kingdom of Jordan. It is important to remember that by this move my grandfather without doubt saved this large area of Palestine from becoming part of Israel. Remember too that in 1948 Jordan had an army of under 4,500.

The King held elections on both sides of the river and enlarged the Chamber of Deputies so that Palestinians were properly and equally represented. In a matter of months, Jordan changed not only in size but in character. Nearly one million Palestinians had been added to the original 400,000 Jordanians. Amman in three years swelled from 30,000 in 1949 to about 200,000 people.

But despite the wise and far-seeing offer of citizenship—a

gesture no other Arab country offered to its helpless brethren —there remained, and still remain today, a million refugees, over half of whom are in Jordan.

Today (according to the official census of refugees in July, 1961) there are 590,822 refugees in Jordan registered with UNRWA (United Nations Relief Works Agency), of whom 416,113 are drawing rations and 224,453 living in camps. Another 182,000 live in frontier villages; 15,988 of them are drawing half rations. UNRWA now has forty-seven food centers in Jordan, one hundred seventy-four milk centers, one hundred seventy-one schools. UNRWA and the Jordanian government run two hospitals for refugees, thirty medical clinics, three mobile clinics and twenty-one clinics administered by volunteer physicians.

We pride ourselves that the refugees are better cared for in Jordan than anywhere else in the Arab world, and one thing we always seek to give them—their human dignity. Our approach to the refugee problem has been simple. If we are to keep their spirits alive and not allow them to wither, since we must try our utmost to uphold their pride and their reason for living, they must be treated as human beings, not merely be left in camps just to survive. It is possible to be alive and dead at the same time, and this we cannot allow to happen. Because of our different approach to the refugee problem, we have been consistently attacked by some other Arab states. They even accuse us of trying to solve the Palestine problem by settling Palestinians and giving them a chance to live so that they forget their cause and lost homeland.

But what we are doing for the refugees is no real solution. It is at best a palliative. While the refugee problem is mainly the most obvious result of some Western powers' abandoned principles, it is a result only, and I do not believe that a policy directed solely toward solving the refugee problem will necessarily achieve a real solution to the original problem—that of ousting the inhabitants of a country which for two thousand years has been Arab.

There can be no solution to this problem unless all the parties concerned genuinely desire a solution. There must exist a real wish to find a general area of agreement from which progress toward a just and honorable solution can be made. Honesty compels me to state that at the present time it is difficult for me to perceive such an area of agreement. Without doubt the State of Israel is doing everything to consolidate its position in a manner as nationalistic as that by which Hitler drove the Jews from Germany. The Palestine Arabs, on the other hand, seek the right to return to their homeland, but Israel's nationalistic ambitions are so passionate that it regards not only any appreciable repatriation of Arabs as a threat to its internal security but even Arab presence in the Jewish-occupied part of Palestine as a threat to the very fabric of its being.

By contrast the Arab world has as its objective a broader nationalism which, while preserving the integrity of the various Arab states, looks toward the eventual amalgamation of them into a larger whole. In fulfilling this aim, we cannot logically ignore the area formerly know as Palestine, where an unresolved issue, involving over a million displaced persons, remains as a living illustration of a grave injustice and of the Zionist threat in the heart of the Arab world. With such divergent aims, what basic area for agreement can there be?

I realize that some Western nations support the principle of "repatriation or compensation." But until this principle (which is at variance with Israel's aims) is completely applied (the Arabs, not the Israelis having the choice), the refugee issue, to say nothing of the other aspects of the Palestine problem, will remain unsolved. Success in solving this problem depends, in my opinion, on a joint international effort.

We are threatened not only by the physical presence of Israel itself, but by the effect which Western support of this presence has had on the attitude of many Arabs and their leaders toward the major powers of the free world. This difficulty has unquestionably influenced the national policies of Middle Eastern countries since the end of World War II, and in some instances it has caused Arab states to establish what may be unbreakable ties with the very forces the free world so steadfastly opposes.

We in Jordan have determinedly resisted this course and shall continue to resist it with all the means at our disposal. Quite obviously, our continued ability to resist, and with it our ability to contribute to the over-all struggle, will hinge, to an important degree, upon the attitude and policies of the West toward Israel. It must never be forgotten that the Middle East is one of the most vital spheres of influence in the cold war today. Napoleon called it "the crossroads of the world," and he was right.

The Palestine issue cannot be divorced from the greater fight for freedom that confronts mankind today. If the West wants stability in the Middle East, if it wants the friendship of all Arab states as a bulwark against communism, then the free world must finally take the initiative with a plan for

Palestine soundly rooted in principles of political and economic justice. And if the struggle for freedom is lost here, it will be because of our failure in the free world to put those principles into practice.

Where there is a gap between principle and practice, there is confusion and insecurity. This provides the crevasses into which the enemies of freedom are only too ready to drive their wedges. Our greatest need as a free world is that our actions be consistent with the principles on which our freedom is based.

9

The Dismissal of Glubb Pasha

"The most important day of my life."

MY DISMISSAL on March 1, 1956, of Sir John Bagot Glubb—or Glubb Pasha, as we always called him—after twenty-six years of service in Jordan was an event of such importance that I have decided to set down for the first time the full and exact facts behind my decision.

There are always moments in the battle for existence, perhaps more so in small countries, when personal feelings must be stifled, and the impersonal takes command. So it was with General Glubb. His dismissal created consternation throughout the world and many were the people who blamed me bitterly for such an extreme step. Not only that: many also saw my action as a calculated slap in the face to the Western allies and jumped much too quickly to the conclusion that because I had requested General Glubb to leave my service it automatically followed that our friendship with the British had ended and possibly even our alignment with the free world. This theory, ardently propounded in the popular Western press, is as farcical as suggesting that if an ambassador becomes *persona non grata,* a request for his withdrawal means antipathy to his government. This is not necessarily the case and was not so with Glubb.

What most people did not realize is that the dismissal of General Glubb was a strictly Jordanian affair, since Glubb was the commander-in-chief of its army, employed by the Jordan government. My main motive in dismissing him was because frankly we were in disagreement on two issues: the role of Arab officers in our Army and strategy in the defense of our country. Since one of my duties as monarch is to ensure the safety of my people and my country, I felt I would have been failing in this duty had I not sought to replace him.

What was done had to be done; and I think now, after conversations with Glubb Pasha since that day in 1956, that he probably appreciates and even sympathizes with this point of view.

He was well aware that behind the many influences which brought the clash between us to a head lay the ghost of my grandfather. He was a man from whom I had learned the fundamental precepts of Arab independence, in which he played such an outstanding role. He believed, and I believed with him, that the greatest of its principles is that all Arab peoples must be masters of their own affairs.

Even if my grandfather's dreams did not all materialize, he never swerved from this dedication. Neither have I, so that here was a fundamental issue on which the General and I were inevitably at loggerheads. It was my express desire to have more of Jordan's officers in high army posts, to take over gradually all commands in accordance with a realistic plan which could be implemented. But this was against the prevailing British policy, and their counterproposals were, to say the least, ridiculous. (Under the Anglo-Jordanian Treaty, Jordan received approximately $36 million a year of British financial aid, and Britain supplied officers to "train" the Arab Legion. In effect, they virtually ran it.)

As the servant of Jordan, I always endeavored to give Jordanian citizens increasing responsibilities. Even more so, I wanted to give them the confidence in themselves which was their right. I wanted to give them pride in their country, to get them to believe in it and its future, and in its role and duty toward the greater Arab homeland. Obviously one way was to gain for them an increasingly bigger voice in the country's affairs, including particularly the Army. Glubb, on the other hand, despite his love for Jordan and his loyalty to my country, was essentially an outsider, and his attitude did not fit at all into the picture I visualized. Yet, since the Arab Legion was the single strongest element in Jordan, he was, paradoxically, one of the most powerful single forces in our country. Consequently, to be blunt about it, he was serving as my commander-in-chief yet could not relinquish his loyalty to Britain.

Throughout the Army this led to a fantastic situation in which the British dominated our military affairs to a great degree. Around me I saw junior Arab officers who would obviously never become leaders. Some of them were men lacking in ability and force, men prepared to bow to Whitehall's commands (transmitted by senior British officers), men who had no spark, men without initiative and who could be trusted not to cause any problems. These were "officer material."

Those with nationalist aspirations, who hoped for a Jordanian Arab Legion, never had an opportunity for promotion, and when they did they were assigned to unimportant positions with no promise of advancement. It was bitterly frustrating to young men. Time after time I demanded that the British should prepare more Jordanian officers and train them for the higher echelons of the armed forces. Time after time my requests were ignored. The highest active post a man could hold was regimental commander.

It did seem to me that, after months of patient negotiation, I had won one small battle, when the British authorities finally agreed to submit a plan of Arabization which "in due course" would give more opportunities to Jordanian officers.

Here was a victory! At least I thought so. Imagine the excitement when I told my Cabinet. All that remained was to discover what "in due course" meant. But my elation was short-lived when I was gravely informed that the Royal Engineers of the Arab Legion would have an Arab commander by 1985! Was it possible that any outside government could be so unrealistic? It was—because the British government at that time was incapable of realizing that one cannot brush aside a nation's aspirations and say, "We will talk about it in thirty years."

I am the first to admit that it was probably not Glubb's fault, and that he was presumably mainly taking his orders from Whitehall. Indeed, on many occasions he tried very hard to help us.

But our overriding problem remained unaltered—somehow we had to give our own men a chance, especially in a country like Jordan where the Army is not only an instrument for defense against foreign incursions but is a part of everything

Jordanian. To Jordanians, with their martial history, it is and has always been an honor and a privilege to be a soldier. No man in the Arab world held his head higher than did the troops of the Arab Legion. But for the officers it was very different, for they saw in a profession to which they were devoted no hope of rightful progress.

This, however, was not all. There were far more personal problems. Glubb, who was now only a month away from sixty, had been with us so long, it was hard to imagine what life in Jordan without him might have been. He had been a part of the Arab world since 1920 when, at twenty-three, he served in Iraq. He first came to Transjordan (as it then was) in 1930 to command the Desert Force and had been in command of the Al Jeish al Arabi—to give the Legion its Arabic name—since 1939. The Bedouin nicknamed him Abu Hunaik ("Father of the Little Chin") because of a disfigurement of his jaw. His cherubic face beneath its silver hair and his brisk figure jumping in and out of his Land-Rover were as much a part of the landscape as the great Mosque of Amman. Politicians held sway and slid into oblivion. Ambassadors came and departed. But Glubb went on forever—efficient, energetic, good-mannered, unchanging. But one thing had changed. The times.

Twenty-six years is more than a third of man's allotted span, and in this period General Glubb had been largely isolated from the outside world. To be quite frank, it was my impression that he smacked too much of the Victorian era. He has said that I was young and impetuous, while maintaining that he himself was older and more cautious. That is true. But Jordan is a young and impetuous country, and we were, and still are, in more of a hurry than Glubb was to achieve our national aims. And because of this very vitality, the last thing I wanted was a cautious army. Although a fine soldier, Glubb at fifty-nine was old-fashioned in many ways. I disagreed, as he well knew, with many of the strategic plans he drew up for the defense of the country, above all his military line of defense against Israel. This was the second facet of our disagreement.

One must always remember that Jordan has a longer frontier with Israel than any Arab state—nearly four hundred miles out of six hundred seventy. In 1948, when Israel was created, the Arab world received a severe check to its aims. Its troops were humiliated, largely because many were untrained and many were poorly armed, and because there was little proper co-ordination and planning of the Arab effort. Jordan, in fact, was the only country that did well. Though the Arab Legion consisted of less than 4,500 troops, it managed to told on to the greater part of the Arab Palestine. It achieved the impossible in keeping for the Arab world a large section of Jerusalem, and saved the holy places of all believers.

The reaction by the rest of the Arab world to our role in the war was astonishing. Instead of thanking us, most of those leaders who in fact were responsible for the Arab defeat immediately turned on Jordan. Activated by jealousy and the need for a scapegoat, they twisted the truth unbelievably and let loose a barrage of propaganda blaming us for losing the war! In the lead was Egypt.

They seized especially on the fact that the Arab Legion was commanded by Glubb. It was very convenient for those Arab states which had done almost no fighting. However, we had learned our lesson in the war and we in Jordan determined that never again would we allow the Jews to take the initiative against us.

If war came, I argued, we should plan to start our defense right on our four-hundred-mile frontier with Israel and accept death with honor if we could not hold it. I realized it would be suicidal to spread our Army over the entire front and fight any war on a purely defensive pattern. We could never hold such a long frontier with such a small force. So we began to train some of the civilian population. At first we named this force "Front Guards," then "National Guards." Their major task was to defend the area in depth, giving the more professionally trained and better-equipped Arab Legion the opportunity to attack selected points in Israel if we were attacked. A start was made with the "National Guard" idea, now a force more than twice the size of the armed forces, and similarly equipped, but it was not enough. To my way of thinking, a purely defensive strategy invited disaster. If the enemy knew that we would hit them as hard as they hit us, where it hurt them most, it would make them think twice before attacking.

I also felt strongly that we should answer with force the Israeli commando attacks against Arab villages. On several occasions the Israelis crept across the frontier, burned houses or even villages, killing defenseless Arabs, then returned to Israel. I argued that every time such an outrage occurred we should select a target on the other side and do the same to them. It would soon have stopped the Israelis. As it was, we accepted these outrages meekly; the people were helpless. The U.N. condemned the Israelis, but that did not stop them. Our soldiers were ridiculed, a great gulf grew between the Army and the people.

In vain I pointed all this out to Glubb. To all my pleas he

advised cautious patience. He advocated at first a withdrawal
that, in the event of attack, would end up on the East Bank,
pending the arrival of reinforcements before we could develop a counterattack. This meant Jewish occupation of the
Palestinian territory Jordan occupied. It meant going back to
the original frontier. It was unthinkable, and though in the
end, as military capabilities improved, a line of defense was
drawn in the West Bank area, nearer Israel than Glubb had
previously planned, it still meant losing a lot of territory before a battle even started.

Glubb, knowing that a million Arabs had already been
thrown out of their homeland by Israel, apparently could not
realize that if Israel ever set foot on Jordanian soil, especially on the rich West Bank, we Jordanians might never be
able to tread that soil again.

I argued with Glubb on this principle of defense. There
were other arguments when I learned that we were short of
ammunition. I realized he had some justification for his theory. But this was not a matter of theory; this was the margin
that separates the honor and the shame of a nation.

When the United Nations armistice first came into operation in 1948, an essential condition was that no side should
increase its power to wage war. Britain, which was under
treaty obligation to supply Jordan with arms, discontinued all
supplies. Israel received all the arms it needed; the embargo
made no difference, and some considerable supplies came to
her from the Communist camp.

"Why can't we get some more supplies of ammunition?" I
asked Glubb. But behind his replies I knew there lay a whole
sequence of tragic events. I knew Glubb had ordered ammu-

nition, and that at one stage in 1948 a fully laden ship had left for our shores only to be turned back by the British and the United Nations. I realized perfectly well that Glubb had urged Britain to send us more ammunition. (In his book *A Soldier with the Arabs* he mentions on page 213, "The British refused to give us ammunition but they agreed to send barbed wire.")

We continued to try desperately to get sufficient reserves of ammunition, without success. Ammunition had to come from Britain, since we used British arms and Britain insisted on implementing what was known as the balance of power— all the vast Arab world on one side and Israel on the other. The Israelis continued to receive shiploads of ammunition from France and other sources, which made Jordan's position ridiculous and made the so-called balance of power even more ridiculous.

Since Britain did not supply us sufficiently, I could not honestly blame Glubb for his unwillingness to commit the Army to battle plans, because for such plans our ammunition depots were virtually empty. In that sense, Glubb was perfectly right in suggesting that we could not defend our frontiers. Thus, though it was not really Glubb's fault, his very presence in our country was without doubt an important factor in the trouble. We were in the hands of foreigners. If Glubb could not stock our ammunition depots, then, as a good general, he was in no position to advise me to fight an honorable battle. Yet, look what has happened since Glubb left. Today our armed forces have grown tremendously; our ammunition depots are full, and the strength of the Jordan Arab Army has stemmed from that one primary military axiom—give a soldier the right arms.

I also tried to build for Jordan its own Air Force. What good was an army against a powerful air-minded foe like

Israel when we were at the mercy of another country for air support? The situation was absurd.

This state of affairs, which he was powerless to rectify, naturally led Glubb to encourage his officers, Arab or British, to accept the view that we must yield territory in the case of attack. On more than one occasion Glubb, in his lectures to officers, asserted that since Israel was stronger than the Arabs, our determination to fight on the frontier was unwise. I remember being extremely angered when he publicly advocated his West Bank theories.

All these problems came gradually to a head. I was determined to build up strong, well-balanced armed forces, including an Air Force, and since this was not possible with Glubb, our self-respect demanded that we fight our battles alone.

One thing led to another. With communism filtering into the Middle East and Cairo branding Jordan an "imperialist power," there was no alternative. Glubb had to go. Let it not be thought that I dismissed an old and trusted friend in a fit of emotional pique. Glubb Pasha is a great man and knows as well as I that this is far from the truth. At the same time I must admit I had disagreed with his strategy. This being so, there was no other course but to carry out my decision. It was a surgical operation which had to be done brutally. I knew I was right; indeed, I would say that if Glubb had been in command of the Army a year longer, it would have been the end of Jordan. The country would have been carved up among the other Arab states seeking aggrandizement.

On many occasions it has been suggested that the dismissal of Glubb Pasha was a sudden decision. One story even suggests that I acted in a moment of anger after reading a story in an English magazine describing him as "the real ruler of Jordan."

What nonsense! The Foreign Office in London knew months in advance of the differences between Glubb and myself. Less than a year before Glubb was dismissed, I visited London. I personally held discussions with the Foreign Office over the subject. I warned British officials frankly that Jordanians had to be given more opportunities in the Legion. I was fobbed off with promises that the matter would be considered, but nothing was ever done.

To suggest, therefore, that this was a sudden decision is a travesty of the truth. I thought long and seriously before I took such an important step. I knew that our Army was so weak that Israel could have overrun us. Other Arab states would hold us responsible for this weakness. I wanted to remain friends with the British—nothing was further from my thoughts than to terminate that friendship—but it was essential to prove our country independent, free to speak its mind, and free to act without outside influence or dictation. We had to build up our power to defend our homeland; we had to preserve our dignity.

I was also not content with a situation where my commanding officer could dabble in politics. Glubb did not deliberately interfere in Jordanian politics, but he had been with us so long and wielded such power that he was incapable of divorcing himself from politics. Glubb operated from a position of such strength that our political leaders tended to turn to him or to the British Embassy before making the slightest decisions.

A classic example of this occurred when the Soviet Union, wishing to establish diplomatic relations with Jordan, approached our chargé d'affaires in Cairo and requested him to transmit a message to me. This message reached Jordan through diplomatic channels to the Prime Minister. When he received it, the Prime Minister did not consult me but took the message, without informing me, to the British Embassy first!

This was just the sort of thing I fought. I wanted Jordan's leaders to stand on their own feet even if they made mistakes.

Events are often determined in a curious fashion. Although I felt Glubb must go, I had not yet fixed the exact time. Then two events occurred. I had for some time felt that our security forces (which included police) should cease to come under Army control (which meant Glubb). How could a police force and an army be run by the same man? Was it even right? Two days before Glubb's dismissal, I tried to arrange the matter with the Prime Minister.

"I feel our security forces should come under the Ministry of the Interior," I told him. He predicted serious repercussions. But what I proposed was our concern only. It had nothing to do with the British. It was an internal affair.

I was really very angry, but I decided to sleep on it that night. The next day—the night before Glubb's dismissal—something else occurred. I was presented with a list of officers about to be dismissed. Their only fault, as far as I could determine, was that they were nationalists and ambitious. How could they be anything else?

Though Glubb was the commander-in-chief, I myself had to sign the papers. I refused to sign the document. I threw the list on the table in my office and told the Prime Minister: "Tell Glubb Pasha I refuse to sign this."

I remained obdurate, for what really made me angry was

the realization that even my own ministers, however loyal, felt helpless to act within their rights.

No sooner had I made this decision than the Prime Minister's final reply to my request regarding the security forces arrived. It was not possible at the time, he said, to arrange the division I had suggested.

As I received the reply, my Chief of Diwan, Bahjat al Talhouni, happened to be in the office. I was quiet for a moment and then, in a burst of rage, I threw the papers I was working on all over the floor and stalked out of the room. Poor Talhouni! I left him for several hours that night wondering what he had done to annoy me.

That night I decided Glubb Pasha would have to go immediately. I have told General Glubb since then that the last thing I desired was to hurt his feelings, nor was it a pleasant task to dismiss a man who had served our country so faithfully for twenty-six years. I pondered the possibility of allowing him to "resign" gracefully with perhaps a little extended leave before the resignation took effect, but I knew that the matter could not be handled this way. I did not believe I could allow any commander-in-chief of my Army, particularly at a time when we were gravely threatened by Israel, to "work out his notice." Such a course would have been ridiculous even with a Jordanian. How much more dangerous when the commander-in-chief was an outsider. No. Though I knew General Glubb would be upset at the brusqueness and suddenness with which this painful episode took place, it had to be done the way I did it.

At 10 A.M. on Thursday, March 1, 1956, I drove with my Chief of Diwan through Amman to the Prime Minister's of-

fice. I was in uniform and, as usual, I was preceded and followed by Land-Rovers containing my escort of armed soldiers. On the way I told Talhouni for the first time what I
proposed to do. And I remember adding:

"This is one of the most important days of my life. I don't
know what its end will be, but one can only live once and
only with honor."

We arrived at the Premier's office, and, as I stepped
through the doors of the white building, I knew that this was
something I must handle myself. My Prime Minister was a
good man, a loyal friend, one who had served Jordan in many
a difficult time, but I could not waste time in arguments.

I had written out the necessary orders myself that very
morning after breakfast, so when I faced the Prime Minister, I put the piece of paper firmly on his desk. (I did not
throw it, as Glubb Pasha said in an article.) Those few lines
ordered the immediate dismissal of Glubb Pasha.

"These are my wishes," I told him. "I want them executed
at once."

The Prime Minister was a trifle stunned, but understood
quickly that things had gone so far that there could be no
backing down. I then told the members of the Cabinet: "I
believe what I am doing is for the good of our country. I
want all of you to be very careful for the next few days.
Keep in touch with my Chief of Diwan if there is any cause
for worry. I am certain this is the right thing to do, but
there are bound to be repercussions. I am ready to take what
comes." I then left my Chief of Diwan at the Prime Minister's office to see that everything was carried out.

I know that Glubb was distressed not only by the sudden

decision itself—it was, of course, more sudden to him than it was to me—but by the speed with which he was requested to leave the country. For when the Prime Minister saw him at two o'clock that afternoon, he suggested that Glubb should leave at four. I sympathize with Glubb's firm retort: "No sir, I have lived here for twenty-six years and I cannot leave on two hours' notice."

I too would have felt angered and, in fact, Glubb did not leave until the following morning. I would like to point out that, though he was dismissed, he was dismissed with full honors. He was driven to the airport in my own royal car. My Defense Minister represented the Cabinet and my Chief of Diwan represented me. They both bade him good-by.

But one thing is certain. The speed with which he left was a matter of vital importance. I knew only too well the pressures that would be brought to bear against me. I knew that should Glubb Pasha remain in the country for another week, the pressure would be too great. I was still very young—only twenty-one—and it was no small thing for me to pit my weight against the whole of Britain. I certainly felt that I would be in a much stronger position to argue with White-hall if Glubb were out of the country, so once the decision had been taken it had to be implemented quickly.

I was right. All that night, while Glubb and his wife were packing, I faced an unremitting barrage from the British to make me change my mind. When the news broke in England it shocked Whitehall as much as it had stunned my Prime Minister. Cables piled up on my desk beseeching me to revoke my decision. Sir Anthony Eden cabled me personally asking me to change my mind. Mr. Charles Duke (now Sir Charles Duke), the British Ambassador, requested an audience in the afternoon. He was deeply distressed and asked

me to see if there was no way in which he could report back
to the Foreign Office that I might change my resolve.

Late into the night I worked with my advisers, planning
new appointments—one cannot leave an army running without new blood to replace the old. I also had to watch carefully for any repercussions. So it was nearly midnight before
I retired. At one o'clock in the morning the British Ambassador telephoned my Chief of Diwan and requested
an audience. He was told that I had retired and that I was
not to be disturbed unless the matter was of great importance.

The Ambassador insisted, so I hurriedly put on a few
clothes including a sports shirt instead of the more formal
collar and tie. I came down to the small study in the Basman
Palace.

It was a tense meeting. The Ambassador, whom I liked
very much, was visibly moved. I had been tired out when I
went to bed, but now, wondering what was to come, I was
wide awake and alert.

At first he did not know how to start and there was little
I could do to help him. He sighed heavily and then said:

"You must be aware, sir"—and I think these were his exact
words—"that the step you have taken has caused a tremendous uproar in London."

He sat there obviously overcome with emotion. He had in
his hand a message from London.

"I must advise you, sir, that Her Majesty's Government
feels that unless you change your decision immediately on
this matter, unless Glubb Pasha is permitted to continue his
work here and we are given a chance to clear this whole mat-

ter up, the consequences, Your Majesty, could be very serious as far as you yourself, the monarchy"—he hesitated—"and the whole future of Jordan is concerned."

These were strong words, with implications I well understood. They made me a little angry, not because I was afraid, but because it indicated that already world opinion was distorting the dismissal of Glubb Pasha—purely a Jordanian affair—into something far more serious.

I told the Ambassador, "I know my country, and I know my responsibilities. I am going to carry out what I believe to be right in the best way I can."

He did not respond, and then I added:

"I believe, Mr. Duke, that what I have done is for the good of my country and I am not going to alter my decision, regardless of any consequences. I would rather lose my life than change my mind. The monarchy belongs to the people; I belong to this country; I know that I am doing this for the best, come what may."

There was nothing the Ambassador could say. He left, presumably anxious to get in touch with London via the radio link from the British Embassy. I returned to bed. At three o'clock the Ambassador returned and asked for another audience. I suppose by then he had received a further communication from London, but my Chief of Diwan told him it was impossible to see me.

"But I must see the King at once!" insisted Mr. Duke.

"His Majesty is resting and won't be disturbed," explained my Chief of Diwan.

"But this is very important!"

Talhouni's English is not of the best, but he was a little irritated. Searching for the right words, he tried valiantly to remember the idiom "So what!"

Instead he came out with a classic substitute, one which must have puzzled the Ambassador:

"And if?" he retorted.

The Ambassador took the hint!

I was under no illusions but that in dismissing Glubb I was playing with fire, but even so I retained the hope that the Western world would try to put the matter into perspective. I was appalled at the wrong interpretation Britain put upon my action. I could understand how dramatic the news must have looked on the breakfast tables of so many homes that morning, but I was bitterly upset that officially Britain did not understand that the dismissal of Glubb had no bearing on my admiration for his country. Nothing could make this admiration of mine more clear than my directive to my Prime Minister on March 6, and I hope the text (which was never originally intended to be published) will clear up the misconception that arose—and arose, I may say, through no fault of mine. This directive read:

> You are no doubt aware that our action in depriving General Glubb of his post was due to loss of confidence in his judgment and the fact that his presence had become a troublesome factor in our country.
>
> But at no time did it occur to us that this matter should lead to any change in the relations between Jordan and Her Britannic Majesty's Government, which are governed by treaty, or that the traditional friendship between our two countries should be affected.
>
> With regard to British officers serving in the Arab Legion, kindly note that Jordan will honour her obligations towards them according to their contracts and to the treaty.

After proper consideration it is our aim that these officers should continue to serve in the Legion, to raise its standard to the level we hope for.

With reference to rumours that we intend to replace the British subsidy by an Arab subsidy, your Excellency is no doubt aware of the existence of a treaty with Great Britain which confers certain benefits on both parties.

Payment of an Arab subsidy, assuming it were to be made, does not in any way annul the effectiveness of the Anglo-Jordanian Treaty.

Nonetheless, Jordan welcomes every form of Arab assistance of a kind she can use to improve her position along the armistice lines where she faces a perfidious enemy and to fill in gaps in her military defence system following the recent transfer of command into Arab hands.

In view of the above I trust your Excellency will do the utmost to emphasise and expound these facts in the interests of the country.

In spite of this announcement, indignation in Britain now seemed to swell into near hysteria. It was certainly in no way allayed by Sir Anthony Eden's statement in the House of Commons in which the Prime Minister said:

The House will have heard with resentment and regret of the summary dismissal of General Glubb and two other senior British Officers of the Arab Legion. The lifetime of devoted service which General Glubb has given to the Hashemite Kingdom of Jordan should have received more generous treatment.

It is right to tell the House that the King of Jordan and the Jordan Prime Minister have told Her Majesty's Ambassador that they do not want any change to take place in Anglo-Jordanian relations, and that they stand by the Anglo-Jordan treaty.

I appreciated the public statement in the second paragraph, but why, then, should Sir Anthony disparage my promise by adding:

Her Majesty's Government have given due weight to the Jordan Government's statement regarding the officers. They feel that in view of the treatment meted out to the British officers who have been dismissed, it would be wrong for British officers in the Arab Legion to be left in an uncertain position. In our opinion officers in executive commands cannot be asked to continue in positions of responsibility without authority. We have, therefore, asked that such officers should be relieved of their commands.

And since the Prime Minister admitted that the dismissal of Glubb was a strictly Jordanian affair, I was perturbed when he added, when discussing the Anglo-Jordanian Treaty:

It is clear from the treaty that its whole spirit is based on the need for consultation to ensure mutual defence, and in this sense General Glubb's dismissal is, in view of the Government, against the spirit of that treaty.

I had hoped for a little more understanding; so much so that I decided to write a long personal letter to Eden, in which I explained in great detail that our disagreement with General Glubb was essentially of a personal nature. I emphasized to Sir Anthony that the dismissal of General Glubb had absolutely nothing to do with the relations between our two countries, and that if the British took his removal as an insult to their country, they misunderstood my motives. The fact that Glubb Pasha had gone—and I was careful to explain this to Eden—had no bearing on the fact that I hoped British officers would remain in the Arab Legion.

I am sometimes tempted to wonder if some governments really understand the countries about which they talk so glibly. While back-benchers in Whitehall were up in arms and newspapers in Fleet Street were screaming abuse, what was the truth? One has only to turn to the columns of *The Times* during that week. In this British newspaper, its special correspondent in Amman, a very acute observer, wrote in part:

> Amman is still *en fête* in celebration of General Glubb's departure and it must be recorded that the pleasure seems to be both universal and genuine. Young Arab Legion officers claim to believe that it will take politics out of the army—on the grounds that General Glubb refused promotion to officers not sympathetic to Western policies.
>
> There are even a few who think it will help rather than hinder good relations with Britain (and many who are convinced that if Britain had voluntarily withdrawn her officers long ago, perhaps incorporating them in a military mission, such an unhappy event would never have occurred).
>
> Western reactions to the dismissal have been read with surprise here. It seems strange that people should be so taken aback at the fact of General Glubb's removal, however affronted they may be by its manner. His position here, for all the years of his devoted service to the State, was an undoubted anachronism. The whole trend of Arab policy for years has been towards the removal of such symbols of Western influence.

Only one thing remains to be said about this unhappy episode. What had to be done was done and it was for the best.

But at the same time, my own personal admiration for the efforts and work that Glubb Pasha put into the Arab Legion remains unchanged. He contributed to our Army's progress in all fields and despite the fact that he left us so abruptly, I am not alone in appreciating the foundations he helped to lay so solidly and on which we have since built an army of which we are proud, an army that has the highest standard both in training and morale in the Middle East today.

Glubb Pasha I still consider as a friend. We have met three or four times, including one evening when, with genuine pleasure, we had a long talk at a reception in London. Occasionally we correspond or send cards; and apart from the work he did for Jordan, I admire him for one other reason. I knew that he was bitterly hurt at what happened. I knew that he felt he had been perhaps unjustly treated. But he is a wise old man, now in his sixties, and his wisdom was never so apparent as in the way he reacted publicly to the whole affair. Another man, less wise, would have become so emotionally aroused that he might have damaged the work he had undertaken for so long and all the success he had brought about. Glubb Pasha acted with restraint and dignity in a great crisis of his life.

When the British press was raving and ranting and putting the most unfair interpretations on his dismissal, Glubb actually wrote a letter himself, which was published in the *Telegraph,* upbraiding those who were magnifying the issue and pointing out this was not an anti-British move but an internal affair. So, even when he left our shores and flew away from the home he had occupied for twenty-six years, he put the interests of Jordan above himself. I hope he will return to visit us one day. He will always be most welcome.

10

A King Against the Government

"I am going to fight, whatever the consequences."

THE TWELVE MONTHS following the dismissal of General Glubb was a period of uneasy experiment. The years during which strong British influence had permeated our affairs were at an end, and though I was delighted that my country should now stand firmly on its own feet (as it had every right to do), I knew full well that the vacuum left by the sudden departure of British army officers must inevitably lead to complications. It was perhaps our misfortune that we had to start very nearly from scratch. First, it was essential to find the right men to lead our country and especially our Army. British influence had been so overwhelming that Arab officers had never expected the opportunity to show whether or not they were capable of holding high rank. Now we had to experiment and inevitably we made some mistakes.

Politically we faced similar problems because for many years our leaders had ceased to think of Jordan as a country standing alone; in any crisis it had become almost axiomatic to go to the British Ambassador for advice.

As the months wore on and the year turned into 1957, the pressures increased until eventually they blew up in the spring of that year—almost exactly a year after Glubb left us—into what has now become known as the Zerqa uprising, in which, thank God, I thwarted, but only by minutes, a deeply laid, cleverly contrived plot to assassinate me, overthrow the throne and proclaim Jordan a republic. Had it succeeded it would unquestionably have meant the beginning of the end of Jordan.

How was it possible that this full-scale revolution so nearly triumphed? How was it possible that I should find myself almost alone in the world, standing between two groups of firing soldiers, so close that I not only smelled the bullets but felt the heat?

The answers to these questions are fascinating, and so is the way in which the plot was slowly unraveled. But one thing I know: the Zerqa uprising, which nearly cost me my life, was ironically one of the great turning points for the better in the history of Jordan. I think of it now, looking back on that awful night when I drove toward a battlefield, as the cleansing of a running sore that had slowly been festering and eating away the hearts of loyal men.

The coup was essentially political, but naturally at that stage in Jordan's development the Army was a force which had to be taken into account. Consequently, paid agents, working with diabolical cleverness, managed to involve the Army in the crisis. Because we were experimenting, it was not difficult. All foreign agents had to do was to look for unstable officers unused to power, and in many cases they were able to gain their adherence one way or the other.

The same applied to politicians. I take full responsibility for that period of experimentation. I felt deeply that Jordanian political leaders had relied too much and overlong on outside help, and it was only natural that these politicians met with bitter opposition from the younger, rising men of ambition, who, like myself, thought it was time to throw off the shackles that had bound us for so long.

I decided, therefore, that younger and more promising politicians and army officers should have a chance to show their mettle in this new phase of Jordan's history. I realized that many were leftists, but I felt that even so most of them must genuinely believe in the future of their country, and I wanted to see how they would react to responsibility.

In the elections which took place toward the end of 1956, the National Socialists gained a party majority. The Ba'ath party and others, even the Communists, had some seats, with Independent members forming the actual majority. The Secretary-General of the National Socialists, Suleyman al-Nabulsi, was actually defeated at the polls, but since his party had been voted into power, he became Prime Minister. (In Jordan, one can hold Cabinet rank without necessarily being elected.) Nabulsi was a leftist, but more so an opportunist. Even then I felt he had to have his chance. At first things went fairly smoothly, but gradually the monarchy and the government began to clash more and more.

It may seem curious that freely elected politicians should enter into plots against me instead of contenting themselves with planning reforms. The fact is that the major "reform" of the Nabulsi clique was to abolish the monarchy and finish Jordan as an entity. For twisted motives, some material, they decided that Nasser and the Communists offered them a better hope for the future. The lengths to which Nabulsi went were really quite fantastic. On December 21, for example, he addressed a big political meeting in Amman. For thirty minutes the Prime Minister of Jordan stood up and glorified President Nasser. Not once did he mention the role of Jordan in the Middle East.

Egypt, Syria, Saudi Arabia and Jordan had become members in the Arab Solidarity Agreement. The Anglo-Jordanian Treaty was terminated, and the three Arab states undertook to assist Jordan's budget with the equivalent of the earlier British subsidy. This was after Suez. Jordan, with myself in the lead, had stood by Nasser in his greatest moment of crisis and had influenced all Arab states to do the same. There was the Arab summit conference held in Lebanon during the Suez crisis. It was brought about by the efforts of my good friend Camille Chamoun, then President of Lebanon. Between us we organized the meeting of Arab Heads of State to rally to Nasser's support. Suez to us was a national crisis requiring an Arab show of strength and solidarity. We almost had to drag the rest of the Arab leaders to the conference, and we forced out of them the maximum support to Egypt that they could offer.

All Nasser's past actions against us were forgotten at that moment of crisis. But soon King Saud, President Chamoun and I (and our countries also) were to become the targets of Nasser's destructive plans. The issue was plain—a choice between freedom and communism.

Nearly four years before Nabulsi came to power, Jordan had passed the "Combating Communism Act" of 1953 which prohibited Communist newspapers in Jordan. Yet on December 31, Nabulsi and his followers passed a resolution allowing the publication in Amman of a Communist newspaper called *Al-Jamaheer*. Nabulsi also allowed the Soviet Tass Agency to set up a bureau in Jordan and distribute its bulletins freely. Soviet films even started appearing.

Presumably Nabulsi thought Jordan would soon be liquidated. And we must remember that propaganda from neighboring countries grew steadily more menacing. The truth became hopelessly twisted over the Glubb affair. I alone had taken the decision to dismiss him, but now it seemed as though every ambitious politician had taken this step himself. It was now they who claimed to have thrown out "imperialism" and brought about the "freedom" of Jordan. Partly due to the struggle for power, partly as a result of bribery and outside influence, but mainly through complete disloyalty to the concept of Jordan, they so distorted recent history that I found myself (I, who had dismissed Glubb!) cited as an "imperialist agent" and the only obstacle to even greater freedom. My stand on Suez was completely forgotten.

It sounds incredible but there it was, and soon the anti-Palace movement spread to left-wing army officers. I do not blame them entirely. The propaganda was terrific. Fortunes were being spent in bribery; the Soviets were openly promising arms to the Army "once the traitor Hussein has gone."

It was hard for me to pin down the moment when I first began to realize the increasingly dangerous turn events were taking. I had been worried for many months and I think it was in the first week of 1957 that I knew we were in for really serious trouble. I was alone in the Palace one night when an army officer from Beirut requested an audience. I knew him well; he had been sent to Beirut on a special mission, and when he came into my study and I asked him to sit down, he said to me:

"Your Majesty, I don't want to make trouble where there might be none, but I am very worried about the way our army officers are behaving in Beirut and Damascus. Time after time I've seen army officers spending fortunes in the night clubs—money they couldn't possibly earn. They always seem to be with Russians or the Egyptian clique."

I asked the officer, who must remain nameless, why he had come to Amman, and he told me that he had requested a weekend leave, ostensibly to visit his family, but actually for the express purpose of coming to see me.

"The only thing is, Your Majesty—I've really got nothing concrete to go on," he added. "It's rather like a detective novel when you can't go to the police because nothing can be proved. But I felt I should warn Your Majesty and I brought back with me a list of names. What do you want me to do now?"

I thought for a minute, and then I told him to fly back to Beirut the next morning and continue to keep watch. I also suggested that one or two Jordanian agents, whose loyalty was unquestioned, should also assist him; and so we continued to observe the antics of some of our senior officers and politicians who were spending large sums of money abroad.

Unfortunately, we had a stroke of bad luck when two agents were arrested while taking the number of a Jordanian car outside the St. George Hotel in Beirut. Both were wearing civilian clothes, but both were found to be armed and had to admit they were Jordanian officers. They were deported, but even so I had by then received serious warnings. They boiled down to this:

Infiltration by Soviet or U.A.R. influence was directed at several key men in the Army and the government. Among them were Shafiq Rusheidat, the Minister of Justice and Education, and General Ali Abu Nuwar, Chief of Staff of the armed forces, and once a close friend of mine. We learned that both were making regular visits to Damascus and holding meetings with the Soviet military attaché there. Another target was Abdullah Rimawi, Minister of State for Foreign Affairs (not to be confused with Foreign Minister; we had both titles in the government). Rimawi was a member of the then Neo-Communist Ba'ath Party. He and the other Ministers drove regularly to Damascus, especially after important cabinet meetings. They returned the following morning. These three all received money. Secret Service agents told my Chief of Diwan, "If the police open their bags at the Syrian-Jordanian frontier post of Ramtha, they will find money in any of their suitcases."

Altogether these traitors brought well over $300,000 in Jordanian money into the country, some for themselves, some to be used for bribery. Yet we never opened their bags—it is rather a serious thing to do with Ministers, so we played a waiting game.

I do not want to give the impression that the entire Army was collapsing, but we had reached a stage when many officers and politicians did not really know where they were going. Some were genuinely nationalistic but felt that Jordan was too small to stand alone. Some decided to offer themselves to other Arab states, which in fact meant offering their services, in most instances, to communism. Thus, our once efficient Army began to deteriorate. Soon it was composed of differing factions, each with its own political beliefs.

Remember, too, that the whole of the Arab world was in ferment. Communist arms were pouring into Egypt, communism itself was beginning to take a foothold in the Middle East, playing the cunning game of apparently sponsoring Arabism when, in fact, as we all know, communism is the worst enemy of any national movement. Without doubt, Communist agents were largely behind the trouble, and as the crisis deepened they instigated riots in the streets. In the early stages they were not serious, except for one thing. The security forces that should have dealt with them frequently refused to interfere.

The Chief of the security forces at the time was Bahjat Tabbara, a loyal man who fought in vain to gain control of this vital department where Cabinet Ministers and the Chief of Staff each had his own agents among the higher officers of the security forces. These officers by and large were completely disloyal and obeyed only the orders of their particular chiefs. The ordinary policeman did not know at all what was happening. He did not, of course, take his orders from Tabbara, but from his immediate superior, often the tool of men like Abu Nuwar. When a policeman was told not to interfere in a riot, his job was to obey orders, not to query them. After Bahjat Tabbara resigned—he objected to outside interference—things got considerably worse.

The spring arrived uneasily. Spring is a beautiful time of the year in Amman for there are splashes of green among the desert-brown buildings; the shaded gardens and the lawns are fresh, and the weather is not unduly hot. Yet it was an unhappy spring. I could sense the atmosphere becoming more and more oppressive. Mobs, often paid with Communist money, roamed the streets, deliberately inciting crowds to riot; the Cabinet was in turmoil; enemy propaganda stirred up ugly passions.

It was always the same story—"Nasser has thrown off imperialism. Follow the savior of the Arab world!" How amazing the ease with which professional propagandists get their message across. It was almost impossible to fight so many enemies on so many different fronts. Facing us was the powerful army of Israel, and who knows if our politically indoctrinated Army could have held them. Despite my faith in my troops, I was apprehensive. We were being stabbed in the back by sister Arab states; our own country was ripe for violence.

Things had gone far enough. I decided on one step. I sat down and wrote to the Prime Minister pointing out in the strongest possible language the dangers of communism as I saw them and I told him without any nonsense that Jordan must take a different stand if our country wanted to continue to defend itself.

In the letter I said in part:

The present cold war between the two world blocs has brought to our country certain principles and beliefs which are in sharp contrast to our own. Strange views have infiltrated into our midst. Unless these unwarranted principles, beliefs and views are curtailed and stopped within certain limits, they will affect all the glory and prestige for which our nation stands. Imperialism, which is about to die in the Arab East, will be replaced by a new kind of imperialism. If we are enslaved by this, we shall never be able to escape or overthrow it.

We perceive the danger of Communist infiltration within our Arab home as well as the danger of those who pretend to be Arab nationalists while they have nothing to do with Arabism. Our ranks must be free from corruption and intrigues. We will never allow our country to be the field for a cold war which may turn to a destructive hot war if the Arabs permit others to infiltrate their ranks.

We firmly believe in the right of this country to live. Its foundations must be strong and built on the glories of the past and the hopes of the future. No gap must be left to allow the propaganda of communism to ruin our country. These are our views which we convey to Your Excellency as a citizen and as our Prime Minister.

We hope that you and your colleagues, the Ministers, will adopt an attitude which ensures the interests of this country and stops the propaganda and agitation of those who want to infiltrate through to the ranks of the citizens. The standing laws and regulations of this country will provide you with ample opportunity to act. The conscience of the people will help you and support your efforts.

As soon as I knew Nabulsi had received the letter, I made it public. The majority of people of Jordan—the honest, God-fearing people who form the backbone of the country—hailed it with delight. Not so my Cabinet. Almost immediately some Cabinet Ministers gave highly distorted interviews to foreign newspapers and agencies, especially to Tass, the Soviet news agency, and the Middle East news agency of Cairo. Within a few hours, newspapers were printing stories of how the Palace and the government were fighting each other.

The day after he received this letter—which was the key to everything that followed—Nabulsi requested an audience. He arrived, accompanied by Abu Nuwar, Rimawi and other leftist Cabinet Ministers. The reason for the conference was simple. They wanted me to modify and "tone down" my letter attacking communism.

"Absolutely not!" I replied. "What I wrote in that letter to the Prime Minister is a directive on policy, not only for this government, but for any that follow."

The meeting lasted nearly an hour, but I refused even to

consider any changes. It was a quiet discussion on the whole, for Nabulsi had one trump card which he was to play sometime later. He was going to initiate steps to recognize Red China and establish diplomatic relations with the Soviets. It is true that I had the power to veto such a move, but Nabulsi hoped that if I said "No" I would be attacked as an "imperialist agent."

In the meantime, my letter caused quite a reaction. It was the beginning of the final battle for Jordan. Syria's Foreign Minister, the Ba'ath leader Salah Al Bitar, actually sent a message to the Jordanian government criticizing our attitude and suggesting that Jordan become more friendly to the Russians and Chinese Communists. My government refused to send him a reply I had prepared for him. I was furious with what I considered a great impertinence. I met him in Cairo, however, and told him my frank opinion of such interference. Nasser also was upset by my attitude. It was the last time Nasser, King Saud, Kuwatly of Syria, and myself met.

On one side were Nasser and Kuwatly for communism. On the other, myself and King Saud. It was nearing the tragic end of Arab solidarity. Incidentally, Jordan never received any of the aid promised by Egypt and Syria.

As I returned to Amman, Nasser and the Communists were firmly behind Nabulsi's group. The issue of diplomatic relations with Russia and Communist China, the fight between the government and the Palace, flared up. The government's move, and my reaction, was followed by riots led by anti-royalist politicians and army groups. Again the security forces refused to stop them. Incredible though it may seem, Nabulsi, the Prime Minister, addressed an enormous crowd in the main square in Amman making fiery speeches, while on his left was Esa Madonet, a key Communist agitator, waving to the people. Imagine the head of a government doing such a thing after receiving a letter ordering him to put a stop to Communist penetration.

By now we had reached April 8 and suddenly I discovered that an armored regiment had moved up and surrounded the capital. They were at strategic points everywhere. Nobody could enter or leave Amman without passing their guns.

I was thunderstruck. I knew things were grave—but an armored regiment! This could only mean one thing—imminent danger to Jordan, a possible attack on the Palace. Certainly it indicated that Abu Nuwar was plotting a military coup.

I sent for him, and trying hard to control my rage, I asked him what on earth was happening.

"It's purely routine," he answered smoothly. "Just a matter of checking the traffic in and out of Amman."

A likely story! However, I suggested the regiment be withdrawn—a suggestion offered casually—and Abu Nuwar agreed and left.

Now I was really alone. I had virtually nobody I could trust, but what was I going to do? Hour by hour the situation was deteriorating. I had few friends to help me and a government openly hostile to me.

The next day the armored vehicles were withdrawn, but I knew this might only be a temporary respite. The time for action had come.

On April 10 I arrived at my office and I told Talhouni, my Chief of Diwan, "It's time to throw this government out!"

I dictated a letter to Nabulsi ordering the dissolution of the government, and Talhouni carried it to the Prime Minister's office. The Cabinet was meeting when Talhouni arrived. Talhouni asked the Prime Minister to leave the meeting. When they were alone Talhouni conveyed the gist of my letter to him, but did not hand him the actual letter, fearing Nabulsi might use it for political propaganda. After a short conversation Nabulsi went back to the cabinet meeting. Then they sent for Abu Nuwar, Chief of Staff, and two other officers. Why? To ask their advice! Abu Nuwar told Nabulsi, "You should resign, if only for one reason. The King will never be able to form another government without you. Do it. Resign! I know how to force the King to ask you back."

A few hours later Nabulsi came to the Palace and submitted his resignation. In his letter he carefully pointed out, "by order of Your Majesty"—doubtless so he could use it for propaganda.

That evening my uncle, Sherif Nasser, came to see me with other members of my family. He was deeply worried about the grave turn of events, though he did not know how close we were to a military revolt.

He was very blunt.

"I hate to say this to you, sir," he said, "but everything seems to be lost and the rumors and reports indicate that you are alone. Are you going to stand and fight or should we all pack our bags? Don't you think we ought to think about our families and their future and try to move them out of harm's way?"

"I can't," I told them. "I must stay. You know I believe in what I am doing; I believe that I can only live once."

It was not only a stubborn stand on my part. I felt that I understood the people of Jordan and I believed in them, despite appearances to the contrary. I had tried to bring about a family atmosphere so that I was not separated from the people and believed that if or when the crucial moment arrived we would not necessarily lose. There had to be some wisdom, there had to be some individuals who believed in Jordan, there had to be some people who would realize we were heading for disaster.

"No," I said to my uncle, "I cannot leave. You know that I believe in serving my country. I am going to stand and fight, whatever the consequences."

11

Zerqa · · · The Final Round

"We are in a race with the morning sun."

WE WERE NOW in the midst of the holy month of Ramadan, the month of fasting and good deeds. Yet right from its first days I had sensed that before the month was over there would be a showdown. The issues were too great, too fundamental to be patched up. But though I felt I had done my best for my people both in Jordan and in the bigger family in the Arab world, I had my first doubts as to whether I, or for that matter, Jordan as a country, would see the feast that heralds the end of the month of Ramadan. I remember when this doubt first crossed my mind. I had motored for a few hours' rest to the Jordan Valley where my uncle, Sherif Nasser, has a small farm. One cannot eat, or even smoke, until sunset during the holy month, and we sat there, waiting for the sun to go down, so that we could have breakfast and a cigarette with our first cup of tea of the day and I suddenly wondered, Where will it all end?

One thing I was sure about. I would fight for my people

to the end. But things had gone from bad to worse. The Nabulsi government with its leftist elements, backed by Cairo's President Nasser, had infiltrated all walks of life. Propaganda and every other device to control and influence people were sweeping the Arab world. To find a job in Jordan one had to belong to a party. Even to pass an examination at school one had to belong to a party! Nasser's Arab nationalism was taking the place of pure Arab nationalism. Communist party meetings were blatantly held in Jordan's open squares. The red flag could be seen many a time in Jordan, despite the fact that communism was banned by Jordanian law.

All parties, each one fearful of the other, distributed arms to their members. But one vital question remained unanswered: Would the real people of Jordan, the great majority, who watched these events apprehensively, stand by their country? It would not be long now before I knew. Events were moving swiftly to a climax. I prayed for my country and people, and I prayed, too, for the strength and stamina to do my best.

But what enemies I faced! For example, just before Nabulsi resigned on April 10, 1957, an open cable was intercepted. Incredibly, it was from President Nasser to the Prime Minister of Jordan. The contents were even more incredible. The cable said in effect: "DO NOT GIVE IN. REMAIN IN YOUR POSITION. SIGNED, NASSER."

The tug-of-war had begun with myself and what I hoped would be all of the genuine elements of Jordan against forces that had ceased to believe in Jordan or be loyal to its concept. Throughout April 11 and 12 I tried in vain to form a new government. I first asked the late Dr. Hussein Fakhri Khalidi, a prominent Arab nationalist from the West Bank, to form a new Cabinet but he soon found it was impossible. I was in constant consultation with all political figures. It was the beginning of many sleepless nights filled with one crisis after another. Nabulsi had made certain that none of his followers would help anybody trying to form a Cabinet.

The supreme confidence of those who were fighting me is best illustrated by a conversation that took place at a night club in Amman where Nabulsi and his group were drinking late into the night, with Ali Abu Nuwar, the commander of Jordan's armed forces. I learned later what had happened. Nabulsi turned to his friends and asked aloud, "Who do the people stand with?" The reply was "With you!" Then he turned to Abu Nuwar. "Who does the Army stand with?" And Nuwar replied, "With you, Your Excellency."

"Then," asked Nabulsi sarcastically, "who has the King got to stand with him?"

When Khalidi found it impossible to form a government, I then received in audience Abdel-Halim Nimer. Nimer, like Nabulsi, was a member of the National Socialists, but I hoped he might be able to form a new Cabinet that would not be too extreme. He himself had been a minister in Nabulsi's cabinet. But the National Socialists and their collaborators refused to let him, except on their own terms. They insisted that he include several well-known Communist sympathizers. This I could not accept. I then thought about Said Mufti, but in the meantime Abu Nuwar and his friends had decided that if they could not have a government headed by Nabulsi then it might be a good move to appear to support Nimer. They were playing for time. They were trying to put me off balance.

It was now April 13, the day of the Zerqa incident; Abu Nuwar soon heard that I was proposing to ask Said Mufti to form a Cabinet. During that day several remarkable things happened. I found out that Abu Nuwar had been in consultation with Egyptian officials and with the Soviet officials in Damascus. In retrospect, the astonishing thing about these events is the matter-of-fact way in which Abu Nuwar began increasingly to take control of the whole political scene. Later that morning Abu Nuwar held a meeting with left-wing politicians, and it was decided to support Nimer. But there remained one obstacle. They knew that I had refused to accept Nimer's complete list of proposed Neo-Communist Cabinet ministers.

It was time for a few veiled threats. Early that afternoon, Said Mufti was summoned to an army camp outside Amman. When he arrived, this loyal patriot was confronted by Abu Nuwar. He was invited to sit down in a private room. A number of senior officers were present. Then Abu Nuwar, as leader of the group, told Said Mufti bluntly:

"You must go to the King immediately. You will tell him that the situation in the country and in the Army is extremely explosive. Inform the King that unless a Cabinet which will be satisfactory to the people and all parties is formed and announced on the radio by no later than nine o'clock tonight, then I and my colleagues will not be responsible for anything that happens."

Stunned, humiliated and angry, Said Mufti left the meeting without a word and drove straight to the Basman Palace to see me and deliver the message. I told him not to worry. It was not his fault that he was the bearer of such insolent words.

I was not going to give in to threats, but I decided to call in Nimer for one last try. We had a long discussion on the formation of a Cabinet. He did not prove too difficult—in fact, he admitted that he himself found his "friends" difficult. I felt that perhaps there might still be a way out of the impasse. He left for more discussions.

Things by now developed swiftly. Abu Nuwar drove to the Palace and had a talk with my Chief of Diwan. Said Mufti was still present and Abu Nuwar declared again:

"If the Army doesn't hear that the Cabinet has been formed by the nine o'clock news, the country will be in trouble and you will be among those responsible for it."

Then he added significantly:

"You must consider this statement a final ultimatum."

Curiously, Abu Nuwar used the English word "ultimatum."

It might have still been possible to form a Cabinet, but then an event followed that changed everything.

Shortly afterward a group of officers from Zerqa arrived at the Palace. They had with them the son of one of the paramount tribal leaders of Jordan. They did not request an audience, but gave my Chief of Diwan an urgent letter to be delivered to me personally.

I opened it, and as I started reading, I forgot everything else. With a stunned feeling of despair I reread the vital paragraph:

"The loyal officers in the Zerqa area are worried, sir, because of the strange orders we are receiving. We have information that some of the units will soon be ordered to surround Amman. Sir, we are full of doubts about the loyalty of those in command and we beg you, sir, to let us have our orders cleared through Your Majesty."

The letter went on to say that some units with reliable, loyal commanders had been sent away to various parts of Jordan, as I well knew. The First Armored Car Regiment was still in Zerqa, but was commanded by Nazir Rashid—a bosom friend of Abu Nuwar. Abu Nuwar's own cousin, Ma'an Abu Nuwar, commanded the Princess Alia Infantry Brigade in Zerqa. I had some doubts about him, but even more about some other unit commanders in Zerqa, Jordan's biggest military camp, the "Aldershot" of our country.

Almost immediately afterward my uncle, Sherif Nasser, who had commanded the First Armored Car Regiment before leaving the Army, came to me. "An officer wishes to meet you secretly, sir, on a very urgent matter," he declared.

I asked my uncle to bring the man—an officer I knew to be loyal—to my private study immediately.

He came in. His name was Abdul Rahman Sabila. He had been delegated by officers, N.C.O.'s and troops of the Armored Regiment to come to me. He was a fine man, a true Arab.

"How far have things gone?" I asked him. In his deep voice, his eyes shining with determination, he began:

"Your Majesty, there are traitors everywhere but not in the First Armored Regiment, sir. Trust us, sir. The officers, N.C.O.'s and men are all standing solidly behind you."

He went on to explain what had happened. The regiment commander had met some officers in his command and explained to them the mission of the regiment. The plan was to prepare to move at short notice on to Amman, to surround and capture the Royal Palace and myself at the sign of the least resistance. And the orders included the sentence, "You will reply to each bullet with a six-pounder shell."

The First Armored Regiment was chosen for this task—and all were promised glory. However, the officers met among themselves and took an oath to remain loyal to King and country. They later advised those N.C.O.'s and troops they trusted, and they all agreed to pretend to remain loyal to the

conspirators, meanwhile advising me of developments. They
would then await my instructions. I thanked God there were
men like this in Jordan, the country in whose service I had
dedicated my life. Jordanians were awake after all and everything was not lost! Incidentally, this was the same regiment
that had surrounded Amman a few nights earlier. It had been
a rehearsal and show of power.

I asked Abdul Rahman to return to his unit.

"Advise your friends and colleagues," I told him, "to be
very, very careful not to show their true colors until the last,
vital moment. Keep in touch. God be with you."

Then I sat back alone and reflected. I was deeply worried.
I was not afraid of death—I have seen it too often and too
close at hand to fear it—but I was very much afraid for my
country and people and for the armed forces which have always been my pride and that of every Jordanian. The big
crisis was near and I became increasingly angry. I went back
to my office and asked Abu Nuwar to come and see me. It
was time to act quickly before things got out of hand. I was
going to have it out with my commander of armed forces
once and for all.

As I waited, I cogitated on the strangeness of mankind.
What was the real motivating force behind the traitorous
conduct of Ali Abu Nuwar? Here was a man who had once
been my friend. I had placed great hopes in him—faith and
trust too. What made him a traitor? Was it simply that he
had given in to the Communists and their Egyptian collaborators? He had certainly fallen increasingly under their control and become deeply involved with them by the time of

the crisis. But was that all? Or was there something else that
drove him . . . the greatest weakness of mankind—the lust
for power?

I knew that if Jordan collapsed it would be the severest
blow to the Arab cause in a long, long time. Israel would
surely strike and the Arab countries—what was left of them—
would be Communist-dominated or carved up among the
victors. If Jordan went, one more obstacle would vanish before the Communist tide that aimed at flooding the entire
Arab world. There were even those who said openly, "Let
Israel take the West Bank. We will be able to recover it with
Nasser's leadership and Communist support."

It was by now nearly seven o'clock. For almost a week I
had had no sleep. I had been working in my office night and
day trying to sort things out, watching and working. When
Abu Nuwar entered my office I looked at this thirty-four-
year-old, dapper man of medium height, with his neatly
trimmed black mustache. I could restrain myself no longer.
Angrily I demanded a full explanation about everything I
had learned that afternoon, about his attitude, about his part
in all that had been happening.

As he started to speak, the telephone rang—a sharp, long
note. I picked it up. It was a very urgent call for Abu Nuwar.
On the other end of the line was Abu Nuwar's cousin, Ma'an,
the commander of the Princess Alia Brigade.

I heard his frightened voice speaking swiftly. Abu Nuwar
went pale and stole a glance at me. Then he shouted into the
telephone, "Prevent them, for God's sake. Stop them at all
costs. What about the artillery? Where is General Hiyyari?"

Quite clearly I heard the voice of Ma'an on the crackling
line. "It's already out of control. The whole brigade believe
that their King is dead, or will be tonight. The officers

couldn't control them. They are trying to move on to Amman. Nothing can save the situation but the immediate presence of His Majesty."

Ali looked at me. I snatched the phone out of his hand.

"I'll be right over!" I cried, and to Abu Nuwar beside me, I added, "You wait here. I'll be back in a moment."

With that, I ran out of the office.

"Get me a car quickly," I cried to Talhouni, my Chief of Diwan.

In the hall I told two aides-de-camp—one of whom was my cousin Zaid, the other the commander of my small personal guard:

"Both of you go quickly. Tell any troops coming to Amman I am alive and well. Tell them to return to their barracks. I will follow you shortly."

I quickly changed into uniform and was back in a matter of minutes. I called to Abu Nuwar:

"Come along, we are going to Zerqa."

I jumped into the front seat of the car beside my driver. It was a Palace gray Chevrolet. Abu Nuwar and my uncle, Sherif Nasser, sat in the back seats. We shot off toward Zerqa. Ali's car and aide-de-camp followed behind. I do not think I have ever been so furious in all my life, as I thought of Jordan's fine Army being jeopardized by conspirators.

Suddenly we met a full army truck at a bridge called the Russeifa Bridge. As both cars and the truck came to a stop I could see the truck jam-packed with troops and civilians, yelling angrily, holding rifles and sticks over their heads. As I jumped out an officer and troops leaped from the truck. Suddenly they recognized me. It was one of the most moving moments of my life. Tears came to my eyes as we all kissed and they mobbed me. "We are your men!" they all yelled. "Thank God you're alive, sir! Down with the traitors!"

I asked them to go back and got into the car. I had not noticed Abu Nuwar. He had evidently stood behind the cover of the car. He got in and, as we started to move, the truck turned and raced behind us. I could hear them yelling and firing into the air. Suddenly Abu Nuwar spoke. I looked back at him. He was trembling with fright.

"Sir, please let me go back to Amman," he begged.

"Why?"

"Sir, I heard them calling for my death. I have a family and children, sir. If I go on with you, I won't live the night."

"Stop the car," I told the driver. I was disgusted. "Get out, go back and wait for me at the Palace."

So the King, without his commander of armed forces, drove into the unknown to deal with an army uprising. Soon we encountered more trucks, more angry troops, more civilians, more shots breaking the peace of the night, more stops, more road blocks. Officers pointed submachine guns, unknowingly at their supreme commander, but not recognizing me until I yelled or jumped out.

"I am Hussein. I am all right. My life is yours. All is well. Back to your camps. I will be there shortly."

The scene was fantastic. Some troops wore steel helmets, some had no jackets; there was even one soldier with shaving soap drying on his face. They all cheered. I could not hold back my tears. At one moment the poor Chevrolet was bumping on its flattened springs. Then the roof caved in. Troops had got on top and as we drove on they would not get down. However, my uncle, an athlete and heavily built,

soon put his shoulder to the roof and pushed it back in place.
We also got rid of some of our passengers.

In the Zerqa camp itself I could find no trace of my two
aides-de-camp, but I later rescued them near Divisional
Headquarters and the headquarters of the Princess Alia Brigade. They had been arrested by troops who refused to believe their story and thought they were conspirators. They
were pretty annoyed by the time I arrived.

At one point burned trucks that had been shot up stopped
our progress and there were more clashes to come.

Slowly the story began to take shape. In the Princess Alia
Brigade, a regiment had been paraded and addressed by the
brigade commander. They were told they were to leave immediately on a long march, an exercise, without their arms.
But the troops had heard strange rumors. They felt that
something unusual was happening.

Suddenly, an N.C.O. had yelled:

"What about the King?" Within seconds the place was in
a turmoil. That regiment, followed by the rest of the brigade,
broke into ammunition depots. Officers they suspected were
mobbed and soon the first troops were on their way to Amman to discover the truth for themselves. I myself found the
brigade commander running on the road alone. I picked him
up, but already some damage was done. The conspirators
had acted quickly. They brought down the artillery units,
telling the artillery troops the infantry were moving onto
Amman *against* the King. The stunned artillery went out to
stop them and so the fighting started, each side believing the
other guilty.

I drove on to Divisional Headquarters, where troops had

smashed everything in their way, then I went to Brigade Headquarters. Here, too, everything was broken, save a portrait of the Princess Alia. I spoke to troops while standing on the car's hood, then from the top of an armored car. At times, heavy machine-gun fire whistled past my head and I could even feel the heat of bullets whizzing past in the dark. I nearly lost my gun at one place where I was mobbed. Only with the greatest difficulty was I able to leave the Brigade Headquarters. Troopers cried, "Down with traitors!" and "Down with communism!" More shooting occurred, and at first the troops refused to let me go on. "They will kill you, sir. We won't leave you!" they cried. I finally left and drove into the artillery lines.

It was a little tricky between the two lines of firing troops, but luckily nothing happened. Although I did not know it, there was another narrow escape that night. A conspirator officer, knowing I was coming, had mined a small bridge and was waiting to blow it up as I drove over it, but a bullet out of the dark wounded him and my car passed safely over the bridge.

Now I found that Abu Nuwar had not gone directly to Amman. He had tried to re-enter the camp area by a back road, but finding troops motoring down toward his car, he turned and then went back to the Basman Palace. No doubt he hoped to find the Armored Regiment surrounding the Palace. He told the Chief of Diwan that I had sent him back to reassure him and my staff that I was well and to await my return.

I spent several hours in Zerqa and it was not until nearly midnight that I drove back to Amman, having established order everywhere.

Driving back toward the capital, I felt a strange exhilaration. That night was a turning point in Jordan's history. The nightmare of Zerqa was over, and now I felt more confident than I had been for a long time. I was dreaming as we drove along, and then suddenly, as we turned into the main Palace gates, I was brought up with a shock against reality. I had forgotten all about the Armored Car Regiment that was supposed to move on Amman and surround the Palace. Two armored cars stood at the gate, their guns pointed outward. As we stopped, troops and N.C.O.'s in their black berets jumped out, eyes shining, crying "Long live our King! Down with Communists and all traitors! If they dare to raise their heads, then by God we will level the place flat."

We kissed and embraced and as I drove up to the Palace, I saw more and more armored vehicles. They were behind every corner.

I ran up the Palace steps to look for Abu Nuwar. The front hall was crowded with jeering troops and I learned Abu Nuwar was in my small study. I was also told what had happened after he arrived. When the troops arrived Abu Nuwar had tried to talk to officers of the Armored Regiment, obviously thinking they were his allies, but a sergeant major had stopped him on the steps, his Sten gun in his hand and, looking his commander-in-chief in the face, said:

"If you weren't in the King's Palace, I would blow your head into a million pieces. Get back and pray that the King comes back safe and sound; then he can tell us what to do with you."

In the small study Abu Nuwar was in a state of collapse. Troops milled around the Palace screaming "Down with communism. Death to Abu Nuwar and all traitors!" Two officers from the loyal regiment came in, and I let them confront Abu Nuwar. Then he retired to the next room. He was crying now, an abject figure. He was a pitiful sight.

What was I to do with this man who had once been my close friend? The past flashed by as I heard the officers shouting at him. I remembered the good companion of Paris days. I even remembered, like a picture, a dinner we had enjoyed at the Colisée restaurant. Then I thought back to the young, energetic helper in whom I had reposed my trust when I was alone. How we spoke of our pride in Jordan. How often I had discussed with him my plans and his place in them. And now—this! A whining man, tears streaming down his face, trembling for his life.

I ordered him into my private study.

"Well," I asked him. "What do you expect me to do?"

Nuwar's black-mustached face was the color of ashes. He begged me to save him.

"But what have you done to justify the faith and trust I once put in you?" I asked him.

Almost collapsing, he pleaded with me again to save him. Incoherently, he mouthed lies, lies, lies. I suddenly felt desperately tired—an anticlimax, I suppose, to a week of crisis upon crisis. And my heart was sick that a man whom I had trusted could behave thus, that humanity itself could breed such deceit.

I could not bring myself to put him to death. I have been criticized for this act of mercy—and Abu Nuwar has certainly been an active enemy ever since—but there it is, I could not do it. Is it past memories that chain one with sentiment? I was so tired, so sick with shame for my fellow human beings, I could not do it.

Though many think I was wrong to spare his life, they

forget one important factor apart from my personal feelings. I could not tell at that time what would happen in the next few weeks and I did have one quite cold-blooded thought in my mind—I would not make a martyr of him. If I had put him to death, his name might have been much more revered than it is today. I said to him again:

"Well, what do you wish me to do?"

He said: "Can I take a fortnight's leave in Italy until things clear up?"

"All right," I said. "Go!"

I knew that once he left Jordan we would probably never see him again. In fact, he spent the night, ironically, at the home of Said Mufti, whom I asked to look after him. He was in a state of collapse, and Said's brother, a doctor, had to give him a sedative. The next day Abu Nuwar and his family left for Damascus. They have never returned.

It was now after midnight but there was no question of sleep. I had two things to do: to form a Cabinet and arrange to tell Jordan the truth over the radio. Our main transmitter was at Jerusalem, and in Amman we had only a small studio and a tiny transmitter, with a range that did not even cover the whole country.

However, our troubles were by no means over and it took us some days before we achieved real stability. In those sleepless days and nights I formed one government that did not last; I appointed a new commander-in-chief who escaped to Syria; and our main radio station did not operate from Jerusalem when most needed because its director and some of his party members on the staff closed it down.

The army units, one by one, pledged their loyalty to King

and country and a great deal of reorganizing had to take place in the disposition of troops. Outside, the pressures were still immense. Israeli troops were concentrated on Jordan's front, ready to pounce. Radio propaganda from all leftist radios in the area intensified their barrage to a point never reached before. Then, while I grappled with these problems, a Syrian armored brigade under the supreme command of Egypt's General Amir, moved toward Amman from its base in the north and completely surrounded the Jordanian city of Irbid. Would our troubles never end?

Two brigades—one from Syria, one from Saudi Arabia—had been stationed with our consent in Jordan ever since Suez. But to surround a Jordanian city! Neither the Syrian President nor the Syrian army commander knew of this move or who had ordered it. However, King Saud rallied to my support at this stage by putting his forces in Jordan under my direct command. It was a good brigade and we did our best to train it into an efficient force.

The day after the Syrian move—which I promptly countermanded—the new Jordanian armed forces commander left for a meeting with the Syrian commander at the frontier. With some misgivings, I had appointed General Hiyyari to succeed Abu Nuwar. After he had taken his oath of allegiance, I went to sleep for a few hours—for the first time in many days. I left my uncle, Sherif Nasser, who was by now back in uniform, on duty. We were so used to crises that when he learned that General Hiyyari had crossed the Syrian frontier and sent his guard back, he did not even bother to wake me up. It was seven in the morning when Sherif came into my room. Hiyyari had left hours before.

"Good morning, sir," he said.

"Good morning," I answered. "What is new?"

"Nothing important, sir, just that your commander-in-chief has escaped into Syria."

"What! Why didn't you wake me up?"

"I did not think it was important enough to disturb your badly needed rest."

I could not help laughing, for we had known Hiyyari was involved with Abu Nuwar and was a weak man. I made him commander-in-chief only because there was nobody else at that stage. My uncle's natural calm amused and cheered me immensely. Anyway, I thought, things cannot get much worse.

I quickly put General Habis Majali, an old and trusted friend, in charge of the armed forces. Then I turned to the political scene. Even the government could not last. It had been formed under Dr. Hussein F. Khalidi and included Nabulsi and representatives of all other groups, but the strains and stresses from within pulled it to pieces. The violent mobs destroyed its dignity. In Jerusalem the leading Communist member of Parliament, Jacob Ziadun, threatened at one stage to destroy and burn the holy places of Islam and Christendom—which he called "the opium of nations"—if the people did not demonstrate against Khalidi.

When the Prime Minister came to offer his resignation he had tears in his eyes. He told me: "I lost my parents, sir, but did not shed a tear. Now I can't hold them back, seeing what irresponsibility is doing to my homeland. I have, however, prepared everything to the best of my ability in case martial law has to be brought about. It seems the only way out. Good luck, sir, and thank you for your confidence."

I thanked him for all he had done. He had been under a

great strain. Other politicians whom I had summoned were
in my Diwan.

It was about 10 P.M. I spoke to them at length, explaining
the critical situation. Among them were my old friend Ibrahim Hashem, who was later to lose his life brutally in Iraq,
and Suleiman Toukan and Samir Rifai, many times Prime
Minister of Jordan. This was no time to mince words. I gave
them the whole clear picture.

"Gentlemen," I said, "this is not a request, this is recruit-
ment. We are in a race with time—with the morning sun!
Either a government is formed before then or it is the end of
Jordan. We need control—quick and firm control. I cannot
do it alone. It is your country, and remember, many of you
helped to build it. This is no time for argument."

A government was formed in record time under Ibrahim
Hashem, with Samir Rifai and others. The radio people were
standing by for my long speech to the people of Jordan. We
imposed martial law, banned all political parties, put troops
in position on a temporary basis.

The morning came. I stood out in front of the Palace,
breathing the fresh air. This was the morning when peace
came to Jordan as traitors ran in every direction, as their
secrets were revealed, as calm and sanity prevailed. At last,
about 10 A.M., I went to sleep. I had lost track of days and
nights, but I slept long and peacefully after praying to God
for all His blessings. Jordan had come through. Zerqa was
the turning point.

The holy month of Ramadan came to an end and the
people of Jordan celebrated with feasting. But I think everybody in Jordan remembered to thank God for His wisdom in

saving our country, whose very existence had been in the balance during all that holy month of fasting.

So ended the final round. As one Bedouin officer had told me, even new flags had been designed for the republic of Jordan. We found two samples in Abu Nuwar's office. He was so sure of success, he had not even bothered to conceal them. Obviously, the plot had been organized from outside. Equally obviously, the final optimistic objective, after murdering me, was probably to establish some kind of federal union with Egypt—and thus make Jordan in effect a vassal state of Soviet Russia.

Looking back now as I write these words, it all seems like a nightmare. The last I heard of Abu Nuwar, he was in Egypt. Nimer, whom Abu Nuwar tried to force on me as Prime Minister, is now a farmer not far from Amman. Nabulsi was kept under house arrest until 1961, but is now free in Amman. Ma'an Abu Nuwar is now a member of our foreign service. After answering for his actions, he studied political science and is a sincere, loyal Jordanian and a hard worker.

It seems hardly possible, looking back, that these men were involved in a coup that was brilliantly engineered and all but succeeded. Only one thing the plotters who wanted to ruin Jordan had failed to reckon with:

The Jordanian people.

12

The Arab Union

··· And a Warning

"Promise me to tell the King of the danger."

ON FEBRUARY 14, 1958, Iraq and Jordan were joined by mutual constitutional agreement to form the Arab Union. It was a historic event, and for me not only the climax to years of struggle but, I hoped, the beginning of a new era for the Arab cause. Based on absolute equality, it was an attempt at a model union between two states. It constituted the first realistic, idealistic step toward the fuller, more comprehensive Arab unity so lacking today. Alas, it was more than some Arab statesmen of the period could stomach. Five months to the day after signing the treaty, my cousin, King Feisal, lay brutally murdered and the Arab Union was to all intents and purposes nothing but a shattered dream. The blame for this outrage will in the main rest on one man—President Nasser.

The reason is simple. Ours was everything a union between friendly states *should* be; a fortnight previously, Egypt and Syria had formed the United Arab Republic—in my opinion, everything a union of states should *not* be. In the Arab Union, Iraq and Jordan were equal partners. The United Arab Republic was an unbalanced arrangement in which one partner, Egypt, had a dominant role, while the other, Syria, was subservient. Nasser possibly saw in our union an idealism lacking in his own plans. Moreover, I believe he was astute enough to know that other Arab states would compare unfavorably what he had done with what we had done. If they joined us, his power would wane. Nasser knew also that Iraq, bordering his eternal target, the oil-rich Persian Gulf, was in itself one of the wealthiest Arab states, and that the Arab Union could easily mean the end of any dreams he harbored to make the U.A.R. a single geographical entity.

The new Arab Union, with a common defense program, had a frontier stretching from Sinai to Kuwait. Nasser might have hoped to swallow up Jordan one day and so form a land link between Syria and Egypt, but now that Jordan was united with Iraq it was not possible. If this was so, it was easy to understand how violently some irresponsible Arab leaders attacked the Arab Union and sought to destroy it. They did not like the fact that for once there was real hope for Arab unity, not merely plans for political domination. For this reason the Union was never permitted the time to develop into more of a threat.

Our union was a natural answer to the growth of communism in the Arab world, especially as King Feisal and myself were both great-grandsons of the Hashemite Sherif Hussein who had raised the banner of Arab revolt against the Turks in World War I—a rising that has not yet attained its full objectives. Both of us had been crowned on the same day, and both of us believed passionately in the real Arab freedom for which our great-grandfather had fought. Here was a real opportunity to show the Arab world how a constitutional democratic system of government could operate between two united, progressive states. All too often royalist systems are easy targets for revolutionaries inspired by communism or pseudo-nationalists. Our union was the answer.

What high hopes we had on the morning of February 14, when the flag of the Arab Revolt—black, red, white and green—was unfurled for the second time. I had worked unremittingly for the unity of our two countries, and if I had had my way, it would have come about much earlier. As I embraced King Feisal, I was already preparing the speech I broadcast a short time later: "This is the happiest day of my life, a great day in Arab history. We are under one banner, the banner of Arabism which our great-grandfather, Hussein ibn Ali the Great, carried in the great Arab Revolt."

With pleasure and happiness I agreed that King Feisal should be head of our combined state with myself as deputy. Baghdad and Amman would alternate every six months as the Union capital. The Union would be open to other Arab states who wished to enter. With our two countries joined as one, foreign policy, finance, education, and diplomatic representation would be unified in the coming months, though each of our states would preserve its independent existence and sovereignty over its own territories and retain the existing regimes.

I had earlier in my reign envisaged some form of nationalist alliance on the lines of the Baghdad Pact, but my hopes had been dashed when the Baghdad Pact was formed with unseemly haste, especially as it included only Iraq, whereas it would have been so much wiser to have an Arab defense pact with all Arab states as members. Even though Jordan did not join the Baghdad Pact in the new Union, I still felt the union of our two countries increased enormously the defensive alignment against irresponsible policies benefiting communism in its penetration of the Arab world. It was a genuine Arab movement, guided by selfless Arab nationalism. If it was against communism, it was because the two can never be reconciled. As for imperialism, we had been the victims and fought against it from the beginning of the Arab Revolt.

We had our problems and differences in forming the Union. No two countries can join themselves together without some difficulties. Some of these arose because of the problems confronting King Feisal. As my cousin, as my schoolmate at Harrow, he was as close as a brother; and how I echoed Nasser's hopes, voiced to me in 1955: "I wish him every success and I have great hopes for him." But the tragedy of King Feisal lay in the fact that he was never permitted to have any success or to fulfill any of his hopes. Nor was he really allowed to handle responsibility properly. When I think back to the day we signed our names for the Union, a host of memories flood my thoughts. They date back to Harrow, Sandhurst and other scenes. And I think it important that these should be recounted, if only to defend the memory of Feisal, my friend and brother in all but name. As I shall relate, I was forewarned of the murder of my cousin. Yet those responsible in Iraq did not heed my warnings and King Feisal seemed powerless to judge or to act. How could such a situation come about?

I even remember long ago at Harrow, where I always enjoyed, despite the discipline, a sense of freedom, being

sorry for the way Feisal was hemmed in, unable to act alone
—almost, one might say, a prisoner of his position. I do not
entirely blame the old-time politicians. The trouble lay in
his relationship with his uncle, the Crown Prince, who was
later, ironically, to lose his life by the King's side in the
Baghdad massacre.

The Crown Prince (the Emir Abdul Illah) had been appointed Regent after Feisal's father, the popular King Ghazi,
was killed in a car crash. Young Feisal was then only a boy.
For years the Crown Prince dominated the political scene as
Regent and guardian to the young King. Eventually my cousin
assumed his constitutional powers. Every Iraqi had prayed
for the day when he would be their King, but it really made
no difference. The Crown Prince had done a great deal for
Iraq, but his relationship to my cousin Feisal was so deeply
ingrained that he still clung to his power. Though he was
not very popular in Iraq he wielded a great deal of power
right up to the time of his death, and I think his influence
must have counted in the casual attitude of the Iraq government to the warning they received of impending disaster.
Somehow his judgment had become faulty.

The Crown Prince and I were, to my regret, never on very
good terms. We are brought up to respect our elders, but
there were times when it was not easy for me to remember
this with the Crown Prince, and I trace our coolness to an
incident at Sandhurst. When I was an officer cadet there,
King Feisal had a house at Staines in Middlesex, which he
used when visiting Britain. On one occasion he was accompanied, as usual, by the Crown Prince and they both came
to visit Sandhurst. The Commandant thought they might be
interested in visiting and touring the College. It was, if I am
not mistaken, a Saturday. Anyway, there was leave in the air.

I had planned to drive to London; but when the visit was over, King Feisal asked me:

"Why don't you drive back with us to Staines for tea? Then if you want, you can go to London afterwards."

I agreed and we all left together. The Crown Prince drove. The aide (who later, at the time of the coup, was the Commander of the Iraqi Royal Guards) occupied the other front seat, while Feisal and I sat behind. My car followed.

One must understand that I loved Feisal very, very much; and it was this deep feeling that had always given me an inner sense of awareness at the way he was treated. I saw, I heard, and felt it, and hated to see him, a highly intelligent, promising, well-prepared monarch of eighteen, hemmed in. I sensed that he knew and could do nothing. During the drive a family quarrel started between Feisal and the Crown Prince. The latter was angry with the King, and though I did not think it very seemly to argue in the presence of an aide and myself, I managed to contain my rising annoyance. Actually I was furious. Such conduct was to me unbearable. The wrangling died down.

As we approached Staines, Feisal asked the Crown Prince:

"Could we make a short detour, please, Uncle? They're making a film somewhere near here and it might be fun just to watch for a few minutes."

The Crown Prince did not even bother to answer.

I was flabbergasted. After all, Feisal was King of Iraq!

Then unaccountably the Crown Prince lost his temper again. Without warning, he launched into a tirade. He told the King off as though he were a naughty little boy.

At this moment my nerves snapped. We were driving along the main road in Staines and I burst out at the Crown Prince:

"Slow down, please!" As he looked around startled, I told him: "I'm sorry to have been present at this family quarrel, specially in this company. I have stood as much as I can. I'm not prepared to listen to any more of this. Kindly stop the car!"

He did, and I got out on the side of the road without another word to him, and slammed the rear door.

That was the end of the Staines tea party. I waited for my car and drove to London. My action was perhaps rash, but it was caused not merely by one quarrel. It was the culmination of a long period of watching my cousin being broken.

The Crown Prince may never have forgiven me. In fact, when my father was King and it was obvious his mental illness was getting worse, the Crown Prince did everything he could to prevent my succeeding to the throne. The Crown Prince happened to be in Amman during the period when the future of the monarchy was being discussed.

"Whatever you do decide," the Crown Prince told the Prime Minister, "don't let Prince Hussein be King. At least not now."

"Why on earth not?" asked the Prime Minister.

"Why not? He's irresponsible. He knows nothing of the dignity of Kingship."

This and a great deal more was said but fortunately the Prime Minister knew better.

I remember one more instance that made by blood boil. I was visiting Baghdad and Feisal and I made a visit to the site of the new Royal Palace and offices.

The two of us led the way, the King of Iraq behind the wheel of a small, rather shabby sports car that looked as though he had picked it up at a used-car lot. I looked around. The Crown Prince and other high officials were following us—yes, in the most luxurious, modern, shiny car that Rolls-Royce could produce.

"Don't you think you ought to have a better car?" I asked the King. Feisal shrugged his shoulders.

I was so angry that when we returned to Baghdad I put in a telephone call to the Palace in Amman.

"Give me Raynor," I asked the operator when the call came through. "That you, Raynor? I want you to be in Baghdad tomorrow. Will you please drive here in the new Aston Martin? I have presented it to King Feisal."

This and many other incidents did nothing to make my relations with the Crown Prince any friendlier. But I mention them because they illustrate why there was such a gap between King Feisal and his people. He was never able to do anything or see anyone without permission—and that, I may say, was not always granted. These instances also show why we had certain difficulties when forming the Arab Union.

During preliminary talks, King Feisal came to Amman without the Crown Prince and the talks went very smoothly. He agreed with the suggestion that he and I should take it in turn to be head of the Union.

Then the Crown Prince arrived. He objected violently to the arrangement, and during one of the most difficult nights of negotiations we argued and argued until finally I was given two choices: either King Feisal could be permanent head of state of the Union, or if we alternated, Iraq would insist on having more members in our joint Parliament than Jordan, and so on down the line.

King Feisal looked discomfited. I felt humiliated. But the only real thing was to get the Union working.

"I don't mind about my own position," I said, "but my country is different. Jordan must have as many members of the Parliament as Iraq and in the government. The whole basis of this Union must be equality."

So I stepped down, King Feisal became head of the Union, and the Arab Union was formed. That was the only thing that mattered.

We were naturally interested in President Nasser's attitude toward the new Union. At first he was all smiles. He telegraphed his congratulations to King Feisal almost before the King had returned to Baghdad. Describing the Union as a "blessed step" to which the whole Arab world had looked forward with great hope, Nasser said he was sure that King Feisal's youth, beliefs and sincerity would constitute a driving force assisting the Arabs to the realization of their great dream of unity. Arab nationalism was proud of this step taken in Amman, the message continued, and there was no doubt that recent events in these "glorious days for the Arab nation" indicated that the day of unity had dawned. "I wholeheartedly congratulate Your Majesty," Nasser concluded, "asking Allah to head your steps towards success and bless your great people."

King Feisal transmitted the message to me, asking for my opinion, and I smiled to myself as I read the cable. Since the violent days when Nasser instigated the Baghdad Pact riots, I had tried to patch things up between our two countries. In fact, it was Jordan that played a leading part in the Arab world at the time of the Suez invasion in 1956. We were the first to stand by Nasser when the Suez was nationalized. We were the first to call the Arab world to stand united in support of Egypt after the attack by Israel and the Western powers. President Chamoun of Lebanon and I had worked together to arrange the meeting of Arab states to discuss support for Egypt. How difficult it had been to rally the Arab world to Nasser's side! Yet, forgiving the past, we had done it. We had even agreed earlier that the armies of Jordan, Saudi Arabia, Egypt and Syria should be united under one command.

Fingering the cable, all these memories came back to me. Nasser knew Jordan had worked hardest for the Union but he had not cabled me and I knew why. It was his way of showing that Jordan as a country and I as a king no longer counted. I do not doubt he entertained the thought that Iraq would control Jordan as Nasser had begun to dominate Syria. He was incapable of swallowing the fact that we were free and equal partners. However, I told Feisal, "You must answer it, of course." But I told him not to take the honeyed words too seriously and explained my skepticism. I was right. From what followed within a few brief months, the leaders of the then so-called U.A.R. obviously felt our new-found strength such a hindrance to their ambitions that they took all possible steps to liquidate it. Diplomacy had failed, so the machine gun was introduced.

Now I come to the tragic manner in which we in Jordan learned that a *coup d'état* was being planned in Iraq, yet could not persuade the Iraqis to heed our warnings. I personally had advance warning of the coup some time before my cousin was murdered. The first inkling came through the arrest of a Jordanian agent of Nasser, Cadet Ahmad Yussef al Hiari, of the Fourth Tank Regiment. Ahmad was in charge of a plot to kill me, my uncle Sherif Nasser, and other officials by hurling grenades at a public function. When arrested, he made a full confession, in which he stated that a *coup d'état* instigated by the U.A.R. would take place in Iraq in mid-July, simultaneously with one in Jordan. Before long, other details of the U.A.R. plans were discovered, and I was not only in possession of many details of the coup but I even had the names of some of the leaders. The events in Baghdad were geared to a plot timed to occur simultaneously in Amman.

The first thing I had to do was warn my cousin. I telephoned him.

"I have some very important information about a *coup d'état* being planned in Iraq," I told him urgently. "Please be very, very careful."

"What do you suggest?" he asked.

"Send somebody over to see me," I replied. "Somebody important. I will explain everything to him. Believe me, this is a matter of the utmost urgency."

King Feisal thanked me and arranged for General Rafiq A'rif, Commander-in-Chief of the Arab Union forces, to fly to Amman. There was no time to lose if the conspirators were to be uncovered, so as soon as he arrived, we held a conference in a study at the Royal Diwan.

I remember the scene so well, just a few days before the murder. I had summoned to the office my Chief of Diwan, the Prime Minister and General A'rif. Also present was the Jordanian Commander-in-Chief. Slowly and meticulously, an intelligence officer read out the damning details we had pieced together. I stole a look at General A'rif now and again. He looked politely bored. As the recital of evidence ended, General A'rif stretched himself and laughed. He had a loud, cheerful laugh, famous all over the Middle East.

"Your Majesty," he said, "we are very thankful for your concern. I appreciate all your trouble, sir, but I do assure you the Iraqi Army is built on tradition. It is generally considered the best in the Middle East. It has not had the problems—nor the changes—your army has had, sir, in the past few years." He paused for breath. "I feel that it is we who should be concerned about Jordan, Your Majesty. This coup applies to your country, and it is you we are worried about. I beseech you to take care, Your Majesty."

At first I was speechless.

"But you must realize, General, that it is equally serious for Iraq!" I cried.

"I do understand," he replied—but I wondered if he did.

"At least promise me, General," I implored him, "that you will convey the full facts to His Majesty in Baghdad. Promise me to tell the King and officials of the danger."

"That I promise your Majesty. The King and the government shall be told everything."

With that, General A'rif took his leave. I had done everything I could. On the Friday before the fateful Monday, A'rif returned to Baghdad.

Left alone with my suspicions, I could only pray that the General's lack of concern would be proved right, and that our dire foreboding and fears were groundless. It transpired later that mine were not the only warnings. The Turks had also warned the Iraqis of the coup.

During the weekend I spoke to my cousin the King once

more. It was the day before he was due to leave on a visit
to Turkey. I wished him well. In his absence I would take his
place as head of state, and I told him I would do everything
to serve the Union. I actually planned to go to Iraq myself
and try to sort things out, but I never went.

13

The Murder of King Feisal

"Would our troubles never end?"

THE MURDER of my cousin, King Feisal of Iraq, on Monday, July 14, 1958, was one of the heaviest blows I have thus far faced. It was, besides, a political disaster of the first magnitude to Jordan, for it disrupted the aspirations of our two countries, so recently joined in the Arab Union.

It was about seven o'clock in the morning when I was awakened by the first telephone call that brought me the news. But much of it that morning was rumor; at one moment the King had lost his life, the next moment he was safe and well, and one report even said he was on his way to Turkey as originally planned. Nothing was clear and definite. We tried frantically to reach Baghdad by telephone, but it was impossible, so we tried to get in touch by radio. That, too, was hopeless. Iraq, no doubt deliberately, was cut off from the world, and it was not until much later in the day that my fears were confirmed.

197

I remember so well thinking to myself, how ironic that my cousin should have been murdered instead of me. I was the one who might have expected death. I was the one who took stands that had made enemies. But Feisal, a few months my senior, never harmed anybody and never had enough control of events to make a single major political decision that could have angered anybody. Yet he, not I, was the one to meet death.

Throughout our short lives we had been so close, united in many ways. Our grandfathers had also been closely bound. On my side was King Abdullah; on his, Abdullah's brother, the first King Feisal, who played a major role in the Arab Revolt and on whose side Lawrence of Arabia had served. As boys we had played together—hadn't Feisal given me my first bicycle?—and later at Harrow, we had discussed so often the problems which would one day face us. Now that he is lost, I believe many, many Iraqis, for or against the monarchy, feel a deep sense of guilt for the brutal assassination.

For in fact, the monarchy had always been popular in Iraq. King Feisal's father, King Ghazi, was a man always accessible to his people, and when he was killed in a car crash, all Iraq hailed the young Feisal as their king. All awaited the moment when he would take power. But gradually any ambitions and hopes he held were frustrated and stifled. I could see it happening, but though I tried to interfere there was too much to deal with. My efforts brought no changes. And now Feisal was dead.

In Amman, the Cabinet met the same day. Many Cabinet members urged me to oppose the new regime with force, since Iraq and Jordan were both linked by treaty. The Jordan Arab Army had never been in greater battle strength. They argued that we should move troops immediately into the

Iraqi section of the Union (which had not been dissolved) and try to oust the plotters and restore order. But I answered, "No." I explained as simply as I could my reasons.

"With our approach to life," I said, "we are not the sort of people who wish to impose ourselves on others. If the people of Iraq have chosen a different way of life, then—whatever we think of it—they must sort it out for themselves. We may move later if we are called for, but not now."

I was influenced by several factors. First, who was there left to save? To the best of our knowledge, the King, his family and many important figures had been lost. The Iraqi people could eventually make their choice of a system of government. Secondly, we did not really know what had happened in Iraq. We could not just send in troops without being able to appraise the total situation. Thirdly, if we marched into Iraq, we should be fighting and killing Arab brethren. It was not their fault this *coup* had taken place. If we fought anybody, it should be those outside Iraq who had masterminded the plot, not their innocent dupes.

I was worried, too, about the threat to Jordan. Whenever Arab nations were in trouble, Israel was always ready to pounce. We could not leave our frontier of four hundred miles unguarded. It would be inviting trouble. And since I felt that Cairo planned to overthrow the monarchy in Jordan as well, we had a double enemy to face. Jordan was now the only stumbling block to communism and the ambitions of the then so-called U.A.R.—ambitions which I believe at that time meant nothing less than the domination of the Arab world.

It is perhaps hard for those who have never visited us to realize what we passed through in that fateful summer of

1958. Not one single road was left open out of the country; our only air corridor to the outside world was blocked by Syrians. So was the railway. Our only port, Aqaba, two hundred miles south of Amman, was not then properly developed, nor was the Desert Road linking Amman and Aqaba finished. We were encircled completely.

Some Iraqi troops were in Jordan at the time of the Baghdad coup and when they heard the news they openly celebrated and rejoiced, possibly expecting that our time was coming soon. There was an urge to deal with them severely at first, but moderation prevailed. A number of Iraqi staff officers were kept in Jordan for a time. We treated them well, but kept them in Amman until I knew that Jordanians still alive in Baghdad would be allowed to return. As it was, we lost many great patriots in the uprising, among them Suleiman Toukan, Minister of Defense in the Union, and the wise old Ibrahim Hashem, a great legal brain and administrator, former Prime Minister of Jordan and Deputy Prime Minister to Nuri es-Said in the Union.

It was very hot and torpid as August came, and a dozen metaphors spring to mind to describe the deadly feeling of inevitability that hung over Amman. Fear was not the predominant emotion, for the essence of the drama lay in the fact that we could do nothing but wait and see what steps would next be taken by the latest Pharaoh across the Nile.

If I was not afraid, and I think I was not, I must admit that many times, alone in the evening in the small study of the Basman Palace, I wondered if I would live the year out. I felt like an actor on the stage in a tragedy so well-known that every audience—and the audience was the world—knew what the final curtain would bring. I was almost alone. I was only twenty-three.

Worse was to come. The friends in the same cause for whom Iraqi leaders had lost their lives—the countries of the free world with whom Iraq had stood four-square against communism—now started to bring pressure to bear on us not to take any action. One by one—as though to legalize this pressure—they recognized the new regime. With what unseemly haste they married after burying the corpse! The murders took place on July 14. Turkey recognized the new regime on July 31, Britain and the United States on August 1.

It was quite a spectacle. As Sir Anthony Eden in his memoirs, *Full Circle,* states, "Within a few days the free nations of the West recognized the Government which had endorsed, if it had not sanctioned, the gruesome deeds. In London, only the initiative of friends, which included Ministers, working against ecclesiastical difficulties, organized a small service in memory of those national figures whose friendship proved faithful unto death. This did not seem enough to mark our country's respect and gratitude."

Our most urgent needs were twofold—fuel and friends. We were woefully short of fuel. The Syrians had earlier closed their frontier against all Jordanian imports and exports and traffic. This meant we could not use our traditional fuel route by land tankers from Lebanon through their country. So we had started importing fuel by heavy land tankers from Iraq. Now, at a moment's notice, this source dried up. Even worse, some of these heavy tankers had been caught in Iraq. We needed fuel for everything. We needed it to pump water to keep Amman and other cities alive, for electricity; we needed it to take supplies to the south, where there had been a bad harvest, and to carry water.

In desperation I appealed to the United States, which had unlimited fuel resources in the region. I asked the United

States chargé d'affaires, Mr. Thomas K. Wright, to come and
see me. I explained the problem to him frankly, adding, "The
position is desperate because of the urgency. Without oil we
cannot survive."

Within a matter of hours the U.S. Embassy received a
reply from Washington.

"My government is only too willing to help, sir," said Mr.
Wright. "You may have as much oil as you require. The fuel
will be flown from the Gulf across Saudi Arabia to Jordan."

What a load off my mind! Within twenty-four hours the
first aircraft were landing outside Amman, and our few re-
maining tankers and many trucks lined up to bring the oil to
the city. Then, just as all seemed well, another blow fell—and
as so often happens, from an unexpected quarter.

Suddenly the hum of the transport planes ceased. With
barely a dozen cargoes of oil delivered, the American aircraft
stopped arriving. What on earth was the matter? I telephoned the airfield. My first thought was that something was
wrong and planes could not land; but no, everything was in
order. Had Washington changed its mind? That was impossible. I thought of a thousand reasons, but never the real
one.

Our friends in Saudi Arabia—on whom we counted—suddenly refused, at this critical juncture, to permit American
aircraft to fly over their country while carrying fuel from the
gulf to Jordan. It was the only possible route they could take.
The unspoken reason was obvious—some powerful advisers
in Saudi Arabia thought this was the end of our country and
they did not wish to anger Nasser.

The situation was critical. I did not wish to tell my people what only a few of us knew—that we had barely enough fuel in the country for a few hours and were completely surrounded by enemies.

Then Mr. Wright came to see me again with even worse news. "I'm afraid, Your Majesty, the Saudis are not only refusing to let us fly fuel to you," he said. "They are also refusing to allow the aircraft already in the Gulf to return—even empty."

Would our troubles never end? This was disastrous. I might arrange an alternative source for fuel, but even if I did, where could we find tanker planes to transport it? I was furious, but I picked up the phone and put in a personal call to King Saud.

It was about three hours coming through, for to put it mildly, Saudi Arabia is not the easiest country in the world to telephone. I pondered, as I waited, on the complexity of human nature. Here we were alone, almost down and out. And why? Communism as an enemy I could understand, and, opposing it, expect no mercy. But with our brother Arabs, it was different. Communism seeks to destroy us, but the Arabs should have been resolved in a joint effort to bring greatness to the Arab world, not to squabble among themselves. My fury increased as I sat there, wondering where our next gallon of fuel would come from and even how long we could exist. I remember thinking, "Where will this cowardice of our Arab brethren lead us? What are we heading for, divided like this?"

At last my Chief of Diwan warned me, "The call is coming through, sir," and a moment later I heard King Saud's voice on the other end of the line. I could hardly control myself.

When I asked him why Saudi Arabia had taken this stand against us, King Saud apologized and said, "If I'd known all these details before, I might have been able to do something else, but I'm afraid it is too late now—the government has already made its decision."

What a shallow excuse, I thought, and then said:

"To the end of my life I will never forget this stand against my country and my people in this hour of need." With that, I slammed down the receiver.

Turning to my Chief of Diwan and others who had been listening, I said bitterly:

"This is probably the first time in history that any government has ever taken any decision in Saudi Arabia, or for that matter, even met!"

We did receive fuel after a short break in supplies, but how it arrived was perhaps the most humiliating feature of the whole sordid business. Our Arab friends had refused to let us fly over their country—the air of brother Arabs—and so, in the end, the fuel came from Lebanon, and every gallon had to be flown over the skies of Israel, the mortal enemy of all Arab states. Where an Arab nation refused, an enemy agreed.

As I was endeavoring to solve these many problems, I called a full meeting of the government in the Palace and we decided to ask the United States and Britain to send us troops. We needed some help—not so much physical as moral help. A token force would be enough—something to take off some of the load for at least a short while. We were in truth stretched to the limit.

We faced plots inside our country. There were troop concentrations on our frontiers. And we were still members of the Arab Union. I was automatically the head of the Union, which had not been dissolved, and as the Iraqi-Jordanian treaty stipulated that either country could help in the internal troubles of the other, we might still have to take military action. Who could tell at that time? If we did, we needed some force to hold off any aggressors who might attack us if our troops were outside the country.

It was a big decision and not one I wished to make myself. When the government agreed that it was necessary, I called a joint meeting of the Cabinet, Parliament and the Senate. I also invited any members of the Arab Union Parliament to come if they wished. I told them the government wanted American or British troops to come to Jordan and I asked everyone present:

"If you have any point of view on this subject, please feel free to speak now."

Unanimously, the meeting approved the step.

Both the British and U.S. Ambassadors were absent from Jordan, so I asked the chargé d'affaires of both countries to come to see me. Mr. Heath Mason of Britain and Mr. Wright of the United States were given a joint audience, and I told them both that we did not require troops to sort out our internal problems but as a proof that a small, free nation in times of trouble did not have to stand alone.

"We do not mind which country sends the troops," I added. "We need them for a limited period only. I look upon this move as a symbol of the ties that bind free peoples in times of crisis."

We had to take this step, for the strain was beginning to tell. There was a genuine fear that Israel might seize this moment for a thrust into the West Bank area. We still did not know what was happening even in Iraq. The threats all around were genuine enough, and each day more spies, with guns or explosives, were crossing our frontiers plotting murder or sabotage.

I had purposely allowed the British and Americans to decide which country should send troops, and the answer came swiftly. British parachute troops would fly in from Cyprus.

On Wednesday, the night of July 16, we rounded up the last of the plotters and conspirators who had hoped to stage a *coup d'état* in Jordan. We were just in time. We had kept a careful watch on the conspirators since our first inkling of the plot. Now we pounced and seized the actual orders to plotters inside Jordan, telling them to move into action the following day, July 17. Jordan was saved by a matter of hours. The original plan was for the coup to take place on July 14, but it was postponed as a result of our precautionary measures.

With the plotters safely in jail, I went to bed at 3:30 A.M. and for the first time since my cousin's murder two days previously, I slept for two hours. I awoke soon after dawn and about 9:30 I heard the drone of heavy aircraft. The British paratroops were already landing.

Only later was I able to piece together the action in Whitehall before the troops arrived and the reasons behind the magnificent response by Mr. Macmillan, the Prime Minister—particularly the speed with which he acted. In every way it was thought to be more suitable to send British rather than American troops. The British had crack forces alerted in Cyprus. They could reach us in a morning. The American

Marines were already engaged in Lebanon. But could the British slash through red tape and reach a decision in time? They did. Almost at the moment Britain received our request for help, their intelligence was given details of the *coup d'état* plot against us. It was the combination of these two factors which enabled the Prime Minister to take what he described as the "most difficult decision" of his career.

The sequence of events leading up to the decision to help us was among the most dramatic in recent history. At five minutes past ten on Wednesday night (July 16) Mr. Macmillan was preparing to go home after winding up the Middle East debate in the House of Commons. He sent his parliamentary private secretary, Mr. Anthony Barber, M.P., to escort Lady Dorothy Macmillan from the gallery so they could go back to No. 10 Downing Street together. But by the time Lady Dorothy arrived, the Prime Minister had discarded all thoughts of home. In those few minutes the intelligence reports of the plot against Jordan and my own appeal for help had been handed to him. Knowing that Jordan's future hung by a thread, Mr. Macmillan immediately ordered a full Cabinet meeting.

British Cabinet Ministers were convinced that if action was not taken immediately, the Middle East situation might rapidly deteriorate beyond Jordan. For if Jordan went the way of Iraq, so might Kuwait, a key oil-producing center, and who could know where it would stop? At 2 A.M. on Thursday, the Cabinet meeting ended and a code message was flashed to Cyprus ordering British paratroops into the air. Speed was vital. There was no time for diplomatic niceties. Britain did not even have time to explain to the Israelis, over whose territory their planes would have to fly, why it was so urgent for their paratroops to reach Amman.

So British troop-carrying aircraft took off before the for-

malities of getting permission from the Israeli government
had been completed. This explains the "buzzing" of British
air transports by Israeli fighters as they crossed the coast
early on Thursday morning, and the recall by G.H.Q. in
Cyprus of the main contingent of paratroops. The Israelis
allowed three Beverley transports carrying an advance body
of about a hundred men to proceed across their territory. But
it was not until six hours later, following clearance by the
Israeli Cabinet, that the airlift from Cyprus could proceed in
full force.

Only one trifling incident marred the British parliamentary
proceedings, when a Socialist member of Parliament said
that instead of sending British troops to Amman, "Would
not the King be safer over here where he could be looked
after by a couple of policemen?"

Those words came back to me about a year later when I
was in London. Mr. Macmillan gave a dinner in my honor at
No. 10 Downing Street. When I was called on to speak, I
said: "One member of Parliament has suggested that two
British policemen would be enough to protect me, and that
there was no need to send British troops to Jordan to protect
me there. May I say that I personally have never needed any
protection. It was not me or my country those British troops
came to protect—it was freedom."

14

Surrounded by Enemies

"The Soviets had gained their foothold in Islam."

THE BRITISH TROOPS stayed in Amman until October 29. The last small detachment departed from Aqaba on November 2. The British force was small, but its very presence gave us a chance to breathe. Seeing the famous Red Berets in the streets, the people knew we were not alone, that this was no time for despair. Yet there was still much to be done and we faced grave problems.

Many prominent Jordanians, who were by chance in Baghdad at the time of the uprising, were also murdered along with King Feisal, and it took little imagination to realize that what had happened had been aimed as much at Jordan as at Iraq. We soon received positive proof of this. The next few weeks of crisis were perhaps the gravest in the history of my country, weeks in which, diplomacy having failed to split us, we now faced the machine gun and the bomb and the ever-present blaring voice of radio propaganda.

I would certainly be next on the list and I was deeply worried, not so much for myself or my family but for Jordan —my bigger family. In recent crises every Jordanian rallied behind me in every decision we took. How different it was from the crisis leading to the Zerqa uprising. Then I was almost alone. But now everything had changed. I really had become the head of a large family. They stood by me loyally against all attempts of other states to destroy Jordan.

I knew that if anything happened to me, the whole of Jordan could easily go. It was unthinkable to quit like a coward and leave this family at the mercy of its enemies, despite the by now rather monotonously regular attempts on my life. The people of Jordan—from both banks alike—were my people; I loved them and believed in them and our cause, as I always will. My place was with them as it always shall be. I had accepted a challenge, not only as King but to carry on the ideals of the Arab Revolt. I knew the dangers, but accepted the risk of death to myself and many others. Never would I leave Jordan unless I was of no more use to my people.

My main problem now was desperate: What should I *do* for these people who had shown their trust in me? This was no internal political problem to be solved by forming a new Cabinet. We were faced with enemies who would stop at nothing to strike me down and destroy Jordan.

Looking back, it is obvious that 1958 was the climax to three years in which Jordan was subjected to a merciless war of propaganda, subversion and infiltration by Communist-dominated agents in sister Arab states. Their propaganda was brilliant. Traveling over even the remotest parts of Jordan, it was impossible to escape its voice. While Cairo had powerful modern stations, Amman Radio at that time had a strength of only five kilowatts. Its radius was hardly more than thirty miles. We did our best to combat the lies that poured in, by presenting the more outrageous ones in the newspapers and on the radio every day. People who had passed a normal, quiet day in Amman roared with laughter when they heard and read the text of Cairo Radio's outbursts:

"Troops clash in Amman, blood ankle-deep in its streets!" And so forth.

It was easy to deal with but naturally many distortions and exaggerations filtered through to the ordinary people of the country. One did not prevent them from listening.

I remember one evening I drove out with a friend, just to "get away from it all" for a few hours, and we came to Mount Nebo from which Moses first saw the Promised Land, and in this era of the portable radio set, I heard the voice of Cairo say, "We shall fight until we exterminate the criminal King of Jordan." In Jerusalem, on the occasion of an unexpected visit, I even heard the then Egyptian-controlled Damascus Radio hurling insults at me near the foot of the Mount of Olives in the city where Christ died for his people.

Not only were Cairo and Damascus pouring out propaganda night after night, but civil disturbances were traced to agents from Syria and Egypt. I was convinced that Communist agents were running a vast system of bribery in Jordan, and there are the weak in every community. They had organized infiltration of enemy agents on a wide scale, there had been dangerous smuggling of arms into the country along frontiers hundreds of miles long and it was impossible to patrol every yard effectively.

It became so bad that we even had to withdraw a good portion of the troops from the Israeli border because we needed them to guard our frontiers against sister Arab states. How ironical! But it was incredible to what lengths they were determined to go. Nor was this anything new. It had been going on for months, if not years. Two cases stand out in my memory, as examples of their techniques. The first case involved the Egyptian military attaché to Amman, Major Fouad Hillal, who made contact with a trooper, Safout Shukair, of the Jordan Arab Army. Shukair worked in the legal department at Army Headquarters, and the Egyptian military attaché tried to bribe him to assassinate me.

Plots against my life no longer deeply worried me—so long as I discovered them in time!—but this was something new and decidedly unpleasant. It was not merely enemy activity behind the scenes, but out in the open, from a "friendly" protected Embassy in my own capital. What impertinence!

An intelligence officer outlined the plot to me:

"We don't know yet, sir, how it was going to be done. Shukair was told to wait for another rendezvous with the Egyptian."

"What did Shukair do?"

"He immediately sought an interview with the Chief of the General Staff and told him everything. His evidence was recorded on a tape machine, Your Majesty."

This was as far as the matter had gone. What next? At a conference the following morning we decided to ask Shukair to keep his appointment at the Egyptian Embassy, but to carry a small tape recorder hidden in his clothes. Unfortunately, the Cairo espionage system was so thorough the Egyptians heard about the tape recorder. It was frightening to think how walls could hear at that time. Shukair kept his appointment, but when he entered the Embassy he was pounced on by two members of the staff, searched, his recorder and his weapon taken from him.

He was held for the night, beaten up, tortured and threatened with death. Being an intelligent fellow—who knew his innocence was established by his previous tape-recorded evidence—Shukair signed a "confession." With this in his hands the Egyptian chargé d'affaires told the police that a suspicious Jordanian had been found attempting to break into and rob the Egyptian Embassy. We asked the Egyptians to hand over the man and his belongings. After some hesitation, Shukair was handed over to the police, but not the tape recorder or his gun. It was after this that we requested the Egyptian government to withdraw its military attaché from Amman.

Following this affair, nineteen more persons were arrested and the subsequent trial revealed that the Egyptian Consul-General, Mohammed Abdulaziz, had been organizing sabotage gangs and smuggling arms into Jordan from the Gaza Strip. Very convenient for Egypt. He, too, had to leave.

The other typical case took place a long time before the murder of my cousin but soon after the Zerqa incident, when we were still striving to live in peace with our neighbors, and when we even experimented with a joint army command between Jordan, Egypt and Saudi Arabia. Even then Egypt was plotting against us. I was in the Palace one evening—I had been out flying and was about to dine quietly—when a top army official requested an audience. My aide told me he was extremely agitated and I knew he was not one given to hysterics.

He walked into my study and, putting a gray envelope on

my desk, said without preamble, "I beg of you, sir, to read this."

It was a letter written by Colonel Yusri Kunsowa, the Egyptian representative on the joint command of our armies, and it had been discovered in Kunsowa's safe at Army Headquarters. One glance was sufficient to prove Egyptian complicity in an attempt to take over Jordan and eliminate me. The letter was addressed to Brigadier Mohammed Hafez Ismail, at the Egyptian Army Headquarters in Cairo. It told him that ex-General Hiyyari (who had fled Jordan following the Zerqa uprising) would "follow the same lines" as those laid down by Abu Nuwar who had also plotted my death at Zerqa. Hiyyari was still in Damascus. The letter added that plans had already been laid with the connivance of Abu Nuwar to overthrow the throne. It also gave a list of loyal Jordanians whom Kunsowa considered "traitors to the cause" and others who were considered "loyal" to him.

We acted quickly. Arrests were made and at a trial which followed, seventeen defendants admitted they had been sent in from Syria to blow up bridges and roads and eventually lead attacks on the Palace. They had also organized smuggling of arms.

At this time you could buy a Soviet gun anywhere. There was even a glut on the market. Some came from Sinai where they had been abandoned by the Egyptians during the Suez wrangle. One of my Palace officials actually bought a machine gun over a coffee table. It was sold to him by a complete stranger, loyal to the Crown but who never thought twice about dealing in smuggled arms.

My official had gone for a swim in the Dead Sea. On the way back he stopped in Jericho for coffee. Here, where the richest stories of the Bible were enacted, life has changed little since the days of the Disciples. Sharing a table with my colleague was a striking Bedouin, his handsome, bearded face like a picture from the past.

Knowing that I am always anxious to discover what my people think of me privately (they are often too shy to tell me to my face), my official asked the Bedouin:

"What would you do if the enemies of the King rose against him?"

The Bedouin knew nothing of intrigue or even of the plots that might well have been hatched against me at that very moment. He looked astonished and replied:

"Why! Fight for my King, of course!"

"What with?"

He looked genuinely puzzled. "This—naturally!" And he pulled out a modern submachine gun made in Czechoslovakia. Then he added: "Do you want one? Are you for the King? If you are, you can have this one if you like—I can always get another quite easily. Anyone can buy them in the *souk*."

What better proof could one require of Communist interference, albeit through puppets, in the internal affairs of another country? My official bought the gun and brought it to me at the Palace, where I tried a few bursts. It was an excellent weapon.

The trouble was that after the Egyptian arms deal with Russia, the Soviets had gained their foothold in the world of Islam. Like the salesman who pushes his foot in the door and refuses to leave when the housewife insists she does not want anything, the Soviets were there for a long, long time. I dare say, taking the most charitable view, that the Egyptians may not have relished having hordes of Russians and Czechs around, but one cannot ignore the basic fact that if one buys complicated and modern machines from a country, one must be dependent on that country for spare parts and for servicing. The fact that the Egyptians bought Soviet MIGs was only the beginning of the story. The real trouble lay in the fact that, having bought the MIGs, the Egyptians allowed the Soviets to send technicians (or agents) into their country; they chose to associate with them in more than arms deals; and the Egyptians *had* to buy spare parts from the Soviet bloc and *had* to reorganize their economy to find the money.

The Arab leaders who attacked us so ruthlessly at this period were really the tools of Moscow whether they realized it or not. I stood firmly behind my belief that communism could never help the liberation of the Arab peoples—which I wanted quite as much as the other Arab leaders, if not more —because the ultimate end of communism must be a form of slavery and obedience to Moscow. Communism could never be an ally of nationalism because nationalism is a major threat to communism. This I strove to tell my people on every occasion when I addressed them but, alas, I could never hope to speak to them as often as the enemy radio, or in the same tone.

In retrospect, now that the Middle East is a little calmer and its voices less strident, it is like looking back on a horrible nightmare. I remember one night particularly. I slept fitfully, with a feeling of impending disaster, then finally dozed toward dawn, only to wake up desperately tired. I wondered, Where will it all end? What's going to happen today?

Perhaps it was most difficult for my Army, whose loyalty was never in doubt during those dark days or ever since. They were not politicians, only men of action, yet the enemy against them was a constant intangible quantity. My soldiers would have fought to the death against an enemy they could see, for we take pride in having the finest army in all the Arab lands. But we were striking at the unseen.

My main personal difficulty was of another sort. I had my fears, my worries, my suspicions, but these I could never show by even a flicker of emotion. This left me utterly alone, for I had to "put on a good face," I had to prove to my people—who have come, with the help of God, through those somber days—that I had sublime faith in our future. But can I be blamed if on occasion, late at night, I sometimes wondered how it was all going to end?

I am not ashamed to say that at times I felt even death itself would be a welcome relief. But then, one had responsibilities and one could never abandon them. And so each day I was up with the dawn, usually after a miserable, sleepless night. I would dress quickly, neatly, and would take care to include in my dress a smile of confidence in our future.

15

The Syrian MIG Attack

"At this moment I felt my time had come."

BY THE END of October, I felt the crisis had abated sufficiently to enable me to take a short holiday. Consequently I decided to fly my Dove aircraft to Europe. It was a flight which was almost to cost me my life.

I took off from Amman at about 8:20 on the morning of November 10, 1958, in the old twin-engined De Haviland Dove which had been my grandfather's plane and now belonged to the Air Force. In the cockpit beside me was Colonel Jock Dalgleish, at that time Air Adviser to the Royal Jordanian Air Force. My passengers were my uncle, Sherif Nasser, two Jordanian Air Force pilots who were to fly the plane home again, and Maurice Raynor, whom I had known since my days at Harrow. The Syrian Nasserite authorities knew long before I left that I would be a passenger and I planned to stay three weeks in Lausanne with my mother, Queen Zein, my daughter Alia, and the rest of my family. I also planned to celebrate my birthday on November 14. Rooms had been booked at the Beau Rivage, the same hotel in which I had received the fateful telegram which proclaimed me King.

I had gone out of my way to inform my people that I was taking this little holiday. Not only was this publicly announced but I even gave a farewell speech the evening before my official departure from Amman airport which the diplomatic corps attended in full force.

It seemed perfectly simple to fly across Syria and Lebanon to Cyprus, our first stop, and then on to Athens and Rome. This was the shortest and the most usual way, and we had every right to chart this course to Europe.

It was a cool morning when we took off. There was an overcast sky and we climbed to about 9,000 feet, flying toward the Syrian frontier. Very soon we were in broken cloud and then we contacted Damascus by radio. We reported our position at the frontier and got clearance from them to continue.

If one is to follow what happened subsequently, it is vital to understand that it was Damascus Airport that had given us the right to proceed. I myself was listening through my headset on the V.H.F. radio when this clearance came through, and as a result we continued flying to a specified turning point well inside the Syrian territory where we were due to report our position and altitude to Damascus. This we did. We were asked our estimated time of arrival over Damascus and gave this information. Then we got the first inkling of trouble. A few minutes later Damascus called my aircraft again and told us, "You are not cleared to overfly. You must land at Damascus."

We replied, "We are not cleared to land at Damascus. We are proceeding to Cyprus."

Damascus told us: "Stand by."

Dalgleish and I thought there must be some mistake. We flew on and were not more than fifteen miles out of Damascus, which we could see occasionally through broken cloud, when they called us again and said, "You are not cleared to fly over. You will land at Damascus." Almost immediately, they started to give us the landing instructions and asked us to report when the airfield was in sight.

I looked at Dalgleish. Without another word we turned the aircraft in the direction of Amman. We replied, "If those are your final instructions we must contact Amman and advise them."

Thoroughly alarmed, I called Amman up and told them what was happening. The anxious but clear reply came back, "You are to return to base immediately. Remain on this frequency. Do not acknowledge any further messages." And then significantly the voice added, "And good luck to you."

I opened again on the Damascus channel. They asked, "What is your position?" We replied, "We are orbiting, awaiting your final instructions." This time the Syrians were even more definite. Again they gave us the order to land.

I replied briefly: "Sorry, this we can't do!" and switched back to Amman.

We were already heading toward the nearest point of Jordanian territory. We did not bother to return by the same route we had taken from Amman. We took the shortest cut to the frontier! At this moment the cloud broke completely. We were flying at about ten thousand feet and I had a sudden idea. I turned to Jock and said: "Why don't we go down and fly at ground level?"

I put the plane into a dive at about two hundred forty air miles an hour, the most the poor old Dove could take, for I felt that once we were flying at ground level the possibility of picking us up by radar would be reduced, while the possibility of spotting us would be made more difficult, especially as jets do not maneuver well at low altitude, nor do they have a long fuel endurance.

We reached the ground—it seemed to take hours—and hedgehopped at zero feet as we approached the Jordanian frontier.

Suddenly one of the Air Force pilots in the back of the plane came up to the cockpit and shouted:

"I've just seen two MIGs flying at height in the opposite direction."

This meant they were flying toward us from the Jordanian frontier, even perhaps from inside Jordan's air space. Dalgleish looked at me. We understood the significance of their position. These were not aircraft sent up since we had refused to land at Damascus.

I think both Dalgleish and I felt a real shiver of fear, but I told the pilot to go back and keep me informed if he saw them again. I glanced at Jock and both of us tightened our safety belts.

Two minutes later the two MIG 17's of the United Arab Republic Air Force passed us on our starboard wing. Almost at our level, they turned across our path, gained height, and dived at us in what is known as a quarter attack.

I felt my time had come. I really believed that this was the end.

I tore the old Dove around in a turn. I thought to myself, If I go, at least I'll take one of them with me. It looked as though we were almost finished, so I made up my mind to ram the first MIG, since it was obvious they meant business.

What a way to get rid of us! No one would ever know what had happened in that uninhabited lava-covered area!

As they tore into the attack, Jock took over the controls and managed to avoid their first pass by tightening his turn. Their tactics were simple. They dived at us in turn, from the port side, slightly forward from our position, screaming down toward us at speed, banking toward our nose. Time and again they attacked. We could do nothing but watch out for them and wait for them to come in. Only one defense was possible. We had to turn inside their circle at the precise moment they began to get us lined up in their sights. I knew that a MIG could not turn as tightly as our slower Dove, which could turn in a much smaller circle and at as slow a speed as ninety miles an hour. So when we turned in to meet the MIGs, they were forced to overshoot every time.

But our biggest fear was not seeing them as the attack developed. Both of us were straining our necks looking out for each new attack. We were flying the poor old Dove as fast as she could go, with full power, exceeding all engine limitations, but she held together. As we twisted and turned I hated to think what it was like back in the cabin. It must have been a shambles. Somehow my uncle struggled to the cockpit and shouted, "What on earth's happening?"

I yelled out, "We're being attacked!"

His reply was characteristic of him.

"Give me the radio," he cried, "and let me tell them what I think of them."

"This isn't the moment," I answered. Nevertheless, his attitude cheered us up enormously.

Before long the attacks intensified. Jock shouted, "I think you had better call Mayday in case we're forced down."

I myself gave the S.O.S. call on the Amman frequency, but unfortunately—or perhaps fortunately for their peace of mind —it was not picked up by Amman, doubtless because of our very low altitude.

Then came the moment, the split second, when we almost crashed. Jock was at the controls, watching one side for a possible attack, while I looked out of the other side. We turned our heads at exactly the same instant—as we seemed to be flying straight into a hill. Frantically, we yanked at the controls. The old plane lurched, staggered, hesitated under the strain, and as the nose went up we skimmed the top of that hill by inches.

That was perhaps the worst single moment of the flight. No doubt it would have elated those who had been sent after us.

The battle was not over. By turning into them at the moment of attack we had foiled them because of our slower speed, so now they tried different tactics. They gained height, and then simultaneously attacked from both sides.

This was even more frightening. I cannot describe it except to say that it was like playing tag in the air at fantastic speeds. They were chasing us and we were compelled to dodge. It was dangerous for them too. We managed to avoid one MIG which then shot right up as the other dived steeply from the other direction. They almost collided head-on.

Attack after attack continued until we crossed the road from Mafraq to H.5—the main road to Iraq and well inside the Jordanian frontier. Suddenly it was all over. The MIGs flew away and we lost sight of them as they headed back toward Syria. At first I could not believe it. Dalgleish and I waited for the next attack, wondering where it would come from. All sorts of possibilities flashed through my mind. It seemed hours since the first attack, though I suppose it was only minutes.

We flew on at a very low altitude for a long distance. They *might* have gone, I thought, but we were still worried. If we gained height, Syrian radar might pick us up again and other fighters might be close at hand.

At last we felt the danger had passed. We climbed. And at that moment my uncle came to the cockpit holding out a cigarette for me—the best I ever smoked.

He gave me the thumbs-up sign. "Well done!" he said. "Don't we passengers deserve wings?"

I shouted back: "It looks clear now. Can we have breakfast?"

Alas, there was no breakfast to be had. The food was an unholy scramble. However, we did have a hot drink. Throughout all the twisting and diving, with everything thrown about during the battle, Raynor—British to the core—had held firmly on to a thermos and now produced two cups of tea.

Tea and a cigarette—what more could one ask! And as music to go with it I could now hear the welcome and angry voices of the Jordanian Air Force jet pilots.

As I sipped the hot tea, I looked at Dalgleish. He was in his element. A huge grin filled his weatherbeaten face.

"That was close, sir!" he shouted. And as we flew sedately on toward my capital, all danger past, I reflected just how close to death we *had* been. And I wondered, too, what madness had prompted the Syrians' wanton attack.

There was never a question of "mistaken identity." My Dove was well known and could not have been mistaken for any other aircraft. It had the royal Jordanian Air Force markings and carried the royal coat of arms and the royal flag. It had flown to Damascus several times, once with me on an official visit.

Even now we do not know why they made the attack. I do not believe for a moment that they were merely trying to turn us back. There is an international code by which planes in the air order another to return. There is a whole sequence of procedure, and only after going through this does a fighter have the right to consider you "fair game" if you do not choose to respond to his instructions. Every flier learns this almost before he can fly. The MIG pilots knew this as well as I did but they came right into an unmistakable attack. And never once did either plane appear in the least friendly.

The Syrians have always been touchy about their air space. In the months preceding the attack on my aircraft, there were others. Some months before, they had caught a Lebanese civil aircraft over Damascus Airport and opened up with anti-aircraft guns at point-blank range. The pilot, a New Zealander, dived just as we did and got away to Beirut. There were other incidents, too, in which the motives seem obscure.

However touchy, this was no excuse for deliberately attacking an unarmed aircraft on a perfectly lawful passenger flight. Only one conclusion was possible. They had hoped to kill us. My death, three months after King Feisal's, could have virtually ended the Hashemite Kingdom. And if it had been an "accident," how easy it would have been to lay the blame on my stubborn insistence on learning to fly.

But so many questions remain unanswered. Who were the pilots? Whose voice was it in the control tower that countermanded the first order for us to proceed? What drama might

have taken place in the control tower at Damascus before
one man took the place of another?

We have never had a satisfactory answer to these questions
from the then U.A.R. authorities or to others in Jordan's official protest over the incident. Despite repeated requests, they
have never told us on whose orders the Damascus Airport
authorities and the Air Force planes were operating.

After serious consideration, we decided not to proceed
with a case to the United Nations. I preferred to consider this
a personal matter rather than a national issue.

I was more than recompensed by the loyalty of my people,
from the moment we landed. Anxious officials had congre-
gated at the airport. Huge crowds rushed to surround my
plane as we taxied to a stop on the apron. When I reached
the Palace, the enthusiasm was unbounded. I was tremendously excited. Through the door of my study where I stood,
scores of officers and troops from the Army, men from the
desert in white and brown robes, and—or so it seemed—people from the streets came to pay me homage. I was almost
mobbed. I could not prevent them from embracing me, shak-
ing my hands and crying, "Thank God! Thank God you are
alive!"

Machine guns were being fired outside, and rifle shots and
shotguns also were echoing round the hills. In one place an
excited soldier found nothing else to use but a tear-gas bomb
—and hurled over the heads of the crowd. It seemed as
though the whole town had gone wild. Men of my Army tore
past the Palace gates up the hill, some of them in Land-
Rovers, firing their rifles into the air as they headed toward
the Palace. The crowds grew as army units stationed outside
the city started rolling into Amman to congratulate me. It
was a wonderful, wonderful day, and it made me change my
mind about a holiday in Europe. At first I had thought of

refueling and finding an alternative route to Europe, but when thousands of men, women and children begged me to stay, I could not leave. My place was with these loyal people, some unashamedly weeping as they embraced me.

My scrape with the Syrian MIGs was a hair's-breadth escape from death, and I must admit that at one time I felt—to use Air Force jargon—that I had "bought" it.

Times have changed since those bitter days of 1958 when tragedy ripped the Arab lands asunder. Even so, the Syrian MIG incident was an attack upon a head of state as yet unparalleled in history, and it will take me longer to forget it than it has taken me to forgive those responsible.

As chance would have it, exactly one year later—the same hour, the same date—I flew over the same spot, on my way to London, and took the opportunity to mark privately the anniversary of that attack. From the cockpit I looked down as I followed the course I had taken the year before with Dalgleish. Then I had been defenseless and flying at zero altitude. Now the Jordanian Air Force was soaring at height and in strength along our frontier. It all looked so calm and peaceful. On the H.5 road, like a straight black ruler leading to Iraq, there were only a couple of trucks. On the desert, with its lava-covered hillocks where we had so nearly crashed, a camel train moved slowly toward the frontier. At the proper moment I called up Damascus to report my position, thinking back to that first enigmatic reply just a year before. It was different this time! Politely, an impersonal voice gave me leave to proceed. There was not a MIG in the air.

How strange life is—and how strange are memories, especially in the loneliness of the skies. I could hardly believe that over those same low black hillocks of lava I had just a year before hedgehopped, fighting desperately for my life, waiting for each new assault as the MIGs attacked. I strained my neck looking out of the cockpit remembering them.

One of my entourage entered the cockpit. Did I need anything? I shook my head. No, I needed nothing; nothing except a moment of privacy to pray silently to God for the gift of life.

Then I busied myself with my instruments and set course for Cyprus and the West.

16

My American Tour

"I was eager to meet the people."

FOR A LONG TIME I had wanted to visit the United States. My impressions of it, like those of everyone else who has never been there, were made up from books I had read, American magazines, and above all, the movies. Of course I did not expect to find cowboys and Indians stalking each other on the Western plains or gangsters shooting it out in the streets of Chicago. But I really had no idea what to expect, beyond having the pleasure of visiting the greatest free nation in the world, and one I had always admired. I was eager to meet the people of the United States and learn what I could from them. I looked forward to my first visit with even more excitement than I had as a child when I first went to Alexandria or later when I first went to London.

Arrangements were finally concluded in the spring of 1959 for me to make a lengthy tour of the country. I flew by way of Formosa, where I broke my journey for a few days. Here

I paid an official visit to its great leader—and my good and
wise friend—Generalissimo Chiang Kai-shek and his brave
people. Then I flew on.

Altogether, I spent about a month in America. It was the
most exhilarating, exciting, and exhausting journey I have
ever made. The Americans are so generous, so enthusiastic
about their country, I had to see everything. Indeed, I wanted
to, for the major purpose of my trip was twofold. I hoped,
in a series of major speeches and meetings, to explain Jordan's
policy, principles, beliefs and traditions to the American
people.

After all, the United States, through much-needed financial
aid, had placed great faith, and I believe, great hope, in Jordan. And I wanted, if I could, to assure the people that their
faith was not misplaced, and that their hopes for us would
one day be justified. At the same time I wanted to see everything I could and learn as much as possible about the most
powerful country in the world. I did not know, but I suspected, that I might learn something that would find application in my own country, different though the two countries
are in almost every physical respect. Above all, I wanted to
meet the ordinary people of the United States. I wanted to
talk to them without any barriers or protocol.

I landed first at Honolulu on March 17 and spent several
days there. This was a wonderful interlude. The weather,
as always, was perfect, and I stayed in that pink rambling
landmark of Waikiki Beach, the Royal Hawaiian Hotel. I
tasted every conceivable kind of Hawaii's wonderful food.
Never had I seen such variety—Japanese, Chinese, South
Seas, with the ever-present pineapple almost given away.

The Governor and his wife and the people of the new state

were very kind. I spent as much time as possible being an ordinary tourist. I wore Aloha shirts. I wandered through the "International Village," where they have in a tree a restaurant that seats only two people. I lazed on the beach and was sorely tempted to try my hand (or rather feet!) at stand-up surfing. I could have stayed in Honolulu much longer, but on March 22 I had to fly to San Francisco to lunch with the World Affairs Council.

Here I had my first view of America's skyscrapers. Like every tourist, I went to the "Top of the Mark" for the fabulous view of San Francisco and the bay and its bridges. I share with everyone who has seen that panorama the opinion that this is truly one of the magnificent sights of the world. After lunch I managed to slip off unattended, except for a couple of friends. I wanted to walk, unobserved, up and down the streets that climb as steeply as those in Amman.

Here I entered my first drugstore. I could hardly believe my eyes. In Amman, drugstores confine themselves to selling drugs. In this shop, I could have stocked a fair-sized house. But like a good Arab, I merely sat at a counter and had coffee. Next door was a vast supermarket, second only in wonder to the skyscraper as an American invention. I moved up and down the aisles, amazed not only at the variety of products but at the variety of brands. Then suddenly I became *cognito*. A mother shopping with her children gave me a stare of recognition. Perhaps she had seen my photographs in the morning papers. She had two children with her, and one of them, a little girl, noticing her mother's intent look, asked loudly, "Who is he, Mummy?"

"Hush," the mother half whispered. "He's the King."

In a very loud voice, the daughter asked, "What does a king do, Mummy?"

It must be hard to find a more beautiful city than San

Francisco. I was intrigued to notice how often in different American cities the people asked me, "Have you seen San Francisco?" They are rightly very proud of it.

The next day I flew to Washington for my official reception. On the flight from San Francisco, there was considerable discussion about what I should wear when the plane landed in Washington. My own inclination was for a dark suit, but the State Department people, who were to be my constant companions on my visit, suggested that a uniform would be more appropriate. Apparently they thought it would make me look more like a king. I have never given much thought to what a king should look like, but I thought, If that's what they'd like to see, that's what they shall see.

I was glad I did wear my Air Force blues uniform, because after I had shaken hands with those who had come to meet me at Washington, the attendant band struck up the Jordanian national anthem. As I saluted, a lump came to my throat, hearing our anthem played on foreign soil. I remember thinking how proud I was to be a Jordanian, and only wished that my people back home could know how proud I felt for them at that moment.

Though this was not a state visit, I was met at the airport by Vice President Nixon and Mr. Christian Herter, then Acting Secretary of State. I did not have much opportunity to get to know Mr. Nixon, though my first impression was of his cordiality and kindness. I was greatly impressed with the charm and dignity of Mr. Herter, an impression that was confirmed on the several other occasions when we met.

In Washington, I had long separate talks with President Eisenhower and Mr. Herter. From their side there is no doubt they wanted to form an opinion about the free Jordanian people and their servant and leader, whom the United States government was helping to support. On my side, I was deeply anxious to explain to the President and others in high office some of the misconceptions about so-called Arab nationalism that I believed existed in the West. I wanted to reassure them, if they needed reassurance, of Jordan's determination to fight communism, in whatever guise it appeared in the Middle East.

I found Mr. Eisenhower most receptive. He was generous and warm-hearted. I could understand why Americans saw in him the so-called "father image." He immediately made me feel that he was aware of the gravity of our problems in Jordan and encouraged me to discuss them at length. What is more, I felt he understood the underlying factors causing dissension among various Arab states that should in reality have been closely united.

He said to me, "We in the United States are very concerned about the spread of communism in the Middle East. The threat of Soviet infiltration into the Arab world is one of our most serious problems today."

"This, Mr. President, is what we in Jordan are fighting," I replied. "But we are a small country. We need, perhaps more than anything else, the feeling that we do not stand alone."

"You don't, Your Majesty," said the President, firmly. "Our country knows what you have done. Believe me, we shan't let you down. Both of us—Jordan and America—are fighting the same battle."

Meeting the President was one thing. Meeting the National Press Club in Washington was very different. American newspapermen do not pull their punches, and their questions are almost always "loaded." I talked at some length after an excellent lunch, again stressing the misconceptions that arise in the West over what constitutes Arab unity and Arab nationalism.

"Whatever form Arab nationalism will and must take, it must grow out of the spirit of the Arab people," I declared. "We will fight, God willing and God guiding us, even though the struggle may be long and the price may be high. Arab nationalism has much to offer the world. It will one day, as our forefathers did in the past, make positive contributions to the well-being of man, and we will take our rightful and equal place in the family of nations. That is our interpretation of Arab nationalism, and we ask you, as Americans, to understand the true meaning of Arab nationalism and not to be misled by the distortions into which it has been cast."

And since I was always trying to drive home my message that Arab nationalism and communism can never live together, I added:

"Communism has recently gained strength in the Arab world, but any policy of collaboration with the Communists who claim to further Arab interests and solve Arab problems can only result in the greatest danger to Arab nationalism."

I had been warned about the tough questions I would be asked but they were not as bad as I feared. Most of them naturally concerned Israel, and many reporters asked me if the Arab world could live with Israel in peace. To this type of question I could only state what I have stated so often—that we all hope for a just solution to the Palestine question one day, adding, "Maybe it will come sooner, once people all over the world actually look at the question and understand it properly and work for a solution."

As I have said, one of my reasons for visiting the United States was to give people a picture of Jordan and what we stand for. How little many people know about countries other than their own. At this luncheon one reporter, presumably intelligent, asked me, "Are Christian pilgrims allowed to worship freely at the Christian holy places under the control of Jordan?"

It seemed almost unnecessary to reply that Jordan is the guardian of the holy places of all true faiths and that all pilgrims are welcome to worship as they wish. We feel that these holy places do not belong to us but to all those who believe in God.

Before leaving Washington, I also appeared on the American television program, "Face the Nation," in which I was interviewed by a panel of prominent newspapermen. This, too, was not as bad as I had been led to expect. All I had to do was tell the truth. Americans have some odd notions about royalty and I think the panel was a little surprised when I outlined in one sentence my views on the subject—something to the effect that "The monarchy is only worth preserving when it works for the people."

After six days in Washington I set off on my coast-to-coast tour of the United States. It was fascinating, but hard work. I averaged two or three speeches a day. I spent many nights in flight, and as I can never sleep in a plane I sometimes only had two or three hours' rest. I started the tour by writing out all my major speeches, but as it progressed I did not have time to do this. The Americans—avid workers—are rigid in keeping to their schedules; many times I had to hold conferences at breakfast. It was my only spare time. In one way

I benefited from this tight schedule. I *had* to learn to speak in English without preparation. Before the end of my American trip I was speaking regularly without having written a speech previously, except in important statements of policy. I found I could do without writing my speeches, but I could not do without any sleep.

After visiting the U.S. Naval Academy at Annapolis, and the American naval base at Norfolk, Virginia, I went to Williamsburg, Virginia, and here I felt for the first time a deep awareness of the value Americans place on tradition. All too often foreigners tend to imagine America as a busy industrial nation with no time to think of anything but work or financial affairs. How wrong they are! I found on this trip that the average American has a profound respect for his past even though it is briefer than that of some other countries.

Williamsburg, the reconstructed capital of eighteenth-century colonial Virginia, was steeped in tradition, even to the horse-drawn carriage in which I rode. And I could hardly fail to be impressed with the city that had once been the home of Patrick Henry, the man who said, "Give me liberty or give me death." Those words exactly echoed my own sentiments.

I was not only surprised by the American respect for tradition, but I remember thinking, as I drove around Williamsburg, that there was a lesson here for many other peoples. Here was a nation forged out of many nationalities, yet preserving its history, immortalizing those great men who had made the United States what it is today. Do not many other parts of the world—and I include some Arab lands—tend to forget at times those who have given us greatness? Do we always look after our heritage, the good in that which our forefathers have left us, as well as we should? Americans certainly do.

What a change the next day when I journeyed to Knoxville, Tennessee, to inspect one of the forty-three giant dams of the Tennessee Valley Authority. Here was the America of today, just a stone's throw from the past, so gigantic in concept and size it seemed to belong to the world of tomorrow. It was like stepping across time, from Williamsburg to Knoxville, seeing in detail a perfect example of the engineering skill that has made the United States the greatest technological country in the world.

And then Los Angeles! And my memories of it are not only of the movie sets or Disneyland, both of which I visited and enjoyed immensely, but also of the world of jet aircraft where I felt at home. At the Lockheed plant in Los Angeles, I took an hour off in one of the latest F-104D supersonic jets. I flew at 52,000 feet above the Mojave Desert, broke the sound barrier and touched more than twice the speed of sound. I had to slow down considerably that evening when speaking to the World Affairs Council at a dinner in my honor!

Yet it was not only very pleasant, but a most important function, for before me were men vitally interested in world affairs. I planned to outline to them some of the problems we face in the Middle East, and I meant every word when I started by saying:

"It is significant that this association is not called a Foreign Affairs Council but a World Affairs Council, for in a very real sense there are no longer any foreign affairs, they are the affairs of the world and of us all. The warm reception I have received during my stay in the United States has touched my heart. The many kind words that have been said to me by the distinguished leaders of the great American people and by others who have been good enough to entertain me while I have been here, will enable me to take back to my people a message which I have previously preached among them. We are not alone. It is a real satisfaction not to feel alone in this world of ever-present difficulties. I am not referring to the security that nations seek in critical moments, but to the security that comes only from respect and common interests. I feel that this exists and will continue to exist between my people and the people of the United States."

In Los Angeles, I had my first serious encounter with the victims of Nasser's propaganda. At Los Angeles Airport there were a few pickets, with placards saying, "Go home, Imperialist Agent!" However, the next morning while I was resting in the Ambassador Hotel, one of my entourage told me that a delegation of Arab students—between fifty and a hundred strong—was crowding the lobby, demanding an audience. The American security officers advised me not to meet them.

"Don't worry," I told them. "I'll go and talk to them."

I did not go out of bravado. If I was in America to put my views before bodies like the World Affairs Council, surely it was equally important to put them before Arab students who apparently believed in Nasser to the point where they echoed his accusations that I was an imperialist agent. I feel one must always speak frankly to people who have differing opinions. A free exchange of views is vital.

The crowd jammed the lobby. I shook hands with many present and then asked them, "What language should I use in addressing you, gentlemen?"

They roared out, "English, please!"

I was sorry I could not speak to Arabs in Arabic and I told

them so, but there it was. I spoke to them of my mission, of Jordan, of conditions in the Middle East. I told them what we are trying to do. I was entirely alone among them and I permitted them to ask questions to which I replied candidly.

The result was gratifying. The demonstrators who had wanted me to go home seemed suddenly to change their minds. They cheered me and then demanded a souvenir photograph of us all together. They had arrived with pamphlets. They threw them away. How easily young students can be led astray by irresponsible leaders who seek to twist their minds with propaganda for their own ends—and how criminal it is. It is important to use every opportunity to tell them the truth. In Detroit the same thing happened. I met a group of more than five hundred local Arabs, many of them pro-Nasser, and I was able to tell them the truth—perhaps it was the first time they heard it—of Jordan's stand in the Arab world.

After Los Angeles I was scheduled to visit the Air Force Academy near Denver, Colorado. I had received a message from a young girl whose fiancé was a cadet there. She wished me a very special kind of welcome. In her message she explained that the American military academies had a tradition (as I discovered when I visited Annapolis Naval Academy) whereby all those confined to quarters or disciplined in other ways were granted an amnesty whenever there was an important visitor—that is, if the visitor requested it. Apparently her fiancé was in just such a fix. And she wanted me to exercise my privilege when visiting the Air Force Academy, which had only recently opened.

As luck would have it, we ran into a heavy snowstorm as

we reached Denver airport. The pilot sent back word to me
that he was sorry, but we would have to change our schedule
and divert to another airfield.

I went up to the cockpit to talk to the pilot, and told him
that I thought we ought to circle around awhile and try
again.

"If you say so, Your Majesty, but I don't think we'll have
much luck."

We made three different passes at the airport, but with no
success. We could not see a thing. Each time we were
ordered away by the control tower.

"I'm afraid I'll have to give up, sir," the pilot said.

"Very well, but those cadets are going to be very disappointed in me."

The next day, when the weather still had not cleared, we
went on to our next stop—Chicago. I sent back a cable to
the Commandant of the Academy. I forget just what I said,
but in effect, it went like this:

"Tried three times to come into Denver airport and even
got down to 200 feet. Although I am aware this is not strictly
a visit to the Academy, I believe my good intentions should
be counted as a visit and that the cadets being subjected to
discipline according to academy tradition should be granted
amnesty. Hussein I."

I do not know whether it had any effect. I hope so—particularly because later I read that after the cadet had gradu-
ated, he married his sweetheart, but on their honeymoon she
was killed when their car overturned. She sounded so happy
and hopeful in that message that I have always prayed I was
able to give them a few more days in their brief lives together.

My trip was drawing to a close. After Detroit I visited

West Point, home of the United States Military Academy, and lunched with the cadets there. Then to New York with its fabulous skyscrapers. In New York the late Dag Hammarskjöld, one of the greatest men of our time and a friend of Jordan, gave a dinner in my honor. But I shall have more to say about him in a later chapter.

I had four crowded, wonderful days in New York to wind up my tour. Mr. Henry Luce gave a small private dinner for about fifty businessmen at the Union Club in New York, and what he said has always stuck in my mind. Before toasting me, he said (these are roughly his words): "I wonder how many of you here realize the number of countries that are our friends and allies that are royally ruled." He then went on to name Britain, the Scandinavian countries, Holland, Belgium, Thailand, Iran, Saudi Arabia and so on, and finally came around to Jordan. He believed, he said, that there must be something in training for leadership from childhood. It was a speech that touched me deeply.

The following day I had a memorable luncheon with Cardinal Spellman, a man of God for whom I have deep respect. My uncle, Sherif Nasser, did not accompany me on this visit. Later I learned that he had gone to the races at the New York track. My uncle is one of the greatest horse breeders of the Middle East. He knows horses better than any man I know and I was not surprised to learn that even though he knew nothing about their form he picked four out of the six winners merely after watching the horses parade.

I wish I had had a little more free time in New York. It is, after all, one city in the world that can truly be called unique. But the Americans believe in working you hard! I still enjoyed every minute of it. In my four days, I spoke at the Hammarskjöld dinner, at a Reader's Digest luncheon, to the Council on Foreign Policy, and to a private Wall Street group. Then I made a major speech at a dinner at the Waldorf-Astoria given and attended by all societies interested in the Middle East, such as the Islam Institute, the American Friends of the Middle East, and the Middle East Institute.

All this prevented me from spending as much time as I would have liked to see the people of New York. Yet I did manage to get about a little and those five weeks certainly crystallized for me a definite set of opinions about the United States and its people. I felt one thing above all else. The Americans have many qualities, but the most impressive of all is their genuine sincerity. I felt I could believe everything they told me. One can get along with them so easily. They have an insatiable curiosity. They want to know as much as possible about other people and other countries. They want to share and help. They have hearts that are open, and because their free and easy manners knock away all barriers, I felt very close to them.

I know one thing about my visit to the United States. I believe my experiences there have made me a more broadminded monarch. The inspiration and example of people hard at work impressed me a great deal. It made me realize how much hard work counts. This being so, I came away from the United States believing even more strongly that, even with its limited resources, Jordan can become an economically viable country if our people work hard enough. It was this inspiration that led me to start broadcasting my "Build the Country" programs.

This much I learned. There were two things I hope I achieved: first, that I had explained Jordan's position and role in the Middle East. Second, that the leaders of the United

States had accepted me, I felt, as a serious, hard-working servant of my country and dedicated to it above all else. Too often newspapers have portrayed me differently. It is understandable. I like dancing and fast cars and jet planes, but the newspapers tended to seize on these hobbies and forget that I only indulge in them after a hard day's work.

Now I come to one last recollection of my American tour. I do not suppose a single person outside those very close to me knew—or knows now—that during the entire five weeks I spent in the United States I had with me in my entourage a man who was a conspirator. I knew it. We lunched and dined together, he was introduced to many of the American leaders, yet all the time, behind every smile for five weeks, I knew he was the ringleader of a plot to overthrow the regime in Jordan.

The man was General Sadiq Shara', Chief of Staff of Jordan's armed forces. Why was he with me? Just as I was about to leave on my American tour, strong evidence reached me that Shara' and several other officers planned, with outside help, a coup against the throne while I was away. Later we learned that they planned to take over the army headquarters, assassinate the Commander-in-Chief and open up with guns on the Zahran Palace, where my family was living. Shara' was not a man for half measures, for he had told the plotters, "When you have to fire on Zahran, don't bother with rifles, open up with the artillery!" And he added, "The Second Infantry Regiment stationed there will get it too."

Our information had come from an officer who, on my instructions, still pretended to support the conspirators but kept us informed of every step. It is hard, however, to pin down and prove conspiracies until the very last moment; and when the time came to leave for Formosa, although we knew the plot was being hatched, we could not deal with it.

What an awkward dilemma! With the plot moving forward and with my absence for such a long period, anything could happen. Then I had a brainstorm.

"All right," I announced. "I'll take Shara' with me as part of my entourage."

It put him in a difficult position, for he could not refuse my wish, though he tried his best to get out of it by claiming that he had fallen in his bath and had badly hurt his ribs.

I insisted, so he had to accompany me to the United States, leaving behind conspirators who regarded Shara' as their leader.

I hope it does not sound vengeful if I admit to rather enjoying the situation. By the time we reached the United States some of the conspirators had already been arrested and Shara' became more and more worried. His only information came from the American newspapers, for I had given instructions before leaving Amman that in no open cables was his name ever to be mentioned. In any event, he never saw any cables.

His anxiety increased. He bought paper after paper, reading the news of the arrest of his close companions, and doubtless wondering if any of them would implicate him. By the time we reached Chicago he *had* to find out some more details. I do not know what he did, but he vanished from my entourage in Chicago for a few hours and I said to my Chief of Diwan, "I fear that Sadiq might leave us—might try to run away now."

But he turned up in due time. In Washington and New York he tried to find fellow Jordanians who had perhaps received letters from home. Our days were filled with official engagements but he asked to be excused, on the ground that he was not feeling well. His request was ignored and he stayed with us.

Finally, we flew from New York to London. There, almost beside himself with worry, he said he needed an urgent operation and begged leave to remain behind when the time came for us to return home. Obviously he was going to bolt, so I refused permission but blandly promised him that as soon as we reached Jordan and the trip was over I would, if necessary, arrange for him to make another trip to London for the operation.

He was arrested shortly after our return and sentenced to death, a sentence I later commuted to life imprisonment.

17

The Murder of Jordan's Prime Minister · · · And Plots Against My Person

"We suspect an attempt to poison you."

so CUNNING and varied have been the plots against my person, and so constant, that sometimes I have felt like the central character in a detective novel.

In my own mind I class plots in two different categories. The first is the major coup, such as that at Zerqa, which has as its objective the overthrowing of the monarchy and the downfall of Jordan. On such occasions my assassination is important to the plotters but only as part of their general strategy.

The second type is the attempt on my life, divorced from any major political coup. If these have increased, I believe it is because those who wish to see the end of a free and democratic Jordan know now that it is not as easy as they anticipated to foment revolution in my country. They cannot, as they once hoped, buy off large sections of people whose loyalty and faith are above all price. The only alternative is to smuggle in assassins to kill me and other important leaders, in the hope that such a deed would in itself lead to that conflict, bloodshed and even civil war so ardently desired by the Communists and those adopting their strategy.

On no occasion have I felt I was indispensable to Jordan. I am its servant, not its master. Invariably I have been at pains to build up a family feeling in Jordan so that I may be, if you like, the father of a large family just as much as the king of a small country. My sudden death at this stage would doubtless lead to strife.

One of my narrowest escapes was when I discovered an attempt to kill me with deadly acid. But before I describe what happened, I must retail the events leading up to it, for this was the second lucky escape I had had within twenty-four hours.

On the day before—August 29, 1960—the worst outrage in the history of Jordan shattered the warm summer peace of Amman. On that day, Hazza Majali, the Prime Minister, and twelve other Jordanians were killed by explosives planted in the desk of the Premier's office. Hazza Majali was a man of great courage, a man with a big heart, a believer in freedom, and one of the most popular figures in the country. To think of his death even now saddens and angers me.

It was a Monday, the day when the Prime Minister invariably threw open his office to all comers to listen to their ideas, their requests or their problems. The day of the plot was chosen, as was discovered afterward, because the plotters were certain he would be there. Even more, they knew that he was a great personal friend of mine. In the opinion of most people, with which I agree, the plotters who sent their men to plant the explosives during the night of Sunday relied on the fact that when I heard of my Prime Minister's death I would immediately rush to his office. There they had planted a second bomb.

As fate would have it, I had been overworked. A sinus condition was troubling me and I had been advised to take a rest on Monday. I had checked on Sunday night with the Prime Minister, little thinking that I would never speak to him again. He reported delightedly on the results of the recent Arab League Foreign Ministers' Conference in Chtaura, Lebanon, and that agreement had been reached to remove all causes of the strained relations between the Arab states. All the member states, he added, had finally drawn up a satisfactory plan to bring this about. In addition, Jordan's stand at the Arab League meetings in Chtaura had stopped the U.A.R.'s attempt to force Arab states to break relations with Iran, which had been unrealistically accused of dealing with Israel.

So on that Monday morning around eleven o'clock I was still resting at my farmhouse at Hummar when the telephone rang. The head of the Premier's Information Office wished to speak to me and said it was urgent.

I was puzzled. What, I wondered, could have prompted him to phone me in this way? Then suddenly his anxious, distressed voice came on the line and without any forewarning he blurted out: "Sir, the Prime Minister's office has been blown up and Hazza Pasha is dead . . ."

At first I could not believe it, I just could not take in his words. Brusquely I said, "Get hold of yourself, man! What the devil are you talking about? Now—tell me exactly what happened."

He told me again. I still could not believe it. Stunned, I asked the operator, "Get me my Chief of Diwan." To my dismay, he replied that the Chief of the Diwan and other Palace officials had left for the Premier's office.

That was one of the most awful moments of my life. It could not have happened. Why Hazza? Hazza, my friend— the friend of every Jordanian. Hazza, the man who, though Premier, opened his office doors each Monday so that anybody who pleased could come to see him.

I slammed down the telephone and as I dressed hurriedly, I remembered how happy he had been the night before when telling me of the end, at last, of plots and counterplots between the Arab states. What about Chtaura and its resolutions now? I thought bitterly. Poor Hazza. How dared they do this?

I ran out to my car, making doubly sure that my submachine gun was on the seat next to me. I told two guards to get in the back and drove toward Amman.

Those few miserable, apprehensive minutes as I raced the fifteen miles toward the capital seemed interminable. As I swerved around corners I was thinking not only of the grave loss to Jordan but of the dangers that the country might have to face before the day was out. I watched the road carefully, for experience had taught me quite enough to beware of the possible dangers on the route to Amman.

I had just reached the outskirts of the city when a car screeched to a stop in front of me. Out jumped the Minister of Defense. Behind his car was another with the Army Commander, General Habis Majali, a close friend of mine, and a cousin of the murdered Premier.

One of them—I forget who it was—said, "Your Majesty, it's all over."

"In no circumstances can you go, sir," said General Majali. "If you could serve any useful purpose, of course we would not stop you, but it's all over and I am sure there is a grave danger of another attempt being made."

"What happened?" I asked.

"Half the building is demolished," replied Majali. "The roof of Hazza's office crashed in on him."

"Have you found him?"

"Not yet, sir, but the building is partly down and rescue work is going on. It must have been in his office."

I still hoped for a miracle, that this could not be the end of Jordan's Hazza Majali. I had warned him so often, "Take care. It could be you or any of us."

"You take care, Your Majesty," Hazza had smiled. "You are the one Jordan needs. The rest of us are all expendable."

General Majali and the Defense Minister refused point blank to let me pass their cars, but the Minister of Defense suggested that I go to the Palace and begin to pull things together.

How fortuitous that the danger was sensed, for less than forty minutes after the first explosion, a second one occurred. It caused more damage and loss of life, mainly among the men trying to rescue those trapped inside the building. My Chief of Diwan was actually leaving the wrecked, torn Prime Minister's office when the second bomb exploded. I shall never know whether it was intended for me or not.

I was sick at the perfidy of it all, for among those killed was a ten-year-old child, a man of seventy, and an old woman calling on Majali with a grievance. Majali himself was so honest, so God-fearing, that he had consistently spurned the advice of security officials who begged him not to allow so many people into his office after a previous plot against him had been uncovered.

But now, the most urgent problem was to get things under control as swiftly as possible, for I knew that this spark could start a roaring inferno. Soon enough the radio "Voice of the Arabs" from Cairo came to life, praising the so-called heroic deed, extolling the way "an imperialist agent" had been killed by the people, and promising in no uncertain terms a similar end for the rest of us in Jordan.

Shortly after I reached the Palace, still awaiting news, a report came in that the Prime Minister had been seen walking out of his office toward the hospital next door with only head injuries. He was said to have been holding his head.

With a lump in my throat, I rushed out of my office to see if it were true. Alas, it was a mistake. Soon afterward the body of Hazza Majali was found. He had died instantly at his desk in the explosion.

I ordered an immediate Cabinet meeting. Whatever happened, I had to form a new government with all speed. I was sick with shock as the members of the Cabinet filed in, each as dazed as I. I sorely missed Hazza Majali. There was never a truer Jordanian patriot, nor a more forgiving man. How insane could one's enemies become? To replace him would be difficult. I thought quickly and then I knew the man I wanted—Bahjat al Talhouni, my Chief of Diwan.

I cannot remember my exact words, but I recall well my meaning. When the Cabinet was seated I addressed them:

"Gentlemen, it is essential that we have a new government immediately. Our enemies are ready to seize advantage from this wicked murder. Without leadership we may be unable to deal with developments. They have got Hazza. They have struck a cruel blow. But, gentlemen, they have not got Jordan."

Amid dead silence, I went on:

"As men, we must not let his work be lost. Nor our country. We who are alive must carry out our responsibilities toward the Arab homeland. We will avenge Hazza—with greater determination than ever to make our lives worth living, and to save our nation from those criminals who seek to destroy it."

Palace servants brought in coffee. I paused. The respite was welcome, for I knew what many of them must have been thinking. When the servants had gone and the doors were closed, I continued, choosing my words carefully:

"We have lost a great Prime Minister, but even in adversity there is some solace and I am happy that so many of my Ministers have been spared and that I can speak to you now.

"It is my wish that you all remain in the posts you have filled so well. I would rather have no changes at this moment. Our country has prospered under this government and all of you must share the credit. I ask you now to remain in your present posts and I have decided that my Chief of Diwan will become Prime Minister."

I asked Talhouni if he were prepared to assume office and he replied after a moment's hesitation—for Hazza was his closest friend—that he would be honored. There was a moment's silence that seemed very long to me, but then came murmurs of assent from most of the others, and I knew that my instinct had been right. Some Ministers resigned on the spot, but they were replaced immediately.

Within a few minutes, agreement was reached and I invested Talhouni, who had served Jordan magnificently as Chief of Diwan, as Prime Minister. In these days of political squabbling and interminable discussion, I am rather proud that we in Jordan formed a new government within two to three hours after the assassination.

Already investigations had proved that two employees of the Prime Minister's office had crossed that morning into Syria, at that time the northern part of Nasser's U.A.R. I knew then what I had already suspected.

When the capital was a little quieter I drove back to my farmhouse to pick up some of my belongings and decided to lunch there before returning to Amman. I was halfway through the meal when Sherif Nasser, my uncle, telephoned me.

His voice was urgent. "I'm speaking in the presence of Habis and the chief of the political intelligence." (Habis Pasha was commander-in-chief of the armed forces.) "We have found evidence that there will be an attempt on your life through somebody on your personal staff—it could be at the farm or at the Palace. Please stay there. We are coming right out."

Within a few minutes their cars drew up at the door. The intelligence chief carried with him a tape recorder.

"Just listen to this, Your Majesty." He started to thread the tape through the machine.

"Who is it?" I asked.

"One of my men has become," he coughed discreetly, "a very close friend, sir, with a member of the United Arab Republic's Embassy here."

We sat down to listen, with rising horror, to a conversation between our intelligence agent and the U.A.R. man. After a few preliminaries, the latter said:

"Within a very short time Hussein will get the same treatment. We've recruited somebody in his residence to finish him off and it won't be long now. If he only stuck to a proper routine, we would have got him days ago."

For a moment I was speechless. Then I cried, "It's incredible! I can't believe it!"

"It's true, all right," said my uncle. "You'd better not stay at the Basman Palace tonight."

I finished lunch rather hurriedly, and left for Amman. On the way, thinking things over, I decided to spend the night at Maurice Raynor's house, which he and his family occupied in the Palace grounds near my office. This would give the security forces a chance to make a careful investigation into the lunchtime story and thoroughly search the premises.

When I got to the Palace I asked Raynor if I could use his spare room. I then told him what clothes I wanted and asked him to arrange for them to be taken to his house.

"And you'd better take a new unopened medicine kit with you," I added. "My sinus is troubling me. I might want some of my drops. Kindly ask Mrs. Raynor to get rid of the old supply just in case."

Since my youth I have suffered from sinus trouble and indeed I was operated on in England when I was a cadet at Sandhurst. But the only real cure is rest. Rest, however, is out of the question in Jordan, as anyone who has read this much of my story will readily concede, so I find the easiest way to gain relief is to take more drops. I certainly felt I needed them that night. But to this day I wonder what instinct made me suggest that Raynor get a new supply.

Just before dinner, I went into Raynor's house and when I asked for my phials, Mrs. Raynor cried:

"Sir! Come and look, please!" She led me to the sink in the bathroom. On the edge of the basin stood a half-empty phial —the one I should have used. In the bottom of the basin were some of the drops. To my horror the liquid was bubbling.

I poured out more drops. The liquid looked as though it were alive; it hissed and bubbled and frothed, and as I watched aghast, Mrs. Raynor cried, "Look at the sink, sir!"

I did. By now the chromium on the basin fittings had peeled off.

"Thank God you poured the stuff away!" I exclaimed.

"Maurice told me what you said," she replied. "I didn't honestly think, sir, there was anything wrong—but look what's happening!"

The bottle contained a strong acid. Somebody in the Palace, somebody close enough to have access to my bathroom, had poured the harmless drops out of the bottle and filled it up with acid.

We never did discover the culprit. It pained me to have to suspect my personal servants, particularly the non-Jordanians. Some of them had been with me for a long time, but my security forces could not prove anything. Nevertheless, I had to find some servants—and acquire an entirely new medicine chest.

The plot of the acid nose drops was cunning, but even more weird and frightening was the incident of the poisoned cats. Amman abounds in cats, mostly strays that know no barriers and can slip through any barbed wire. My grandfather loved cats and a large floating cat population in the Palace grounds has always been tolerated.

Walking in the grounds I came across the bodies of three dead cats. Poor creatures, I thought. I assumed they had starved. I happen to like cats and wished to find out whose fault it was.

As I entered the Palace, an officer was waiting for me. I told him I would be with him in a minute, adding:

"I'm just going to tell the servants to bury some dead cats."

"What dead cats, Your Majesty?" He looked alarmed.

"Over there," I indicated the general direction.

"But how many, Your Majesty?"

I wondered what on earth was wrong with him.

"Does it matter?"

"It does, sir, it does indeed," he replied earnestly. "Your Majesty, yesterday we found six dead cats in the grounds. The day before we found seven."

Now it was my turn to become alarmed.

"Is all this true?" I asked incredulously.

"Indeed, sir. They were poisoned."

"But why haven't I been told about this?"

"We didn't want to alarm you, sir, until we were sure. We suspected a man in the kitchen so we made certain he never had anything to do with your food, sir. There was no danger to you."

"Who is he?" I asked.

"We received a report a few days ago from the military attaché in Beirut. He said the U.A.R. Deuxième Bureau in Damascus had been in touch with an assistant cook in the Palace kitchen named Ahmed Na'naa. We've been waiting, sir, and now we're about to arrest him."

What had happened? Only Na'naa's confession could tell the incredible story. He had a cousin in Damascus who worked with the Syrian Deuxième Bureau. This cousin, knowing Na'naa worked as an assistant cook, had recruited him with the idea of poisoning my food. He was to be paid a large sum when his assignment was completed. But Na'naa was no expert in poisons and so, he said, he had been experimenting on cats in order to find out what constituted a lethal dose. He admitted readily that the only reason no attempt had been made on my life was because he could not judge the dose. None of the cats, he said, had died quickly enough. Na'naa made the mistake of letting the cats wander off into the Palace grounds to die, otherwise we might never have discovered the plot.

Na'naa went to jail, but he is now free. Some time later, on the occasion of one of our great Moslem feasts, I was driving from the Mosque after praying. A young girl pushed her way to the car in which I was driving. She was carrying a copy of the Koran. She implored me to release her father, this same Ahmed Na'naa, who had attempted to poison me.

What can one do at such a moment, on the way from praying to God for the very gift of being alive? The Chief of my Diwan was sitting beside me.

"Arrange things with the authorities," I sighed, "and let him go free." Na'naa was freed to celebrate the feast with his family.

Before 1956, Jordan's Intelligence Service was very small, since our country was almost totally free from the plotting and machinations that haunted so many other areas of the Arab world. There were occasional plots, but in most cases these were discovered through the loyalty of individuals both in the Army and in other walks of life. The loyalty of man is often wonderful. I remember we discovered one plot when a father informed against his own son after the boy arrived from Syria on an assassination mission. On that occasion it was a plot to shoot Majali, or my uncle Sherif Nasser, a few weeks before the Prime Minister's office was blown up.

I myself not only dislike but deeply resent being hemmed in by security measures. Yet, as communism and our enemies increased their attacks on Jordan, we had to build up a tight net against all possible subversion. Now we have a better security force, one of which I am proud. It stands in the face of attempts that continue to threaten Jordan's peace.

How many attempts on my life, or the lives of prominent Jordanians, have we uncovered during the years! They have tried everything from direct shooting to the use of bombs and poison. We have had some very lucky escapes.

My uncle, Sherif Nasser, and I had one particularly lucky escape a few months before General Glubb left Jordan. It happened like this.

Several times during the warm summer evenings I drove to my farm for dinner with friends, always at about 8 P.M. I had not then built the house I now occupy with my wife, but used to stay in a small one which had belonged to my grandfather. I always traveled unescorted in those days. It happened that both my uncle and I had similar Buick convertibles at that time.

On this particular evening, he traveled to the farm when I was supposed to be doing so. Instead, I was driving back from Jerash, the ancient Roman city where I had spent the afternoon supervising arrangements for a dinner party I was giving the next evening for foreign diplomats. I was late and was returning to Amman prior to going to the farm as usual. It was just past eight as I sped up a hill toward Amman when I saw my uncle's car spanning the road with the front wheels in a ditch. I braked to a stop and jumped out, to find my uncle walking toward me visibly shaken, his clothes covered with dust.

"What happened?" I asked.

He replied, "It was a puncture. Don't worry, sir!"

Then as I looked more closely, I saw to my horror two bullet holes. They had shattered the windshield just above the steering post. In all we counted nine bullet holes in the car, and one that had punctured the left front tire.

I did not wait to find out more. The car with the would-be assassin had raced toward Amman barely ten minutes before I arrived. My uncle gave me a description of it and I started out at once to catch it. It was, he thought, a pale blue car, but I was unable to trace it. We never did find those responsible.

They had waited on the side of the road facing Amman and as my uncle's car, which looked exactly like mine, came up the brow of the hill, they flashed bright headlights in his face, so as to make sure which car it was. As it came closer, they opened fire from two guns at point-blank range. My uncle threw himself on the seat and out of the car as it came to a stop on the roadside. He managed to shoot twice at the tail lights of the attacking car as it disappeared in the direction of Amman. The assailants obviously had mistaken their target.

18

I Fly to the United Nations

"I did not travel all these miles to utter platitudes."

IN LATE September, 1960, barely a month after the murder of Hazza Majali, I decided to fly to the United Nations to make a speech there. This was not an impulse. I thought the matter over very carefully, and there were several reasons why I went.

The United Nations itself was under bitter attack by Khrushchev and the Communist bloc. Khrushchev was trying to get rid of Hammarskjöld and substitute his "troika" system. I felt strongly that the Communist countries—and the so-called neutrals—were dominating the speeches so much that a distorted picture of world thinking was emanating from the U.N. It seemed to me, reading the reports in Amman, that the friends of freedom were being out-propagandized by the friends of communism. I was particularly worried about the effect of this on the newly admitted African states. Furthermore, the United Nations means more to the smaller nations of this world, wherever they are.

As far as the Middle East was concerned, I did not like the way in which Arab world opinion was being put forward, it seemed, by only one man—Nasser. Nasser did not, and does not, represent all Arab thought. I felt it my duty to alert the U.N. to the problems of the Middle East, particularly the renewal of tension between the then U.A.R. and Jordan, as symbolized by the bomb plot that killed our Prime Minister. I thought, too, that a free Arab nation like Jordan should voice its opinion on the Algerian and Israeli problems.

I knew my voice would be small compared to the booming of Khrushchev and the raving of Castro, but nonetheless I decided that, whether or not they listened to me, I would go.

It was not so easy to fly there as I thought, for once again the then U.A.R. interfered with my plans. The B.O.A.C. airline did not at that time have its Comet service stopping at Amman and there was no way but to ask if they would land their plane at Amman on its way to London from the Gulf in order to pick me up. This they agreed to do.

As the plane had to fly over Syria, they notified Damascus that I would be a passenger, and of their change of schedule. The Syrian authorities gave the usual permission. Then at the last moment they flatly refused to allow the plane to fly over Syria if it changed its time of flight. In other words, it could not land to pick me up. I had to cancel that plan. Instead, I had to charter an Air Jordan plane and fly with my entourage south over Saudi Arabia and down to Khartoum. From there we continued on over Libya to Malta and on to London. A trip that should have taken about seven hours took twenty-three hours.

From London I caught the next plane to New York where I was met by representatives of all the Arab governments, and then had my first police-siren drive from the airport to the Waldorf-Astoria. Each day while I was there, I had a police escort with sirens going full blast. With so many heads of state in New York, this incessant noise must have disturbed New Yorkers, but if it is any consolation to them, it annoyed me just as much.

Though I was very, very busy, it was a good feeling to be back in New York, for it is my favorite city in the world. The New Yorker is a very special person, compounded of so many races, so vitally proud of his great city. But what fascinated me most was the friendly curiosity behind the New Yorker's unceremonious "Hi'ya, King!"

The Waldorf was filled with visiting heads of state, and at first I thought the New Yorkers were merely displaying normal inquisitiveness about famous personages. I was genuinely astonished to find, after I had made my speech, that those who talked to me knew what I had said, were aware of what I and Jordan stood for. They were not just gazing at celebrities. Theirs was a genuine curiosity, aimed at discovering facts about another part of the globe.

I noticed this too when I went to watch a football game at Yale. They were playing Brown. When I stood in line for lunch in one of the college cafeterias, my mind went back to my earlier thoughts of university life. But I hardly got any lunch. Half a dozen boys brought their trays to my table, and I spent most of the time before the game answering questions. I was very much impressed by the atmosphere of Yale, and I remember wishing that I could have attended such a university.

At the game I sat next to one of Yale's former football stars, who explained the fine points of the game to me, at the same time, offering unheeded advice to the coach and the man directing the play on the field.

On the way back to New York, the son of one of my friends, a former Yale student who had attended the game with us, said to me, "I want to thank you very much, Your Majesty."

"What for?" I asked.

"That's the first and probably the last time I'll ever sit on the fifty-yard line!"

That day, as a matter of fact, was the only day of relaxation I had during the entire visit, and a very happy one at that. In the evening, a group of us went dancing at the Plaza Hotel in New York, and we stayed until the orchestra put covers on their instruments.

I liked the young people of America, boys as well as girls, and I look forward some day to visiting them with my wife and meeting my many friends again. Their thirst for knowledge impressed me. If they did not know about anything, they never hesitated to ask.

The morning after I landed in New York, Mr. Hammarskjöld visited me at the Waldorf to welcome me. It was a rare privilege—I am told I was the only head of state he visited—and I was deeply moved. I had always had the highest regard for this quiet, unassuming Swedish diplomat who has laid down his life in the cause of freedom. His death is a bitter loss to the cause of human rights. He was a true and great friend to Jordan.

I had a great deal of trouble preparing my speech. I had less than forty-eight hours to work on it and, unlike some heads of state with their groups of secretaries, I had to do most of the work myself. I was under heavy pressure—from some of my own government people among others—to "tone down" my speech. But as I told one anxious diplomat, "I did not travel all these thousands of miles just to utter a few well-worn platitudes." I felt, as I do now, that the small nations look to the U.N. for protection, for peace and progress, and, with those sentiments in mind, I decided to say exactly what I thought. There was absolutely no point in playing down the tensions in the Middle East. If I did that, I might as well have stayed at home.

On October 2, the night before I was due to make my speech, I discarded all draft suggestions that did not fit in with my ideas. Some of my group felt that I should avoid mentioning "neutralism"—this was the popular thing to do at the U.N.—but I *had* to mention neutralism. As I have said so often, there can be no neutralism in the life-and-death struggle between freedom and communism, and though I respected the choice of others and their right to make that choice, I had to state my own views clearly.

That night I worked on my speech until nearly four the next morning. By 9:30 A.M. I was at the U.N. Headquarters. I should have spoken at ten o'clock, but Khrushchev somehow got in first. He bitterly attacked the U.N. and various aspects of our life in the free world. He scornfully derided all we believe in. It was a remarkable coincidence, but my speech could have served as a direct reply to his tirade. If I had studied his speech in advance, my reply would have been the speech I composed before I knew what Khrushchev was going to say. Khrushchev and the U.A.R. delegation got up and walked out as I began to speak, but that did not matter. It was not to them I was addressing my words but to world opinion.

Since this speech was made only a few months before I started writing this book, it still represents my views on the United Nations, neutralism, and the problems of the Arab world. For this reason, I have decided to include the text in this chapter. As this book draws to its close, my speech represents a summing up of all I have learned since I first ascended the throne of Jordan. After the preliminaries, I said:

There are four reasons why I am here today. First, I was deeply concerned over what seemed to be an obvious attempt to wreck the United Nations. Second, I wanted to be sure that there was no mistake about where Jordan stands in the conflict of ideologies that is endangering the peace of the world. Third, as the head of a small nation, I felt that it was my duty to the other small nations of the world, particularly to the new members of the United Nations, to share with them our experience in preserving the freedom for which we, like they, fought so hard to win. Fourth, and finally, I believe it to be my duty also to express my views on three vital problems in the Middle East affecting the peace of the world—namely, the growing tension between Jordan and the United Arab Republic, the independence of Algeria, and the still unanswered problem of Palestine.

It is needless to affirm that the United Nations represents the only hope of peace and freedom to humanity. This is of major significance to all the small nations of the world. Yet the Soviet Union has sought to destroy the United Nations, to hamper its deliberations, to block its decisions and, by rowdy tactics and petulant walk-outs, to demean the reputation of the Security Council and the General Assembly.

The most recent illustration of this has been its performance at this Session, the attempt to weaken the powers of the Secretary-General, and the proposal to move the site of the organization's Headquarters. These are only slightly concealed efforts to destroy the United Nations itself.

No one who has followed the deliberations in the General Assembly for the past two weeks can fail to be aware of the significance of this meeting. The problems that confront us are not new problems, but as they have remained unsolved they have so grown in magnitude that their continued existence threatens not the peace of the world but our very life. I have no major plan for the solution of these problems. As a country which owns no nuclear weapons and which can only suffer from nuclear warfare, Jordan merely beseeches the powers involved to resume their labors and strive even in the face of all obstacles in their path to find a formula. Or better, perhaps, to find a way of truth that will not only save them, but save us all.

There are other problems, too, and one would indeed be blind if he did not realize that almost on every vital issue that confronts this body, the nations of the world are being offered a choice. And there is no secret about what that choice is—it lies between becoming part of the Soviet empire, subservient ultimately to the dictates of the Supreme Council of the Soviet Union, or standing as a free nation whose sole external allegiance is to the United Nations itself. That is the choice, and it is there for each and every nation to decide. And may I say at once, with all the strength and conviction at my command, that Jordan has made its choice. We have given our answer in our actions, and I am here to reaffirm our stand to the nations of the world. We reject communism; the Arab people will never bow to communism, no matter what guise it may use to force itself upon us.

Communism will never survive in the Arab world because if it ever did it would have replaced Arab nationalism. There would cease then to be an Arab nation. I believe that Arab nationalism is too deep-rooted in the love of God, the love of freedom, and the concept of the equality of all before God, to

I Fly to the United Nations 267

be ever supplanted by a system which denies the importance
of those ideas. Moreover, it is my firm belief that all nations
which believe in God should meet in counterattack against the
common challenge to their very existence. Not even the emotional power that comes from love of country, or the resistance
offered by material well-being, or the spiritual strength to be
drawn from the concept of freedom—none of these singly or
alone can meet the threat to peace presented by the totalitarian
conditions of communism. Not until those who honestly believe in God and in his dictates of love, equality and social
justice translate those ideas into actions, will communism be
defeated and peace restored to the earth.

In the great struggle between communism and freedom,
there can be no neutrality. How, then, can we be neutral in
our attitude towards two systems of government, two philoso-
phies—one of which challenges these concepts and the other
which denies and stifles them? In taking our stand with the
free world, however, we do not forget our long struggle for
liberation. Nor could we support existing injustices being
committed by some members of the free world; but in the
setting sun of the old imperialism we are not blinded to the
new imperialism of communism, one far more brutal, far more
tyrannical and far more dangerous to the ideas of free people,
to the concept of nationalism, than this world has ever known.

While we reject the doctrine of neutralism for ourselves, we
respect the right of any nation to choose its own course of
action, but we are wary of the use of neutralism to exploit the
division between communism and the free world. And we are
also wary of the danger of Communist expansion under the
guise of neutralism.

I come now to the problem of the Middle East, so vital to
the peace of the world, and of major concern to the United
Nations. In our part of the world I look to the problems of
Algeria and of Palestine. There now exists a situation of which

the General Assembly should be aware. I will not dwell upon it in unhappy detail, for to do so might increase, rather than decrease, the danger of internal conflict. Yet to let it smolder unnoticed by the United Nations would be equally dangerous. I feel, therefore, that I must discuss the tensions which exist between Jordan and the United Arab Republic.

With other and more world-wide problems facing the General Assembly it may seem to some rather presumptuous to introduce what may appear to be a local issue. However, no issue is entirely local, and as the world has now learned no conflict of ideas or threat of physical conflict stops at the borders of those directly involved. Moreover, the principles which underline, as well as those which must be used to solve it, are applicable throughout the world and as new independent nations find their freedom in increasing numbers, the effective application of these principles becomes of ever increasing importance.

For me to remain silent, then, would be to encourage the continuation of a situation that could destroy the Arab nation and in the process lead to the involvement of the major powers and thus produce a world conflict.

It all began several years ago, and at a time when Jordan, having just completely achieved its independence, faced the new and more formidable threat to freedom in the form of Communist penetration into our area. Our warnings to the people of Jordan and to the Arab nation as a whole caused Jordan to be subjected to abuse, subversion and external pressure of many kinds, so intense we can only believe the aim of our sister Arab state was our destruction. Its Government, one would have supposed, would be as strongly dedicated to the goal of Arab unity as Jordan is. In fact, the United Arab Republic's attacks on us were so constant that on August 21, 1958, the General Assembly endorsed an Arab League resolution by which the United Arab Republic pledged itself to cease its campaign against us. Unhappily she did not follow her pledge. The attacks were resumed; incitements to overthrow our government and assassinate our leaders were daily broadcast over their government radio. Borders between us were closed to damage our economy and convicted traitors were encouraged, or at least permitted, to engage in subversive acts against us. The situation once again became so grave that the Arab League, of which the United Arab Republic and Jordan are members, passed a resolution calling upon its members to refrain from all activities that would disturb fraternal relationship.

The day following the close of that session, Jordan's Prime Minister, Hazza Majali, was killed by a bomb placed on his desk, along with eleven others, including a child ten years old. I would restrain myself, and I assure you it is with the greatest difficulty that I do so, from saying any more on this subject. However, I would like only to add that I find considerable significance in the fact that our troubles with the United Arab Republic date from the time that I denounced the growing menace of communism in the Arab world. Moreover, I detect a significant parallel between the tactics that have been used against Jordan and those employed by communism all over the world.

It is no secret that the policy of the Soviet Union is to split friend from friend, to divide nation from nation, in order to achieve its own goal of total world domination.

The point I wish to make is this: If, as the creation of the United Nations suggests, our hope is for more freedom, more co-operation, and what we often refer to as a better world, and survival lies in the adherence to mutually agreed ways of dealing with one another, then we must find better ways than we now have to bring our combined weight of opinion quickly and effectively to bear upon any nation that transgresses these agreements. I do not suggest that there is any-

thing new in this idea, it is simply the idea of government by
law applied to the actions of sovereign nations. Yet to me, as
the leader of a small nation much beset by outside pressures,
it is a concept which is worthy of re-emphasis at this time,
for I believe that it is in the successful application of this idea
that the survival and progress of my and so many other small
nations in the end will be decided. The United Nations is the
only instrument capable of applying this idea successfully.

Before I go on to the subject of Algeria and Palestine, a
final word about the United Arab Republic. While Jordan
would naturally welcome evidence of U.N. support of its position, which it believes to be based on the principles on which
progress toward better relations between nations must rest,
Jordan does not expect or request any United Nations special
or immediate response to what I have said. If we can collec-
tively devise and carry out better means than we now have to
assure the integrity of smaller nations and to guarantee their
ability to improve their lot, free from outside interference,
then I believe we will have progressed. If what I have said
contributes to this end, then it will have been worth saying.

The tragedy of Algeria remains grave and shows signs of
becoming graver. To me again, the problem is that of refusing
to recognize the right of the people to determine their own
future. This is the very essence of freedom. The United Nations
cannot afford to take a passive position in this matter, any
more than it was passive about Korea or about Hungary. In
one sense the problem is far more serious, because a party to
it is a member of the free world. We appeal to France to uphold what she seems to have neglected, her own tradition for
liberty, freedom and equality. There is no doubt that a large
and impressive number of the French people are wholeheartedly in favor of permitting our Algerian brothers the
choice of their future. May the French government issue and
reflect by its actions the same belief, and extend to the Al-

gerians the right of self-determination promised by the President of France. By such action, France will win back its place among nations who will fight for freedom. There will never be a better world if principles continue to be compromised. We must put an end to useless bloodshed. Enough wrong has already been done.

The third problem in the Middle East is Palestine. The world's conscience seems to have closed its eyes in a rather shameful manner and for far too long on this tragedy of humanity. So serious is its magnitude that over a million Arab refugees from Palestine have lived for twelve years ignored by a world that has not yet seriously attempted to help them return to the most essential and sacred right in life—human dignity. The original failure of the United Nations to permit the people the right of self-determination in 1947 has left in its wake an unresolved situation. There is no question in the mind of any just and impartial observer that the Arab people of Palestine were wronged by the partitioning of Palestine and by the subsequent establishment of the State of Israel. As it was already wrong and politically unjust then, it is no less so today. The world is too prone to accept a *fait accompli* as a basis of policy.

As everyone here is well aware, there still exist various resolutions, those of 1948 and 1959, for example, yet nothing has been done to persuade Israel to live up to them. The United Nations must enforce its will upon a member who refused to abide by its decisions. There will be no real peace in the Middle East without an honorable, just solution to the Palestine tragedy, and complete restoration of the rights of the Arab people of Palestine.

I said earlier that we in Jordan are not neutral between right and wrong—or our belief in God—and I ask the God in whom we believe to send down on this General Assembly his

blessing and that from it we may have the courage to decide
wisely and fearlessly the questions that lie before us.

.   .   .   .   .

I was very deeply touched, following the speech, to receive a letter of congratulations from President Eisenhower
and also the congratulations of Mr. Macmillan, the British
Prime Minister, and many other delegates. Even Mr. Nehru
applauded my speech, but I was mainly affected by the reaction of the people of the United States during my short
stay.

The President later invited me to the White House and we
had long and valuable talks together. Mr. Hammarskjöld
held a private dinner party for me and then this great man—
so busy, and so vilified before his death—took time off from
his never-ending duties to come to the Waldorf-Astoria once
again to bid me good-by before I flew home.

19

The Economy of Jordan

"It is important to answer speculation."

THERE MUST BE many people who wonder what Jordan is like and what are its prospects of surviving both economically and politically. Some observers suggest it lacks several factors —such as sufficient size, population, economy—necessary to survival. It is important to answer speculation of this sort.

A nation's spirit and ability to survive are not determined by its size or population but by the will of its people, their faith in their country, their causes, and their determination to make their lives worth while. Jordan aims at setting an example to the world of what a model democracy should be like. We try to base our lives and our work on all the previous heritage of Islam, by learning from experiences of other nations, and by keeping ever before us the symbol of freedom to which the people of Jordan are dedicated.

Jordan's economy today is healthy and it is developing. Before judging it, consider the pressures and heavy burdens

273

Jordan has had to face. Consider the brevity of Jordan's existence, and then see how rapidly it has developed.

Jordan as an independent country was born only in 1946. The Hashemite Kingdom of Jordan *as presently constituted* has existed only since 1948 and came into being after one of the most devastating upheavals in history.

Although divided arbitrarily by politicians in the early 1920's, Transjordan and Palestine have always, geographically and historically, constituted one economic unit. Highlands and lowlands, hinterland and coastland, river streams and lake reservoirs, were formed by God's will into a near-perfect entity.

True enough, most of the thirty-seven thousand square miles of present-day Jordan receives less than five inches of rain a year, and is, therefore, mostly desert. This seems to have been caused by atmospheric shifts over several thousands of years, and no human action could have halted the process. Such hardy and industrious peoples as the Nabataeans (an Arab race) and the Romans made signal contributions to civilization during their abode in our land, and before they were caught in this ruthless process of nature.

But having said that, it would be a mistake, which I regret many outsiders make, to describe Jordan as a desert kingdom without any hope of economic development. If this were true, men would never have settled in such places as Texas, California and the Nile Valley where, despite desert land, civilizations flourish.

So it is in Jordan. The major groups of people are found in rain-fed areas of the plateaus or along the banks of abundant (or potentially abundant) waters in the valleys.

When the Palestine refugees were granted citizenship and the hill regions of Palestine became the West Bank area of

Jordan, our population increased threefold, but our arable land was increased only by one-third. Of the millions of people suddenly added to our country almost half were "physical" refugees uprooted from their homes and means of livelihood. They needed jobs. Many thousands were "economic" refugees, who had lost lands, businesses, industrial establishments. They needed businesses to run.

Many brought with them great skill and knowledge. Normally such a massive addition to a country's population could be turned to economic advantage in increased productivity and purchasing capacity, but this was not the case in Jordan. The problem which faced my people was not one of reconstructing assets destroyed by war as happened in many countries after World War II, nor was it one of changing from war to peace, or modernizing obsolete plants. Our problem was essentially one of creating, almost from scratch, an economy capable of supporting overnight a vast influx of people. The task was colossal by any standards.

The situation was doubly difficult because the Palestine upheaval smashed, with a shattering blow, traditional trade routes and communications on which this part of the world had depended for centuries. Before 1948 trade was oriented westward. Goods flowed to the Mediterranean coast with its modern ports, airports, roads and railways. Suddenly Jordan was faced with the gigantic task of improvising new trade routes. Not only did we have a million extra mouths to feed, we had to build new roads, ports, airports.

A country's roads and railways—the arteries of a modern state—normally grow as the country grows. Communication facilities invariably grow steadily through many generations as a country flourishes. Yet because of the abnormal situation facing us after the war which created Israel, the work of generations had to be telescoped into one decade.

I am very, very proud of my people for the way they accepted this challenge and overcame it, especially in view of the underlying psychological factors at the time. For it should not be forgotten that Jordan was never reconciled to the creation of Israel, imposed *de facto* on the Arab states in 1948. Jordan and the other Arab states firmly believed, as they do today, that a situation so starkly unjust could never last—and believed passionately and still believe that the world's conscience would sooner or later rectify the wrong by a just and satisfactory solution. Nothing is more dampening to an all-out reconstruction effort than the belief that a situation is only temporary.

Moreover, the machinery of government on which success or failure ultimately hinges had its own problems. The Palestine civil service had been wrecked, while the government of Jordan was hardly equipped to cope with such a drastic situation. We had, before anything else, to fuse the best brand of old and new Jordan, of East and West Banks. It was a task both stimulating and complementary. The East Bank had a more established tradition of government at the policy-making level, having enjoyed independence longer; while the West Bank had a more highly developed sense of administration, Palestine having enjoyed one of the best civil services in the Middle East.

That was the situation which confronted us in 1950.

We first set our minds to the problem of transportation. After 1948 we were denied direct access to the Mediterranean and could only reach it by driving two hundred twenty miles across Syria, and over the Lebanese mountains and down to Beirut. Quite apart from difficulties and delays when crossing international boundaries, the cost was an impossible drain on our meager resources. When I came to the throne, I remember one of my earliest shocks—that it cost us $3 million a year just to *transport* petroleum imports.

I could hardly believe the figure in front of me. That huge cost was an overriding consideration in our decision to build our own oil refinery.

Furthermore, I agreed entirely with our experts that Jordan could not prosper unless we had access to a seaport of our own. Hence we built the Desert Road to Aqaba on the Red Sea—two hundred twenty miles of asphalt road which, I am happy to state, is now in operation. At the same time we constructed a modern well-equipped port at Aqaba. This has immediately allowed us to expand our exports—particularly minerals—to the Indian Ocean and the Far East. Aqaba, incidentally, could be very useful to other Arab countries, particularly Iraq and northern Saudi Arabia, and we hope they will take full advantage of it in the future.

We have only one major railway in Jordan. It runs from Amman to Ras el Naqab, fifty miles north of Aqaba. It would make all the difference if we could continue it to our only port, and a team of railway experts has been studying the possibility. In view of our mounting exports, the railway will one day have to come.

We now have about 2,000 kilometers of asphalt roads and 1,500 kilometers of non-asphalt roads. One highway links Amman to the Syrian border across the beautiful and historic mountains of Ajloun and Jerash; another runs between Amman and Jerusalem across the Jordan Valley. And of course the Desert Road from Aqaba is a triumph of engineering skill. Incidentally, the Desert Road follows one of the oldest trade routes in the world, the "King's Highway" of the Bible, the road over which the people of Edom (South Jordan) refused to allow passage to the Israelites.

One of my dreams has been a big international airport for Jerusalem. We have two airports—at Amman and Mafraq—capable of accommodating modern medium-sized jets, but the Jerusalem runway is only 6,500 feet long, and of course the city is one of our greatest tourist centers.

We have been too inclined to take our Holy Land for granted, unmindful that the rest of the world is unaware of it. Almost all the holy places of Christianity and important Moslem holy places are in Jordan. In a matter of hours a tourist can see such precious sights as the walled city of Jerusalem, the Holy Sepulchre, the Way of the Cross, and that magnificent masterpiece, the Dome of the Rock. A few miles to the south lie Bethlehem and the Church of the Nativity. In less than an hour a tourist can drive to Jericho, probably the oldest city in the world, visit Elisha's Well, and cross the River Jordan, where Christ was baptized. Farther on is Mount Nebo, where Moses stood when he looked across to Canaan.

The traveler in search of novelty can float on his back and smoke a cigarette in the saline water of the Dead Sea. This is the lowest point on earth—1,200 feet below sea level.

In the heart of the Jordan Valley, the Dead Sea shimmers like a burnished bowl with the mountains of Judea and Moab enclosing it. As the sun sinks one can sometimes see in the far distance the spires on the Mount of Olives, tiny black lines against the red sun.

Farther afield there are equally impressive, even astonishing places to see. For myself, the most amazing sight in Jordan is the rose-red city of Petra. I never tire of taking this excursion to an ancient city, unique in all the world.

You leave the hard-surfaced desert highway at Ma'an and turn onto the smaller road to Wadi Musa, where a police outpost equips visitors for the last lap of the journey.

Horses or mules are necessary for the hour's ride through the narrow defile that for centuries kept the Nabataeans of Petra safe from invasion, at the height of their splendor, which started around 300 B.C. This is a deep crevice in the rock, so narrow that successive handfuls of men held it against all armies for four hundred years until the Emperor Trajan captured it for the Romans in A.D. 105.

In this constantly winding, twisting gorge, sandstone cliffs, of varied and striking colors and fantastic shapes, tower three hundred feet overhead, at points that seem to meet.

An aqueduct chiseled from the rock next to the path reminds one that this was an ancient city whose greatest problem was water, the supply of which had to be defended at all costs.

The first magnificent rock-cut tomb of the city appears suddenly, in a burst of strong sunlight. Indeed, rose-red, incredibly preserved in the ageless rock, this is but a forerunner of the splendid array of temples, palaces, churches, tombs and the incomparable treasury to be explored in Petra.

Now that the new road is open, travelers pressed for time may make the trip from Amman to Petra and return in one day, though to do it thoroughly would take four to five days. The drive to Ma'an which used to take up to six hours can now be made in under three. For those who want a taste of the real desert, a drive on to Aqaba will be very revealing.

The Desert Road now passes through some of the wildest country in the Middle East. In this region Lawrence with the Arab troops harried the Turks in the campaign that drove them from Aqaba to the north.

The capital of our country, Amman itself (called Philadelphia in Greco-Roman times), has a magnificent Roman theater, while the Roman city of Jerash in the north—on the new highway to the Syrian frontier—comprises without doubt the most complete remains of a Roman provincial city anywhere in the world.

These are household names to Western civilization, most of them with Biblical associations known to everybody from childhood. This—if it is not unbecoming to place an economic interpretation on its significance—is an area where Jordan is second to none in what it has to offer. While Greece and Italy have had a huge and ever-growing tourist income, Jordan has hardly tapped its potential. I believe that when our tourist program really starts properly—and we shall shortly be opening offices in several major cities—then the tourist income to Jordan may well equal the fabulous oil revenues of other Arab states.

Admittedly, all tourists are not interested in religious and historical relics, but here again Jordan has failed so far to publicize one of its most important tourist assets, its exciting and variegated scenery and above all its fantastic changes of climate within small distances. In winter, when the cold wraps Jerusalem and you need central heating, you can in half an hour drive to the Jordan Valley and swim. From

Amman, where I myself have many a time helped motorists out of snowdrifts, you can drive to the Dead Sea in less than an hour or fly in an hour to the beautiful tropical beaches of Aqaba. In the hill cities like Amman, Jerusalem, Nablus and Ramallah, the evenings are always cool. Jordan, in fact, always has the weather you want, twelve months of the year.

I have described at some length our tourist potential, not only because of its economic value, but also to correct some of the misconceptions that persist about my country, in the hope that some of my readers will know a little more of a land which, perhaps more than any other, stands as a living embodiment of their deepest spiritual beliefs.

One of my most cherished dreams is to see every boy and girl in Jordan at school. Already it is nearly realized. We have started a full educational program so that many secondary schools give vocational training in agriculture, industry and trades to students who complete their elementary schooling. Ten years ago we had only a hundred or so Jordanians studying abroad. Today there are almost seven thousand Jordanian students in universities throughout the world and the number is rising sharply. The time must come soon when we shall establish our university in Jordan, possibly in Jerusalem.

Educational progress is best illustrated by figures. In 1950–1951 we spent over $400,000 on education, but in the 1960–1961 budget the figure reached nearly $8 million.

In the field of public health, allocations have quadrupled within a decade from about $750,000 in 1951 to $3 million in 1960–1961. Malaria, endemic particularly in the Jordan Valley, has now been virtually eradicated. Hospitals are increasing and there are more doctors every year.

Every section of our community is forging ahead. Our latest survey in 1959 showed remarkable progress over the previous survey of 1954; national income had increased by sixty per cent; mining and manufacturing more than doubled; construction was more than four times as high in 1959 as in 1954; transport increased by one hundred twenty per cent, wholesale and retail trade by eight per cent, public administration and defense by seventy-seven per cent, and services by one hundred per cent. Available supplies of goods and services within the kingdom increased by seventy-five per cent from about $200 million to over $370 million, or close to $200 per capita.

Expenditure on consumption and gross capital formation increased from approximately $200 million to nearly $350 million during the same period. Private consumption increased by seventy-three per cent, government current expenditure by ninety per cent. Private fixed capital was nearly six times as great as in 1954, while government fixed capital was more than one and one-half times as great. Exports increased by forty-four per cent while imports more than doubled from $60 million to just over $120 million.

One of the priceless attributes of the human race is its insatiable aspiration for a better life, and this spirit animates my people so that the achievements made thus far must be regarded merely as a beginning. And since the future is what counts, here is what I hope Jordan will achieve in the decade ahead.

Several months ago, I began a series of what President Franklin D. Roosevelt used to call "fireside chats." Throughout all of them runs the same theme. In Arabic, it is:

"Fal Nabni hatha albalad wal nakhdem hathihi aluma."

The best translation I can find for it is "Let us build our country and serve our nation." In the talks my aim is to inspire our people to create in Jordan a model Arab state, and to build for ourselves the kind of life that we sought when we threw off the yoke of the Turks and began the Arab Awakening.

I am happy to say that my people are with me in this effort, and that the progress we have made will be exceeded by the progress we shall be making in the future.

To begin with, the government, with the assistance of the Ford Foundation, has formulated a Five-Year Program for a fuller development of the country's resources, approved and encouraged by international experts at a seminar held recently in Jordan. The program visualizes doubling our national income in ten years, narrowing the gap in the balance of trade to no more than the investment requirement of the country. This expanding economy should provide almost full employment even though we expect our population to increase half a million by 1969.

This program is likely to cost about $40 million a year for five years, from private and public funds, and includes an expansion of our phosphate production which is well under way, and I hope that production will be nearly two million tons by 1970. (Jordan possesses inexhaustible resources of high-grade phosphates, an important ingredient in raising food productivity for the galloping world population.) We are planning full development of the Dead Sea minerals, including the production of 250,000 tons of potash before 1965, production of bromine, magnesium, heavy water—if a market could be assured—and other by-products.

I will not dwell on the many industries, chiefly medium and small, which are under active study for the program, but I would like to mention our plans for agricultural irrigation, particularly in the Jordan Valley where, thanks to the climate, we enjoy advantages unique in the Middle East for growing fruits and vegetables during winter.

Towering above all my other hopes is the great Yarmuk Project in the Jordan Valley which would bring 150,000 acres of land under intensive cultivation, increase our national income by at least $60 million a year and produce substantial electric power for agricultural, industrial and domestic use.

The total cost of the project is $150 million. Permit me to explain briefly the up-to-now sad career of the Yarmuk Project, and how it was born by chance in the brain of a brilliant American hydroelectric expert.

The Yarmuk is a tributary of the Jordan River and flows through Jordan and Syria except for six miles in no man's land. One day in 1951 Mr. Mills E. Bunger, Chief of the Water Resources Branch of the American Point Four team in Jordan, was flying over Jordan when bad weather diverted his plane over the Yarmuk valley. During a break in the clouds Mr. Bunger suddenly saw below him a point where three small streams feed into the Yarmuk. Below it, the valley narrows and deepens.

The idea flashed through his mind that here was a perfect site for a dam so that the flood water of the Yarmuk could be stored in a reservoir made out of the deep precipitous valley. Experts went to the spot, which is called Maqarin, and confirmed his impressions. A scheme was born. A dam four hundred eighty feet high would provide Jordan and Syria with hydroelectric power and chiefs of the Jordan government, UNWRA and Point Four put their heads together.

The greatest single advantage, in view of our relations with Israel, was that the reservoir would be entirely in Arab territory. UNWRA was delighted, for they had been empowered by the United Nations to spend $200 million on Arab refugee rehabilitation and immediately allotted $40 million toward the cost. The three teams of experts finished their preliminary survey at double speed, my country contributing its share with the others. As one writer put it, "For the first time since 1948 a feeling of real hope and purpose came over the languishing Kingdom of Jordan."

Experts promised that within three years, over a hundred thousand Jordanians would be able to live and work in the area. We concluded an agreement with Syria. We started recruiting refugees for labor.

Then in the autumn of 1953, after two years of hard work and hope, the Israelis protested in Washington and to the United Nations. Their excuse was that they preferred a scheme which would benefit all countries in the area. They even laid claim to a share of the Yarmuk waters. Incredibly, the free world stood behind this action to prevent a humane, strictly internal project, which as long ago as 1956 would have allowed a hundred thousand or more refugees, who had lost their homes because of the Israelis, to earn their own living and regain their self-respect.

Incidentally, I might add for the benefit of those who regard Israel's progress as a modern miracle in "making the desert bloom" that in comparing our progress with theirs, these statistics should be borne in mind. From all sources of foreign aid, since 1948 to the present, Israel has received

$2,200,000,000 while Jordan in the same period has received $400,000,000. They have roughly the same population as we do.

I am convinced that the way the Western world has hesitated over the Yarmuk River project has been one of its gravest errors of judgment, for it has denied Jordan a major artery of life doubly necessary to grapple with the staggering problems bequeathed to it after the Palestine war.

As Mr. Phillips Talbot, Assistant Secretary for Near Eastern and South Asian Affairs, U.S. Department of State, told the Senate Foreign Relations Committee in August, 1961, "Further development of the Yarmuk River, which feeds into Jordan, is desirable because it would further increase the arable land in Jordan."

To which, Mr. Henry Labouisse, Director of International Co-operation and Administration, added that "if it had been possible to irrigate the whole Jordan Valley, both east and west sides going down, it might be possible to find a livelihood for 125,000 more than were then in the valley—if you did the whole operation."

To do this, he said, political agreements would be necessary among Israel, Jordan, the then U.A.R. and Lebanon.

"The engineering, we think, made a considerable lot of sense," he added, "but it is really a political issue."

But is it a political issue? To me, the issues posed by this project are clear-cut. Jordan is aspiring to utilize waters which are undeniably her own and to store the surplus and flood waters within the safety of her own country rather than in the hands of her enemy.

This could be done by this additional dam within Jordan,

and it is my fervent hope that those interested in the stability of this area will give it serious and urgent attention, especially as the Israelis have declared their intention of diverting the River Jordan by 1963, against all accepted principles of international law.

20

My Courtship and Marriage

"A real home for the first time in my life."

I HAVE DECIDED to conclude the story of my life so far with an
account of my marriage to Muna el Hussein because, quite
aside from providing the happy ending, this marriage has
had a profound influence on me. It seems a fitting climax to
my story for another reason, too. In these pages there has
been all too much tragedy and bloodshed, so it is a relief now
to turn to the happy side of the story—and the future.

Before my marriage, my personal life, if not empty, was
made up of endless devices to distract myself. My duties
and responsibilities occupied me for the greater part of each
day, but once the day's work was ended, I knew perhaps as
much as any man alive the dullness and misery of loneliness.
Mine has not, after all, been the life of an ordinary young
man. The many crises that have threatened my life and
throne, the constant attacks of my enemies, our lone stand in
the Arab Middle East against communism, the frequent

betrayal by people I had great hopes for—all these conspired to turn me into what I did not want to be: a man apart.

I was becoming nervous, irritable and bad-tempered. Instead of working with inspiration I was in danger of simply going through the motions, and I have always been afraid that if I *did* things without consideration, it would lead to decisions that did not reflect my true feelings. In fact, I began to be afraid of making decisions. I began to doubt my own judgment. I did not seem able to view my problems with detachment.

I had disciplined myself for years to be diplomatic when I disliked something, to smile when I did not feel like smiling, to encourage even those I did not always believe in, because it was politic, but now I began to shy away from people. I had to force myself to mingle in the evenings with people outside my immediate family.

It was ridiculous. I was far too young at twenty-five to become a recluse. Yet this problem arose because of two contradictions. I needed friends more than acquaintances. But it is almost impossible for a reigning monarch in the Middle East to have close friends, perhaps more so than anywhere else in the world. It is even more difficult if one has come to power as early in life as I did and faced so many difficulties. I did have a few personal friends, but I always had to be chary about seeing them too frequently. I could not attach myself to any group of people. It causes complications at times and leads to suspicion and intrigue. In the end I reached the stage where I did not wish to mix with anybody, and even avoided possible genuine friendships. In a way I was the friend of every Jordanian; but true, personal friendship was a very different matter.

How different it is today! My irritability, I am told, has

gone. I am more at ease. I am happy now and quite astonished at the way I have learned to relax.

There has been criticism abroad of my marriage to a then
non-Jordanian. Many saw it as an excellent opportunity for
my enemies to stir up trouble against me. Whatever the odds,
however, I was never afraid of the outcome, but even had I
been, it would have made no difference. My decision was
based not only on a deep love for the girl who was to become my bride, but on fundamental precepts from which I
shall never deviate.

Above all, I believe in God. I believe, also, that I must live
with myself, I must be able to face myself each morning and
say: "I did my best yesterday, I will do my best again today."
Each man, low- or high-born, has the same duty each day to
contribute to the good of mankind.

I have a simple philosophy about life and death. How
easily it comes and how easily it can end! What man can
afford to waste time? At any moment death can claim anyone, and when it does, death itself is unimportant. The only
thing that matters is the work that one has accomplished.

To these two beliefs, which are my creed, I would add one
more. I believe with all my heart that if a man is to give of
his best he must live the fundamental life of an ordinary man.
One cannot hide behind a title or a position or a throne. One
can be proud of one's responsibilities, just as I am, but one
cannot use titles or position as a shield. I will never work
merely to make a reputation for myself, to be popular for
appearances rather than for what I am. My task is to lead
my country through service. I believe most sincerely that my
marriage will help me enormously in my struggle to remove
the barriers between the ordinary people of my country and

their King, and I believe that by leading with my wife the fundamental life of an ordinary person, I shall come to know my people better, understand more clearly what they need, and so be of more service to them.

I wanted to marry long before I met Muna el Hussein. (I refer to her by her new Jordanian name, although at the time we met she was a typically English young lady named Toni Avril Gardiner, formerly of Suffolk, England.) Not only my beliefs, but my loneliness, led to a perfectly normal desire for a wife who would share my life.

My previous marriage had been unsuccessful, and I knew myself well enough to conclude that happiness did not lie in choosing a person of rank or title. It took me a long time to reach the point when, after the first crisis, I vowed that if ever I married again it would be to a girl with whom I could build a happy personal life. It did not matter to me who she was or from what country she came. Because I sincerely believe I am no better than the next man, all I needed was a genuine person whom I loved. If I could find her, I would marry her. If not, then I would remain single, for I swore that I would never permit any other factors to influence my choice of a wife. If I ever compromised in my marriage, I would be cheating myself and compromising my principles.

For these reasons I was not afraid to marry Muna el Hussein. I know the alliance seemed unusual to many people. Some feared that this time I had gone too far, but I knew what I was doing and my faith in my people was never in doubt.

I am very proud of **my** wife. I first met her about a year before we were married, but during the first few months we saw very little of each other and only at occasional functions. The very first meeting was at an informal private party I

gave in my small winter villa at Shuna, near the Dead Sea.
It was a party for some departing diplomats and their suc-
cessors. I would not say that I fell in love with Muna at
once, yet our first meeting set the stage for what was to
follow, because for the first time in my life here was a girl
who took an interest in me as a human being rather than as
a king. I was deeply touched. So often I have seen a person
laughing gaily at the opposite end of the room, yet as soon as
he or she is presented to me there comes a change; spon-
taneity vanishes as though a curtain had been drawn between us.

Here, though, was a girl of nineteen, respectful of my
rank, but who obviously liked me as a person and who was
determined to treat me as an ordinary man. To be frank, I
was not surprised, for I knew her father well. He was a
British sapper colonel (who later was among the first to enter
the bombed building after my Prime Minister was killed in
1960) and I liked what I saw of him and the family. I liked
their simplicity and the genuine way they lived their lives.

Muna and I met more and more frequently. My fondness
for her grew with each meeting; it was not a sudden emotional affair. At first, most of our meetings were at various
functions. Then I started to telephone her myself and invite
her when we held a motion picture show for my mother and
family in the Palace.

I remember so well the first time Muna had dinner with
my mother. It was after my return from the U.N., and I had
bought her a modest present—a necklace in gold mesh, which
I hoped she would wear that evening. (She did!) I was so
excited, in fact, that I bought presents for everybody—one for
Colonel Gardiner, another for Muna's mother, and I even
bought a rubber ring for Mrs. Gardiner's Pekinese, Mr. Wu.

The gold necklace was really only half the present. I wanted to surprise and amuse Muna, so she received the necklace before dinner, and when this first family evening was over and she was leaving, I gave her "the other half"— a gold watch on a fine gold-mesh strap, which matched the necklace.

It was the Amman Go-Kart Club that really brought us together more informally. This is a private club with about sixteen members, and I drive in races there each Friday afternoon. Muna and her family came to watch and help with timings and so forth, and one day I asked her:

"Would you like to drive a Go-Kart?"

"I can't drive a car!" she replied.

"I'll teach you," I said, and before long Muna was driving in a ladies' race. After that we met every Friday afternoon at the Club. Go-Karting for about two hours a week was a source of relaxation to me. Earlier in my reign we had had regular car races and hill climbs with inter-Arab competitions with the Lebanese. But it was a bit dangerous. Then times changed. Troubles started and there was no chance to go on. However, in 1959 when I returned from a visit to the United States, I found that several diplomats and enthusiasts, including Raynor, had formed a small Go-Kart club. They had hastily imported a few machines from England, and when I saw Raynor spending his time on these apparently childish toys, I was rather dismayed. Raynor had even ordered a machine for me and I remember my first remark: "What the devil is a Go-Kart?"

I was made president in my absence and I finally agreed, mainly because of the way the members suggested by in-

nuendo, "When we raced cars you had an advantage with
powerful machines. Now, every Go-Kart is the same. It's the
driver that counts!"

This was a challenge I could not resist, and once the Go-
Karts had been assembled I tried one out. In a moment I
was roaring over the grounds. I went back to the garage
shouting, "Raynor, it's not bad! When do we start racing?"

That was the birth of Go-Karting in Amman. Now we race
every Friday and my wife loves it as much as I do.

After we had spent a few afternoons racing, Muna asked:

"Would you like to come and have tea with my mother
and father?"

Of course I wanted to.

"Do they know we're coming?" I asked, for I was afraid
they might make too much of a fuss.

"No, I didn't tell them," she answered, "but I'm sure it'll
be all right."

That was what I wanted to hear. When I went to take tea
with her family she did not try to "put on a show." It didn't
matter to her that her father did not live in a house as large
as mine. Even more important, she did not try to explain it
away. I have always liked small houses; I have always felt at
home in them.

I drove Muna to her parents' house where we had a real
English tea. Mrs. Gardiner produced sandwiches and cakes
and the tea was hot and strong. I suddenly realized I was
feeling content and happy. They made no fuss over me. I
was off duty so we relaxed and laughed and had a good time.
When the time came to leave I promised to return.

I had known Muna for several months by now and when I
got home that night I think I knew in my heart that this
girl was destined to become my wife. The possible political

repercussions over my marriage, which I had thought out over a period of time, passed briefly through my mind, but I dismissed them.

I did not see Muna for a week but during that time I discovered that she spent much of her time helping in a welfare center for mothers and young children who needed help. I found that she had a far greater interest in Jordan than I had imagined. It pleased me. I like people who work. I believe that a king or a laborer must toil each day, and I like women who are interested in a man's work and want to share in it.

The week following I returned to the Gardiners' for more tea and cakes, and more fun and laughter. Again I went back alone to the Palace . . . and that night I thought of marriage. I had not spoken a word to anybody about it, but that evening I made up my mind. I surveyed the opposition I would face, the criticism, the difficulties I would have to overcome, and I remember saying to myself, "I must do it. If I fail myself now it will be the first of many failures to come."

The next evening I dined with my mother in the Zahran Palace. She has always been so close to me, of course, that I wanted to speak to her first. When dinner was over, I said to her:

"Everyone is always trying to induce me to marry and settle down. I have a surprise for you. I would like to get married. I imagine you know to whom."

My mother smiled at me.

"I suppose it's Miss Gardiner?"

"Do you approve?" I asked.

My mother embraced me. "Of course I approve, if it means

your happiness. You know, my son, that I have wanted you to marry for a long time. I am glad that you are marrying somebody you love, for it's quite obvious how much you love her."

My mother had met Muna many times; she had dinner with us frequently, and very often they sat next to each other at the Palace movies. I set great store by my mother's wisdom and was delighted when she added:

"Don't worry about any opposition. The most important thing in life is happiness. I know you haven't had much of it and to me it is most important for you to be happy now. But you will never achieve happiness if you marry somebody you don't love."

The next night I asked Muna to dine with us. She arrived about seven o'clock. I was so nervous I cannot even remember what she wore. I waited until after dinner, then asked her:

"I'd like to talk to you. Will you come into the next room with me?"

We sat down on the small sofa and talked a little while of things I cannot remember, and then I said:

"You must know what I am going to ask you?"

"I think I do," she answered quietly.

"What do you say about it?"

She did not speak; she simply nodded.

"It won't be an easy life, you know," I warned her. "Mine is not much of a life to ask any girl to share. It's uncertain and it's dangerous, as you must know."

"You really want to marry me?" she said.

"I've wanted to ask you to marry me for a long time. I first thought it unfair for you, but then—feeling the way I do about you—I know we can make a good life together. There's only one thing that has kept me silent so long. It really isn't a barrier, for we believe in the same ideals and in God. I am a Moslem. Have you thought of that?"

"I understand. I have thought for a long time of becoming a Moslem," she replied. "I know our beliefs are the same. I pray to God to make my life a good and useful one."

"We shall have to give you an Arabic name," I added.

"I suppose so," she laughed. "It's going to be funny getting a new name at my age. What will it be?"

I laughed too. The tension was broken.

"Well, I don't know," I answered. "We'll have to give it some thought. You'll have to choose. And you'd better start brushing up on your Arabic!"

I took Muna back and told my mother that she had accepted me. Then I telephoned the Prime Minister and requested him to come to the Palace.

"I am delighted, Your Majesty," he declared when I told him the whole story. "I'm absolutely delighted."

He thought for a moment, then added:

"I know there are some difficulties, as you well appreciate. You have just mentioned some yourself. But I don't think you need to worry about them, sir. Your happiness means a lot to your Jordanian family. If they know you have found happiness, they will never fail you."

I did not want the announcement of our impending wedding to leak out prematurely. I wanted to make the announcement myself. Muna, at that time, was working as a secretary, so I suggested that she go to London with her mother for two weeks to buy her trousseau and household linen, and get fitted for her wedding dress. This would also give Muna an excuse to give her notice at the office where she was working, and when she announced that she was going home for a holiday, nobody guessed anything. For my part, I missed her greatly. Before she left I warned her, with a laugh:

"Don't you stay one day over the two weeks; otherwise I may fly over to London and fetch you back myself."

When at last we made public the news of our betrothal, what jubilation there was as I broadcast to my people and told them:

"I am happy for the first time in my life."

I thanked them for their loyalty and understanding. I spent the night with my mother in the Zahran Palace and the next morning my Chief of Diwan called me. "Sir, there are hundreds of people at the Palace waiting to congratulate you. Can you come? We can hardly control them. I've never seen anything like it."

"I'll drive straight over," I answered, but it was easier said than done. In the main street of Amman a huge crowd stopped me and tried to lift my sports car on their shoulders.

It was impossible at first to clear the main street. It was jammed with friendly faces wishing me luck.

The warm reception that morning was very different from the chilly forecast by certain foreign critics, who probably needed more time to digest the news. I knew, of course, that many people had hoped I would make a dynastic or political marriage, and I knew my enemies would seize the opportunity for making propaganda out of the match.

Muna had converted to the Moslem faith and become a Jordanian citizen by the time the betrothal was announced, but the world is full of mischief-makers, and inevitably the press were soon sending exaggerated dispatches to their newspapers. I knew it was impossible to make them all understand our point of view. But even so I was flabbergasted at the reports of political upheavals and imminent conflict which appeared in London and Washington.

Even more absurd were the press reports that I had threatened to abdicate if I did not get my way. Nothing could be further from the truth. Neither was there any truth in the suggestion that tension among my subjects forced me to withhold the title of Queen when I married Muna. The truth is quite different. I must admit I had not given much thought to the question of Muna's title. I am not one who thinks highly of titles, but what else could a King's wife be called?

Two days before the wedding, however, Muna asked me:

"Do you remember, you told me once how much more you preferred to be called by the good, kind people of Jordan 'our Hussein' than 'King Hussein'?"

"Of course I remember," I answered. "I feel much prouder when people call me 'our Hussein.'"

"I've been thinking," she continued. "We're going to share our lives and responsibilities, but I, too, like it more when people call you 'our Hussein.' Do you think they will ever call me 'our Muna'?"

"Of course they will. Why do you ask?"

"Well you know," she said, hesitating—she was thinking aloud—"does it sound ridiculous if I say that I don't really want the title of Queen?"

I do not think I have ever been more proud of her than at that moment. This fitted exactly with my own ideals, to a degree which I had never dared to hope. How many girls would give everything in the world just for a title?

I asked her if she really meant it and she assured me she did.

"All right," I told her. "If you feel that way, I'll do as you wish." I sat down that night with Muna and together we composed a letter to the Prime Minister which he received the day before our marriage. Many people were staggered by the news but there was no reason why they should be. It was Muna's idea. As we told the Prime Minister in the letter, kings and queens are not appointed by royal decree, and we will always strive to be accepted by the only family that counts—the people of Jordan.

There is one thing about Jordan: You can be fairly certain of sunshine on your wedding day. Ours was no exception. Both Muna and I had hoped for a quiet wedding but we knew in our hearts that, though the marriage ceremony would be private, we could not keep the press away from the general ceremony.

What a fantastic day! I have never seen such apparent joy in the streets of Amman, except perhaps on my return after that scrape with the Syrian MIGs. But this was different, it was joy born of hope. Everybody was firing rifles and pistols in the air; the bagpipes droned joyously. Even with all the troops in Amman mustered, it was impossible to keep the crowds from breaking over the open car in which we drove through the city.

The wedding was brief and very simple, according to the Islamic rites. It was held May 25, 1961, in my mother's palace, which is set in a quiet garden filled with roses. The entrances were patrolled by Circassian guards. The ceremony was conducted by Sheik Hamzeh Arabi, a senior judge of the Moslem *sharia* who had been my first tutor in religious matters. As is customary, my bride did not wear her wedding gown, but instead was married in a simple blue linen dress with three-quarter sleeves. She wore a chiffon scarf over her head. I wore a gray suit and sat at the head of a low coffee table with Muna on my left.

The senior judge first recited some verses from the Holy Koran before asking both of us whether we intended to enter into marriage, to which we both replied *"Naam"* (Yes). According to custom, I placed a plain gold ring on my bride's left hand, and then gave her a similar ring which she put on my left hand. Both of us then signed in Arabic five copies of the marriage document, which was attested by two witnesses, my younger brother, Prince Mohammed, and my uncle. We kissed and the company called out *"Mabruk!"* (Congratulations).

Colonel Gardiner attended the ceremony in uniform but there were very few others present. Both of us wanted the actual wedding to be private. We felt that the ordinary people of Jordan had been so good, so kind and understanding that it would be unfair if only people of position were invited. So we asked virtually none to the ceremony, though many came to the receptions afterward.

While the legal ceremony was being performed, the male guests were arriving at the Zahran Palace. They assembled in the three downstairs halls, sipping the traditional wedding drink made of rose petals and water and clutching presentation boxes of mother-of-pearl filled with sweets.

When our private ceremony was over we changed our clothes, reversing the procedure of a wedding where the bride changes into "going away" clothes. Only after the ceremony did I change into my official white uniform, and

Muna changed into her bridal gown and veil for which she had been fitted in London. She carried a sheaf of orange blossoms.

Hundreds of guests had now gathered downstairs, and I mingled with them and received their congratulations. While this was taking place more cars arrived with the lady guests and members of the family who were ushered into another great hall where, with my wife, we attended a tea party given by my mother.

Only after these two receptions were over did we then, in uniform and bridal gown, join hands in the great hall of the Palace. Circassians of the royal bodyguard, wearing their long black cloaks, astrakan hats, high boots and silver swords, lined the hall as we walked down the stairs to face the world's television cameras, the photographers and scores of reporters.

Since the time of our marriage, my wife has made excellent progress with her Arabic and has already started to take a much bigger part in the social activities of the country. I hope that together we can do our share in building Jordan and serving our nation.

The birth of our son, named Prince Abdullah in memory of my grandfather, has not only provided the throne of Jordan with a direct heir but it was, from a purely personal point of view, the most wonderful thing that has ever happened to me. The baby was not really expected so soon, but during the night Muna woke me and said she was not feeling well. Like any father-to-be, I was scared stiff! I grabbed the first clothes I could get my hands on, rushed down, got the car ready, and drove Muna to the hospital. Soon afterward, my son was born.

A public holiday was immediately declared in Jordan, and that day I drove back to see my wife along streets so crowded I could hardly force my way through. Every true Arab wants a son, and now that I have one, in addition to a lovely daughter, there is really very little more I can ask out of life.

I must say that I was amused the day after Abdullah was born. Among the stream of visitors coming to congratulate me was one Englishman, who asked me in highly anxious tones, "Sir, are you going to send him to Harrow?" I suppose I will.

A month or two before the baby was born, I had to fly to London for a purely routine medical checkup. I knew I had been working too hard and the strain was undoubtedly beginning to tell. But how easily rumors spread! I was tired and I was not well, but before long the world's press had almost reduced me—in theory anyway—to a chronic invalid. In actual fact I think I can say that I have a very tough constitution.

I was advised during my trip to London to take things easier and to take days off like ordinary people do, and I am trying to do this now. I also had to promise the doctors that I would not indulge in any high-flying jet aerobatics—a pity from my point of view. My sinus trouble was the real cause of my being run down, but it is absolute nonsense to suggest, as some have done, that I am in any way an invalid. I myself was delighted with the doctors' pronouncements during my London visit, and they certainly gave me the most thorough medical checkup I have ever had.

Muna and I live a simple life in our little farmhouse at Hummar. We named it "Daret Alkair," which means "The

House of Goodness and Happiness." It is about ten miles from Amman and has been converted out of the old single-story house where I was resting the day my Prime Minister was killed in 1960 and the day before assassins tried to murder me with acid.

Though things are much more peaceful in Jordan at the time of writing, one still has to be careful, for there are many forces tugging at the Arab homeland. I told Muna when we decided to marry that she must realize being the wife of a king could prove dangerous.

Our low, two-storied house built of white stone is just the right place for us. It epitomizes all that I really believe in. I know that I must endure palaces and big receptions but after all the Palace does not belong to me but to the Government. "The House of Goodness and Happiness" is *ours*. It is the first house we have ever owned, and when I return each evening, it is to a real home for the first time in my life.

It is modest but comfortable. It now contains four bedrooms and two reception rooms. The rooms are simple but airy, and the furniture is modern and comfortable without being showy. We are hoping to build a small swimming pool shortly in the terraced garden. But most important, this is the home of an ordinary, hard-working man. There is nothing ostentatious about it. Two servants manage it comfortably. We have a cook, but my wife is always so busy in the kitchen we hardly need help. Every other morning she cooks my breakfast—eggs or sausages, coffee, toast and marmalade. The other mornings I attempt to do the cooking. My wife also has a long list of recipes she proposes to try out on me in the near future.

We lead a very quiet life. Sometimes we ride in the mornings. Occasionally we have a small informal party. We drive into Amman to dine with our families, or go to a movie with friends at the Palace. And we have the Go-Kart races every Friday. For the rest, I work hard, and so does my wife. I manage to get home for lunch sometimes, as I have a helicopter landing area in the gardens, so that (with another at my Palace) I can pilot myself to my office in about five or six minutes.

Our house stands on the crest of a hill and it has the most beautiful view. My grandfather left me a large area of land when he died, but some years ago I decided that I could not farm it all. Others needed irrigated land, so I gave most of it away and just kept a small plot where I built what I hope will eventually become a model farm. Around me my fellow countrymen till the soil and I can see them working on the land and feel like one of them when I, too, set off each morning to my work.

Since I first started to write my memoirs, many happy events have happened in Jordan and the rest of the Arab homeland.

To the north, our Syrian neighbors are once again a free people, having thrown away the Nasserite imperialism which threatened to destroy not only themselves but the rest of the Arab world.

There can be no doubt that Nasser's concept of dictatorship and Egyptian domination has caused serious setbacks to the unity and dignity of the Arab world. But now the situation in the Middle East looks healthier, despite the problems it still faces and the dangers of future setbacks. I feel that we in Jordan have moved a long way in our determination to set ourselves up as an example and a model to others as a free, progressive country.

As for myself, the birth of a son, who is now the Crown

Prince, has brought overwhelming joy and happiness to both Princess Muna and myself, as well as to our large family—the family of all Jordan.

I hope and pray that we may have in him a true Arab who can live up to his name in the tradition of the Hashemite family and in the service of our nation.

When I thank God for the happiness He has bestowed on me, I pray He will in His wisdom grant all of us—the laborers in the field, whose work is just as important as their monarch's, my wife, myself and my family—a long life to work for the land we love so well, and to prove ourselves worthy descendants of the Hashemite dynasty.

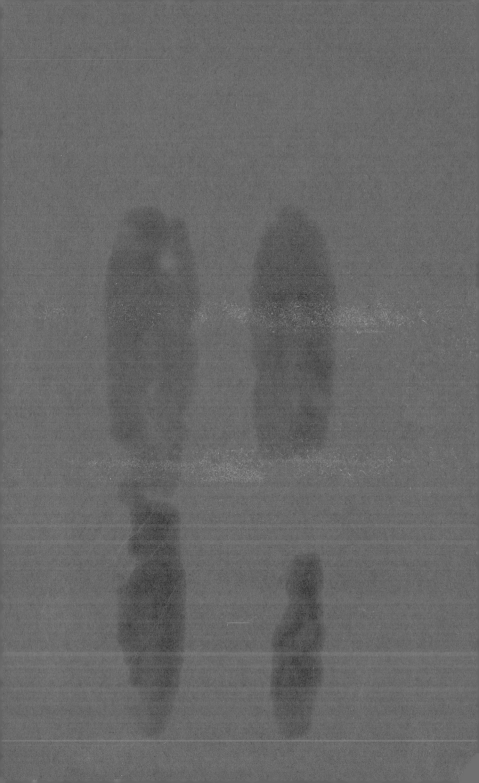